'How Good an Historian Shall I Be?'

British Idealist Studies Series 2: Collingwood

Series Editor:
David Boucher, Cardiff University
Editorial Board:
W.H. Dray (Ottowa)
Gary Browning (Oxford Brookes)
Bruce Haddock (Cardiff)
Rex Martin (Kansas)
Guido Vanheeswijck (Antwerp)
Jan van der Dussen (Open University, Netherlands)

'How Good an Historian Shall I Be?'

R.G. Collingwood, the Historical Imagination
and Education

Marnie Hughes-Warrington

ia

IMPRINT ACADEMIC

Published in the UK by Imprint Academic
PO Box 200, Exeter EX5 5YX, UK

Published in the USA by Imprint Academic
Philosophy Documentation Center
PO Box 7147, Charlottesville, VA 22906-7147, USA

ISBN 0 907845 614

A CIP catalogue record for this book is available from the
British Library and US Library of Congress

www.imprint-academic.com/idealists

Contents

Acknowledgements

Rewriting a thesis is an historical activity. Not only do you have the opportunity to assess how your views have changed; you also have the chance to appreciate the roles that others have played in shaping those views. I would like to take this opportunity to thank a number of people who helped me to complete this project.

To begin, I would like to acknowledge the role of David Boucher and Jill Roe in bringing this work to print. Their unwavering belief in the value of research on the ideas of R.G. Collingwood made the decision to revisit and rewrite my doctoral thesis easy. I would also like to thank those individuals who read and commented on this work in its first form: Nigel Blake, Richard Pring, Martin Roberts and John Wilson. I am deeply grateful for the advice they offered, though of course any errors are my own. Thanks also to Stein Helgeby, Adrian Moore and Bob Purdie, who have been excellent mentors. Kath Evesson also helped to track down some of the materials used in the second part of chapter four.

Two institutions played a large part in the composition of this work. I am grateful to those who assisted with my research at the University of Oxford and Macquarie University. More particularly, I would like to thank the Warden and Fellows of Merton College; the Department of Modern History at Macquarie; the staff of the Bodleian Library, especially Colin Harris and his colleagues at the Modern Manuscripts Room; and the staff of the Macquarie University Library, especially the documents supply staff. I would also like to acknowledge the generous financial assistance of the Rhodes Trust, the Philosophy of Education Society of Great Britain and the Macquarie University Early Career Grants Scheme. Thanks also to Michelle Arrow, who provided valuable teaching relief and to Mary Spongberg, who proves that research and families can mix.

Research is not possible without the support of family and friends. I am indebted to Susan and Grace Durber, who graciously accepted the invasion of their home in the summer of 2002. Helen Verrier, Brad Portin and the folks at St. David's Lindfield have offered many words of support along the way, as did many of my peers at Merton and OUDES from 1992–5. In particular, I would like to pay homage to the role of Marcella, Michael and Claudia in keeping me sane (more or less). But it is to the Hughes and Warrington families that I owe my greatest debt. Thanks Mum, for the offer of the Collingwood premiership memorabilia. Thanks Andrew and Cath, for the phone calls, hilarious emails and afternoon teas. Thanks Bruce, for proof-reading the entire work with scarcely a murmur of complaint. It is just not fair that a scientist can write so well. And finally, thanks to Alice, whose acceptance of a working mum is a wonderful gift. In return, I dedicate this book to her.

Permissions

The author and publisher gratefully acknowledge the permission granted to reproduce the copyright material in this book: Teresa Smith, for generously allowing me to quote from Collingwood's unpublished manuscripts; Oxford University Press, for extracts from Collingwood's published works, particularly *An Essay on Philosophical Method, An Essay on Metaphysics, The Idea of History, The New Leviathan, The Principles of History and Other Writings* and *The Principles of Art*; Blackwell, for allowing me to draw upon 'Collingwood and the Early Paul Hirst on the Forms of Experience-Knowledge and Education' which appeared in the *British Journal of Educational Studies*; Taylor and Francis, for '"How Good an Historian Shall I Be?": R.G. Collingwood on Education', which appeared in the *Oxford Review of Education*; and the R.G. Collingwood Society, for 'History, Education and the Conversation of Mankind', which appeared in *Collingwood Studies*.

Every effort has been made to trace copyright holders and to obtain their permission for the use of copyright material. The author and publisher apologise for any errors or omissions in the above list and would be grateful if notified of any corrections that should be incorporated in future reprints or editions of this book.

For Alice

Introduction
More than a Name

'Must a name mean something?' Alice asked doubtfully.
'Of course it must', Humpty Dumpty said with a short laugh: 'my name means the shape I am — and a good handsome shape it is, too. With a name like yours, you might be any shape, almost.'[1]

Robin George Collingwood's name is familiar to history educators around the world. It has been invoked to validate educational policies and programs and notions of historical scholarship. Yet few appreciate the depth, scope and shape of his views on what it means to be educated in history. The problem is not simply that some of Collingwood's ideas have been emphasised at the expense of others, as was the case with the neglect of his political philosophy.[2] It is more basic and fundamental than that: the Collingwood that educators know is constrained by prevailing assumptions about the territory and boundaries of education, subjects like history and philosophy, and the nature of concepts. He is simply not expected to offer anything more than advice to those who teach and formulate policies on the curriculum subject of history. The time has come to loosen those constraints and look anew at what Collingwood has to offer.

Life and Education

Even the briefest account of Collingwood's life suggests that this was a man whose connection with education was anything but usual. Born on 22 February 1889 at Cartmel Fell in Lancashire, Collingwood was the son of William Gershom Collingwood (1854–1932) and Edith 'Dorothy' Mary Isaac (1857–1928), and grandson of the artist William Collingwood (1819–1903).

---

[1]   Lewis Carroll, *Through the Looking Glass and What Alice Found There* (London, 1871), p. 162.

[2]   For a corrective to that imbalance, see D. Boucher, *The Social and Political Thought of R.G. Collingwood* (Cambridge, 1989).

W.G. Collingwood was John Ruskin's secretary and biographer and a writer, art historian, archaeologist, and painter, and later the Chair of Fine Art at University College, Reading. Edith Collingwood was a musician and a noted painter of miniatures. Collingwood had three sisters, Dora, Barbara and Ursula. Dora became a watercolour artist, Barbara a sculptor and Ursula an art teacher, painter of miniatures and midwife.

Collingwood's education, he tells us, began soon after his birth. In *An Autobiography* he reports that his father took him to an archaeological excavation at the Roman fort of Hardknott Castle at the age of three weeks.[3] From then until the age of thirteen, he was educated at home. Under the guidance of his parents and later his sisters, he was taught to read ancient and modern languages, sing, play the piano, write, sculpt, draw, paint, bind books and sail. He was also encouraged to develop his interest in archaeology, philosophy and the natural sciences. For example, in a letter to Dora, he wrote:

> I have made some gunpowder, and have made a stand to hold a full cartridge. Like this [drawing] The candle underneath red-heats the brass cartridge-shell, and the powder goes off. Next you open the window . . .[4]

His earliest extant letters date from when he was three and a half, and by the time he was eleven he had written, illustrated and bound several books including a guide to Furness Abbey (1896) and accounts of the fictional place called 'Jipandland'.[5] Even his earliest works show a remarkable awareness of writing and publication styles. For example, the first of his books on 'Jipandland' includes the following title page:

Vol. *Jipandland*.
Pictures and stories by R. Collingwood.
Nov 1895. Lanehead.
Part I. Discoveries.
Part II Maps.
Part III A dictionary.
Part IV Alphabet and words.
[Part] V Sketches.
Part V [*sic*] Verbs.
Part VI Stories of Japes.
Printed and illustrated by R. Collingwood Dec. 14 1895.[6]

[3]   R.G. Collingwood, *An Autobiography* (Oxford, 1939), p. 80.
[4]   As quoted in T. Smith, '"This Ring of Thought": Notes on Early Influences', *Collingwood Studies*, Vol. 1 (1994), p. 34.
[5]   *Ibid.*, p. 31.
[6]   As quoted in *Ibid.*, p. 32.

These early experiences, as Boucher points out, provided Collingwood with a model of what education could be.[7] It is a model that he turned to repeatedly in his writings, as we shall see.

In 1902, Collingwood was sent to school at Grange, and a year later he gained a scholarship to Rugby. Collingwood's five years at Rugby were not happy: the curriculum was stultifying, sport was seen as a surrogate for intellectual engagement and the living conditions were akin to a 'pigsty'. He later wrote of:

> ... the frightful boredom of being taught things (and things which ought to have been frightfully interesting) by weary, absent-minded or incompetent masters ... the torment of living by a time-table expressly devised to fill up the day with scraps and snippets of occupation in such a manner that no one could get down to a job of work and make something of it, and, in particular, devised to prevent one from doing that 'thinking' in which, long ago, I had recognised my own vocation.[8]

Here again we see Collingwood's educational views hinted at, views that can be found across his writings. In 1908, Collingwood was 'let out of prison' and gained a scholarship to University College, Oxford, to read *Literae Humaniores* — classics — as his father had done.[9] In 1912 he was awarded a first class degree and a fellowship in philosophy at Pembroke College. With the exception of the years 1914 to 1918, when he served in the Admiralty's intelligence department, and 1931–2 when he contracted a serious bout of chickenpox, Collingwood dedicated himself to his teaching duties and writing projects with incredible energy.[10] And he did both with the same depth and range of intellectual interest that his family encouraged in him as a boy. Out of his lectures emerged major works on religion (*Religion and Philosophy*, 1916), the nature of knowledge (*Speculum Mentis*, 1924), philosophy and metaphysics (*An Essay on Philosophical Method*, 1933; *An Essay on Metaphysics*, 1940), art (*Outlines of a Philosophy of Art*, 1925; *The Principles of Art*, 1938), politics (*The New Leviathan*, 1942) and archaeology (*The Archaeology of Roman Britain*, 1930; *Roman Britain and the English Settlements*, 1937). Collingwood's efforts earned him a number of distinctions in his lifetime, most notably election as a fellow of the Royal Society in 1934, appointment as Waynflete Professor of Metaphysical Philosophy at Magdalen College in 1935 and receipt of an honorary LL.D from the University of St. Andrews in 1938.

---

[7]   D. Boucher, *The Social and Political Thought of R.G. Collingwood*, p. 4.
[8]   R.G. Collingwood, *An Autobiography*, p. 8.
[9]   *Ibid.*, p. 10.
[10] J.M. Winter, 'Oxford and the First World War', *The History of the University of Oxford*, ed. B. Harrison, Vol. 8 (Oxford, 1994), p. 9.

He was, however, unable to collect his honorary degree in person, because he suffered the first of a number of strokes that would contribute to his death at the age of fifty-four. After his first stroke, Collingwood took a year off from teaching duties and embarked on a sea voyage to Indonesia. During the journey, and the three and a half months that he spent in Indonesia, he corrected the page proofs of *An Autobiography* (1939), and worked on *An Essay on Metaphysics* and a manuscript called 'The Principles of History'.[11] After he submitted the manuscript of *An Essay on Metaphysics* to Oxford University Press, he was off sailing again on a voyage that would be described in his *First Mate's Log* (1940). At his death in 1943, Collingwood left few publications specifically on history: a collection of articles from the 1920s that were later brought together by Debbins as *Essays in the Philosophy of History* (1965); a leaflet entitled *The Philosophy of History* (1930); *The Historical Imagination*, his inaugural lecture as Waynflete Professor in 1935; and a lecture given to the British Academy in 1936 entitled 'Human Nature and Human History'.

But he also left behind a large collection of unpublished manuscripts, on topics ranging from history, religion, folklore, and magic to sense perception, archaeology, metaphysics, art and music. T.M. Knox, a former student of Collingwood's, took upon himself the responsibility of guiding some of those writings to publication. First to be published were lectures on the history of theories of cosmology from 1934, 1935 and 1937, which Collingwood began to work up for publication in 1939. These appeared under the title *The Idea of Nature* in 1945. Second was a course of lectures on philosophy of history that Collingwood first delivered in 1936 and revised under the title 'The Idea of History' in 1940. And third was 'The Principles of History', penned in 1939. On the first page of the latter, Collingwood wrote a note to his first wife, Ethel, which reads:

> If this [manuscript] comes into your hands and I am prevented from finishing it, I authorise you to publish it with the above title, with a preface by yourself explaining that it is a fragment of what I had, for 25 years at least, looked forward to writing as my chief work.[12]

Despite these instructions, Knox was of the opinion that a 'good deal of the second and third chapters is contained already in the *Autobiography* and the *Essay on Metaphysics*, and I am not satisfied

---

[11] On the composition of *An Essay on Metaphysics*, see R. Martin, 'Editor's Introduction', *An Essay on Metaphysics* , rev. edn. (Oxford, 1998), pp. xv–xxi.

[12] R.G. Collingwood, 'The Principles of History' [1939], *The Principles of History and Other Writings*, ed. W.H. Dray and W.J. van der Dussen (Oxford, 1999), p. 3.

that we ought to press the wording of a note written in all probability when R.G. Collingwood was unusually ill'.[13] He then combined 'The Principles of History', 'The Idea of History', 'Human Nature and Human History' and *The Historical Imagination* and published them under the title *The Idea of History* (1946). While some editorial alterations to the content of that text have been identified,[14] Knox's influence is most evident in his arrangement of materials. Most problematic is the fifth section, the 'Epilegomena', in which sections of lectures, published essays and 'The Principles of History', which date from 1935 to 1939 are cobbled together in an apparently seamless fashion. Without van der Dussen's introduction to the revised edition of that text, readers would have little clue as to the different dates, purposes and audiences of these writings.

In 1978, Collingwood's second wife Kate deposited many of his manuscripts in the Bodleian Library, Oxford. 'The Principles of History', though, was not among them, leading scholars to conclude that it must have been lost or destroyed. It is hard to convey in words, then, just how exciting it was when in 1995 archivists at Oxford University Press found the missing chapters of 'The Principles of History' and two early drafts of conclusions for what became *The Idea of Nature* (1945). These were published with other manuscripts — including the rough draft of Collingwood's inaugural Waynflete lecture — in 1999. Those manuscripts play an important part in this work.

It seems that we now have a better chance to grasp Collingwood's ideas than ever before. Knox's role in bringing Collingwood's works to publication, though, will continue to be a source of regret as long as his construction of *The Idea of History* remains in print.

Approaching Collingwood

Issues of accessibility to Collingwood's unpublished works have, until recently, formed a major obstacle to the analysis of his ideas. Publication of a number of manuscripts — in the revised editions of *The New Leviathan* (1992), *The Idea of History* (1993) and *An Essay on Metaphysics* (1998), and in *Essays in Political Philosophy* (1995) and *The Principles of History and Other Writings in Philosophy of History* (1999) — has helped to alleviate that problem. Current educational scholarship, though, suggests little familiarity with Collingwood's writings beyond a few sections of *The Idea of History* and *An Autobiography*.

---

[13] As quoted in W.J. van der Dussen, 'Editor's Introduction', *The Idea of History*, rev. edn. (Oxford, 1993), p. xii.

[14] *Ibid.*, pp. xvi–xix.

Rather, educators appear to be highly dependent on the comments of Collingwood scholars, and I believe this dependency has served to reinforce an unnecessarily limited account of his views. This is so for at least two reasons. First, the bulk of scholarship on Collingwood looks almost exclusively to his views on history and philosophy. More specifically, analysis of his directives on re-enactment and 'all history is the history of thought' abounds and shows no signs of abating. This in itself is not a bad thing, for considerable advances have been made in interpreting Collingwood's ideas, advances that inform this work. They have, however, suggested a firmer boundary between history and other mental, social and political activities than Collingwood wanted. It is therefore easy for educators to slip into viewing Collingwood as offering advice only on the distinct profession and curriculum subject of history. History, as we shall see, meant much more to Collingwood. Works that take a wider perspective are not impossible to find, but are still more limited than they need be. Since the publication of Mink's *Mind, History and Dialectic* (1969), for instance, it has become accepted that Collingwood's views on history are better understood in the context of his philosophy of mind.[15] Van der Dussen, for example, has revealed the staggering scope and depth of Collingwood's understanding of history as a form of knowledge and inquiry.[16] Only recently, though, have scholars begun to respond to Boucher's invitation to cast the net even wider and consider Collingwood's vision of history in the context of his social and political thought.[17] Helgeby, for example, has argued for the inter-connection of Collingwood's views on history, epistemology, moral philosophy and civilisation.[18] This work is informed by that same broadening of focus not only because it aligns with Collingwood's own approach to scholarship, but because, as I hope to show, it leads to a better understanding of some of his most discussed and debated ideas.

Second, it is a source of considerable irony that Collingwood tends to be approached by some of the same philosophical methods that he tried to distance himself from.[19] During the period that Collingwood was at Oxford, a varied group of philosophers there and at Cambridge — including Wittgenstein, Austin and Ryle — adopted a

[15] L.O. Mink, *Mind, History, and Dialectic: The Philosophy of R.G. Collingwood* (Bloomington, IN, 1969).

[16] W.J. van der Dussen, *History as a Science: The Philosophy of R. G. Collingwood* (The Hague, 1981).

[17] D. Boucher, *The Social and Political Thought of R.G. Collingwood*.

[18] S. Helgeby, 'Action, Duty and Self-Knowledge in R.G. Collingwood's Philosophy of History', *Collingwood Studies*, Vol. 1 (1994), pp. 86–107.

[19] R.G. Collingwood, *An Autobiography*, pp. 19–22, 56.

style of research and writing that came to be identified as 'ordinary language', 'analytic' or 'Oxford' philosophy.[20] Uniting this loose-knit group was a determination to free philosophical writing from what were seen as the vague and lofty claims of idealists like Hegel and Kant, the almost mystical tone of contemporary continental European philosophy, and neologisms, jargon and technical terms. Philosophy was to be written, as much as possible, in ordinary language. Indeed, Wittgenstein even claimed that philosophical problems were at base due to confusions and distortions in ordinary language.

These stylistic aims accord with Collingwood's own. One of the most appealing aspects of Collingwood's writing is its clarity. This is no incidental feature of his work: in *An Essay on Philosophical Method*, he informs us of his determination to avoid the use of technical terms or jargon in favour of ordinary language.[21] It is therefore relatively easy to slip into reading him as an ordinary language or analytic philosopher, despite, as Dray points out, his own objections to that approach. Interestingly, though, Dray himself clearly feels tugged by an analytic reading of Collingwood, and seems to regret that Collingwood does not meet the standard:

> It cannot be said . . . that Collingwood's writings, when carefully read, are easy to grasp. Although often graceful, they are not always careful. They do not exhibit that exact love of language which analytic philosophers have since made *de rigueur* . . . [22]

So what is the difficulty with this reading of Collingwood? Here we need to turn to Collingwood's own complaints against ordinary language philosophy.

Collingwood's major complaint against his analytic contemporaries was that they were insufficiently historical in their approach to research and writing. In practice, ordinary language philosophers tended to confine their analyses to present-day usages of concepts or to show little concern that past usages might be shaped by very different assumptions.[23] This is a complaint I understand well, having been advised when I first started work in this area that I should work

[20]   See J.L. Austin, 'A Plea for Excuses', *Philosophical Papers* (3rd edn, Oxford, 1979), pp. 175–204; G. Ryle, 'Systematically Misleading Expressions', *Collected Papers*, Vol. 2 (London, 1971), pp. 39–62; and L. Wittgenstein, *Philosophical Investigations*, trans G.E.M. Anscombe, ed. G.E.M. Anscome, R. Rhees and G.H. von Wright (Oxford, 1953). See also C.E. Caton (ed.), *Philosophy and Ordinary Language* (Urbana, IL, 1963).
[21]   R.G. Collingwood, *An Essay on Philosophical Method* (Oxford, 1933), p. 207.
[22]   W.H. Dray, *History as Re-enactment: R.G. Collingwood's Philosophy of History* (Oxford, 1995), p. 27.
[23]   R.G. Collingwood, *An Autobiography*, pp. 58–61.

simply to clarify current usages of the terms 'historical' and 'imagination'. And this ahistorical orientation still persists in some form in writings on Collingwood's philosophy of history. While no Collingwood scholars are as dismissive of history as Collingwood claimed his analytic contemporaries to be, it does not inform their approach to his ideas as thoroughly as it might. A good case in point is the copious literature on re-enactment. Few writers offer anything more than a brief survey of antecedent thinkers, variations in Collingwood's view and or a history of the reception of Collingwood's idea. Typical are Nielsen's careful analysis of Collingwood's use of the term 're-enactment' and its cognates and Saari's critical assessment of various interpretations of Collingwood's idea.[24] Looking at these works, readers are offered no inkling of the relatively long historical context in which the idea of re-enactment may be located. That history is not only interesting, but also helps us to understand the degree to which Collingwood's views were a response to earlier philosophical and literary theories. In particular, it helps us to illuminate Collingwood's judgement on which terms are cognates of re-enactment and which ones *are not*, a point that is relatively neglected in Collingwood scholarship.[25] This is not just a minor semantic issue, as we will see when we look to British policy discussions from the 1960s to the mid-1990s on the role of 'empathy', 'sympathy', 're-enactment' and the 'historical imagination' in history education. Similarly, accounts of Collingwood's views on the 'historical imagination' give readers little reason to believe that any theories existed prior to that of Collingwood. A good case in point is Dray's analysis in *History as Re-enactment*, which includes only a brief mention of antecedent thinkers named by Collingwood himself: Macaulay, Kant and Hume.[26] This is a pity, for a more thorough examination of earlier theories of imagination and historical imagination highlights the breadth and innovative structure of Collingwood's view.

Problematic too are the views of concepts that are commonly coupled with the analytic approach, which are not sufficiently expansive and dynamic to match Collingwood's contribution to philosophical thought. Few Collingwood scholars have read

---

[24] M.H. Nielsen, 'Re-enactment and Reconstruction in Collingwood's Philosophy of History', *History and Theory*, 1981, Vol. 20 (1), pp. 1–31; and H. Saari, *Re-enactment: A Study in R.G. Collingwood's Philosophy of History* (Åbo, 1984).

[25] Rex Martin, for instance, talks of the 'empathetic dimension' in re-enactment, a view that will be challenged in this work. See R. Martin, *Re-enactment and Practical Inference* (London, 1977), pp. 53–4.

[26] W.H. Dray, *History as Re-enactment*, ch. 6.

Collingwood according to his own view of concepts, and even fewer educators have done so. The expectation is that, for instance, the clarification of terms like 're-enactment' or 'historical imagination' will probably lead to the identification of necessary and sufficient conditions equally present in all and only phenomena so labelled, as Frege would have it. Less popular is the more open alternative of Wittgenstein — in which phenomena are connected by a network of overlapping similarities — but this is not a good match for Collingwood's ideas either. To Collingwood, instantiations of a concept are arranged in a hierarchical, cumulative scale. What is remarkable is that Collingwood scholars and educators persist with these views of concepts, despite the many problems they have raised and the promise of Collingwood's own theory.

In sum, then, approaching Collingwood requires the same intellectual breadth and fusion of history and philosophy that his writings epitomise. And cultivating this approach, as we shall discover, is the cornerstone of Collingwood's vision of education and society.

The Shape of this Book

The shape of this book is that of a spiral: it begins with the facets of Collingwood's work best known to educators — re-enactment and the historical imagination — and locates them in the widening contexts of both Collingwood's and earlier writers' views on empathy, sympathy, imagination, education and society. This choice of arrangement is quite deliberate, for it matches Collingwood's vision of the process of education as an 'infinitely increasing spiral'.[27] The selection of re-enactment and the historical imagination as starting points will perhaps generate a groan from readers who are aware of the copious body of scholarship already available on those topics. There is no doubting that re-enactment and the historical imagination are well-worn topics in Collingwood studies. Despite that, I contend that the nature and role of re-enactment and the historical imagination in Collingwood's educational, social and political thought is little understood.

'Re-enactment', the 'historical imagination' and the seemingly related concepts of 'empathy' and 'sympathy' occupy a prominent place in discussions on history education from the mid-twentieth century onwards. Around that time, history education around the world took a turn towards epistemology and educators became increasingly interested in fostering an awareness of both the nature

---

[27]   R.G. Collingwood, *Outlines of a Philosophy of Art* [1925] (Bristol, 1994), p. 95.

and methods of history. For all the attention on these concepts, though, it soon became apparent that educators did not have a clear understanding of what they referred to, let alone how they could be developed. In some places, they appeared in and disappeared from educational discussions and policies with relatively little fuss. In other places, such as Britain, they came under increasing public scrutiny and were used by conservatives as evidence of the emptiness and invalidity of the 'new' ('method-centred') approach to history education. In chapter one I chart the rise and fall of re-enactment, historical imagination, empathy and sympathy in British educational policy and discourse from the 1960s to mid-1990s, identify some of the underlying factors, and note the role of Collingwood as a frequently-cited name in those developments.

Educators commonly associate Collingwood's name with these concepts. This connection is made, however, on the basis of only a slight knowledge of Collingwood's writings. Few educators have ventured beyond page 218 of *The Idea of History* or page 111 of *An Autobiography* to establish whether Collingwood used all of those terms, what he meant by the ones he did use, and whether he saw them as linked. In chapter two, I argue that while Collingwood was not as careful in his writing as Dray would like, he was certainly not careless in his choice and connection of terms. I begin by describing philosophical and literary works on empathy and sympathy that predate Collingwood, and suggest some reasons why he avoided the use of those terms in association with his own historiographical views. Our attention then shifts to an explanation of Collingwood's requirement that re-enactment entails the historian having *the same* thought as the historical agent. Analogical and intuitionist explanations are rejected in favour of the conceptual view proposed by Saari, but to that will be added further evidence from Collingwood's unpublished manuscripts. Of particular interest will be his commentary on Aristotle's *De Anima* (1913–14), his lectures on metaphysics from 1935 and 'The Principles of History'. Moreover, it will be shown that Collingwood's views on re-enactment are best understood in the light of his writings on language, mind and 'reading'. Along the way I identify commonalities in Collingwood and Wittgenstein's later writings on mind and language. This will be the first of a number of occasions where I hope to show that Wittgenstein is perhaps not the ahistorical antithesis of Collingwood that some commentators have taken him to be.

In chapter three, I extend our analysis of the conceptual view of re-enactment, asking what in history is open to it. In particular, I use

'The Principles of History' to refute the common view of
Collingwood as offering a narrow, rational, individualistic view of
history. Re-enactment applies to the reasonable and unreasonable
activities and emotions of both specified and non-specified historical agents. Additionally, I explain why Collingwood saw emotions
as connected with thought. Taking stock of his views, I then draw
out and critically examine the suggestion in Collingwood's writings
that humans might be able to re-enact the experiences of non-human
animals. I then look to Collingwood's understanding of philosophy,
and argue in agreement with Boucher that re-enactment can allow
historians to gain access to the fundamental assumptions or 'presuppositions' that shape the activities of historical agents. Here again
we find concordance between Collingwood and Wittgenstein, not
just on the nature and roles of presuppositions, but also in the
endorsement of a temporal foundationalism. As we shall discover,
though, Collingwood departs from Wittgenstein in being unwilling
to restrict philosophy to a retrospective descriptive role. Points of
similarity and difference between Collingwood's constellations of
presuppositions, Kuhn's paradigms and Foucault's notions of the
epistêmê and *archive* are also noted.

Before moving on to explore the relationship between re-enactment and the historical imagination in Collingwood's writings, in
chapter four I offer a survey of theories of imagination and historical
imagination from Plato to Derrida. This serves a dual purpose,
showing first the context of Collingwood's ideas, and second the
importance of Hayden White's argument for the analysis of both the
content *and* form of theories, including those on the imagination. In
chapter five, Collingwood's concepts of imagination and historical
imagination are unpacked. What we find is neither a collection of
activities bound by an equally present essence nor a network of
overlapping similarities, but a cumulative scale of forms in which
autonomous, dutiful reason is at least minimally present. Looking
across Collingwood's writings, four forms of imagination are identified: imaging, pure or free, perceptual and historical. Importantly,
all of these forms are to be found in the activities of ordinary people,
not just exceptional adults. At the top of the scale is the historical
imagination, for this, to Collingwood, best epitomises autonomous
reason at present. Here again we see Collingwood's affirmation of
temporal foundationalism. Thus for him, I argue, the historical
imagination is the imagination. Further, I show that while
re-enactment might be a part of the historical imagination, it is
certainly not synonymous with it.

In chapter six, our field of analysis widens further as I locate Collingwood's ideas on imagination within his vision of education and society. Collingwood wrote little directly on education, but as I argue, his works are infused with an educational purpose. To Collingwood, education is a process of socialisation that has as its endpoint freedom of the will and an historical civilisation. Students are to be guided through the various forms of experience — art, religion, science and 'history/philosophy' — which embody various forms of rational conduct. These forms of experience and of rational conduct — utilitarian, regularian and dutiful — are both arranged as a cumulative scale of forms. Dutiful action is characterised by autonomous reasoning, a commitment to foster freedom of the will in others and ourselves and freedom from capriciousness and insincerity. Particular attention is given to the experience of history/philosophy and the imagination, which are identified as the epitome and mainspring of rational development respectively. I also stress that history/philosophy is not necessarily synonymous with a particular discipline or curriculum subject, but refers more to a rational, autonomous orientation towards the world and an awareness of the temporal foundations of the human form and forms of life. Experience of history/philosophy is not restricted to institutional education or controlled by professional educators or historians. Everyone is capable of experiencing history/philosophy, but moreover, in Collingwood's view, they have a duty to do so. This is the reasoning behind his request that we should all ask 'How good an historian shall I be?'

After a critical examination of Collingwood's suggestion that parents ought to be the primary providers of education, we then return to where we began, with a consideration of Collingwood's ideas on education in the context of recent educational developments. This time, though, Collingwood is treated as more than a name or the provider of advice on the particular curriculum subject of history. Rather, we look to the influential curriculum innovations of Hirst, Bruner and Bloom and argue that Collingwood's commitment to history, the imagination and the creation of a social, global community is unmatched. In the conclusion, I reiterate Collingwood's challenge to current notions of history education, including public history education.

Chapter I
History in Peril

'The only thing we learned about King Alfred was about him burning the cakes' said Lewis.

'That's something though, isn't it? It's a fact — perhaps it's a fact. But they don't go in for facts in History these days. They go in for empathy, Lewis. Whatever that is.'[1]

History has long been in peril: ancient and modern writers alike complain that we are in danger of losing our connection with the past. Up until the latter half of the twentieth century, these complaints implied that there had been a problem either in the transmission or reception of historical content such as facts. In the 1960s, however, history and history education in the West took a turn towards epistemology, and 'peril' came to signal the potential loss of both specific historical knowledge and the methods of acquiring, organising and communicating that knowledge.[2] History, it was argued, could not be understood without an appreciation of the nature, origins and limits of historical knowledge. Students were thus to be trained to practise history as professionals did: they 'were "to do" history, not merely receive it'.[3] Advocates of this 'new' approach to the teaching of history drew on a wide range of ideas from historians, philosophers and psychologists and wrote not only of historical thinking, skills, understanding and judgement, but also of empathy and imagination. That empathy and the imagination were considered part of the historian's craft was counter-intuitive to many, for these concepts are commonly connected with the emotions, fantasy and invention. Educators from around the world contributed to what became an increasingly lively discussion on the

[1]   Colin Dexter, *The Jewel That was Ours* (London, 1991), p. 364.
[2]   See for example M. Price, 'History in Danger', *History*, 1968, vol. 53(179), p. 342; and M.B. Booth, *History Betrayed?* (London, 1969).
[3]   D. Sylvester, 'Change and Continuity in History Teaching 1900-93', in H. Bourdillon (ed.), *Teaching History* (London, 1994), p. 16.

nature and role of empathy and imagination in history education. It was in Britain alone, though, that empathy and imagination became touchstones for history education. There, empathy and imagination were held up as a test for the validity of curriculum policies and materials and used to designate where educators stood in a perceived dichotomy between 'traditional' ('fact-centred') and 'new' ('method-centred') history. In this chapter, we chart the rise and fall of empathy and the imagination in British educational discourse and policy after 1960 and assess the place of R.G. Collingwood's ideas in that discourse. Although Collingwood is a popular reference point for history educators, it will be argued throughout this work that their interaction with his ideas has only been superficial.

Handbook for History Teachers

Until the 1960s, history teaching in the United Kingdom was underpinned by a 'traditional' methodology in which teachers gave verbal, textbook or blackboard versions of events to students to copy and to memorise. Other methodologies were advanced, but they received little attention.[4] Consequently, advice for history teachers in handbooks took the form of discussions on what content could or ought to be taught, as in the thirty-two-date 'alphabet of history' suggested in the Board of Education's *Report on the Teaching of History* (1923).[5] It is hardly surprising, then, that when William Burston opened his *Handbook for History Teachers* (1964) with a discussion on the purpose of history teaching, he felt it necessary to apologise for writing on 'so theoretical a subject.'[6] Burston was not the first person to write on the purpose of history education. What made his effort different, however, was the suggestion that history education should be shaped in content *and* form by the ideas of historiographers and analytical philosophers of history like Marc Bloch (*The Historian's Craft*, 1954), W.H. Walsh (*An Introduction to Philosophy of History*, 1951), W.H. Dray (*Laws and Explanation in History*, 1957) and R.G. Collingwood (*The Idea of History*, 1946). Burston's own debt to Collingwood — the only one of these authors who focused on the historical imagination — is clear from his conclusion:

> . . . history is essentially an imaginative study — a reconstruction of a past which is gone and cannot be directly inspected or perceived — and

---

[4]   *Ibid.*, p. 12.
[5]   Board of Education, *Report on the Teaching of History*, Pamphlet 37 (London, 1923), appendix.
[6]   W.H. Burston, 'The Place of History in Education', in W.H. Burston and C.W. Green (eds), *Handbook for History Teachers* (London, 1964), p. 1.

... the process of studying it is a process of living in imagination in some past age.[7]

Imagination, he suggested, allows us to recognise artefacts as evidence of a particular event, and to synthesise such evidence into a 'reconstruction of a past'. Imagination was so central to his vision of history that he characterised different kinds of syllabus (chronological, line of development, detailed 'patches' and concept-based) according to the role that it plays in each.[8] In so arguing, Burston not only directed teachers away from competing philosophical writings that modelled themselves on philosophy of science, he also highlighted features of historical knowledge that could be used by teachers and policy makers who were concerned that history was going to be subsumed by the social studies.[9] More specifically, he made teachers aware that there was historiographical scholarship on the 'historical imagination', a move that virtually ensured references to Collingwood in nearly all future educational writings on the subject.

Burston's historiographical approach coalesced well with new curriculum models suggested by the philosopher Paul Hirst and psychologists Jerome Bruner and Benjamin Bloom. In the 1960s, Paul Hirst and Richard Peters argued that education should be seen as a matter of rational initiation into the knowledge and values of Western liberal culture.[10] Sketching out the epistemological component of the theory, Hirst argued that:

... the domain of human knowledge can be seen to be differentiated into a number of logically distinct 'forms', none of which is ultimately reducible in character to any of the others, either simply or in combination.[11]

These forms of knowledge — identified as logico-mathematical, scientific, moral, historical, aesthetic, religious, and philosophical — are not 'collections of information, but the complex ways of understanding experience which man has achieved'.[12] They each have distinctive concepts, ways of utilising and articulating those concepts, ways of adducing evidence in support of propositions and of establishing their validity, and characteristic ways of conducting investi-

[7]   *Ibid.*, p. 11.
[8]   *Ibid.*, pp. 34, 44–56, 64–5. See also id., *Sixth Form History Teaching*, Teaching of History leaflet no. 17 (London, 1957).
[9]   See for example M. Price, 'History in Danger', pp. 342–7; R. Moore, 'History and Integrated Studies: Surrender or Survival?', *Teaching History*, no. 18 (1974), pp. 109–11; and M.B. Booth, *History Betrayed?*
[10] See for example P.H. Hirst and R.S. Peters, *The Logic of Education* (London, 1970).
[11] P.H. Hirst, 'Liberal Education and the Nature of Knowledge' [1965], *Knowledge and the Curriculum* (London, 1974), p. 84.
[12] *Ibid.*, p. 40.

gations, generating hypotheses, and asserting statements. The implications of Hirst's view of the curriculum are fairly clear: syllabuses or courses of study must introduce students to all the forms. As history is one such form, it has a place in the curriculum, but Hirst does not require that it be a separate subject. Interestingly, Hirst's ideas were nevertheless influential in the construction of distinct subject curricula like the National Curriculum.

Jerome Bruner, too, believed that the curriculum should be based on the fundamental principles that give shape to 'history' as historians understand it. His, however, was a more dynamic model. Bruner held that any subject can be taught in some effective form to any child at any stage of development. His 'spiral curriculum' suggested that one can start with fundamental notions about a subject and progressively expand to greater detail, and ultimately to abstract descriptions. This building block approach revisits basic ideas over and over again, building upon them until the student fully grasps the complete process.[13] Benjamin Bloom's contribution was to offer a taxonomy of knowledge and skills that teachers could use to construct history syllabuses that attended to cognitive, affective (emotional) and psychomotor (physical) development.[14] Although there are important differences between the ideas of Hirst, Bruner and Bloom, they are not mutually exclusive, for they have been combined, and continue to be combined, in various ways.

Educational Objectives for the Study of History

The first place we see these theories tied with the historiographical approach suggested by Burston is in Jeanette Coltham and John Fines's *Educational Objectives for the Study of History* (1971), a pamphlet that is still considered influential today.[15] Coltham and Fines aimed to encapsulate the form of history education in a framework of behavioural 'objectives': descriptions of observable behaviours that result from an educational experience. Within the framework, objectives are divided into those describing 'attitudes towards the study of history', 'the nature of the discipline', 'skills and abilities' and 'educational outcomes of study' and are further matched against Bloom's cognitive, affective and psychomotor domains.

[13]   J.S. Bruner, *The Process of Education* (New York, 1960), p. 31.
[14]   B. Bloom, *Taxonomy of Educational Objectives: the Classification of Educational Goals* (2 vols., London, 1956–64).
[15]   J. Coltham and J. Fines, *Educational Objectives for the Study of History*, pamphlet 35 (Saffron Walden, 1971). On its influence, see J. Nichol, 'Who wants to Fight? Who wants to Flee?: Teaching History from a "Thinking Skills" Perspective', *Teaching History*, no. 95 (1999), pp. 6–13.

And alongside objectives sub-categories for analysis, judgement, memorisation and comprehension may be found 'imagining'. The term 'historical imagination', they note:

> [Is] sometimes used in framing objectives; more refined definition of what is required from the learner can help to make objectives, and thence classroom practice, more precise.[16]

Their own attempts at definition, though, resulted in a mixed bag of descriptions. 'Imagining' is described variously as an affective (emotional) motivational behaviour that acts upon the acquisition of skills, abilities and content, a voluntary attitude, the power to entertain mental images, the 'ability to breathe life into an assembly of many small pieces of evidence' and empathy. Empathy is introduced as 'entering into another's personality' and distinguished from sympathy, which is 'entering into another's feelings or mind'.[17] It is not clear what more there is to 'personality' than 'feelings or mind' or indeed what the meaning of 'breathe life' is. Nor is their account of the behaviours that an imaginative student demonstrates any more precise. Such a student, they suggested:

> Describes an historical incident with signs of personal involvement; Constructs a story about a period in which characters are portrayed in the round; Peoples an historic building with characters who are true in action and thought to the particular period; Represents in dramatic form feelings and actions according to human experience and historical evidence; and Identifies with a character under study so as to be able to declare the view-point of this character on problems (etc.) contemporary to him/her.[18]

Readers must surely have wondered what 'portrayed in the round', 'true in action and thought', 'dramatic form' and 'identifies' meant. Further, they were given no indication of how these activities of imagination are related to one another.

Nevertheless, teachers, inspectors and examiners took up Coltham and Fines's taxonomy for history education with much enthusiasm. Frequent references to the framework can be found in issues of *Teaching History* throughout the 1970s. The strength of this approach to teaching history was that the methodological concepts valued by advocates of 'new' history (e.g. historical judgement, understanding, thinking and imagination) were located in a blueprint that teachers could use to construct courses, assess students and clarify their thinking on the aims they hoped to achieve. Despite

---

[16] J. Coltham and J. Fines, *Educational Objectives for the Study of History*, p. 7.

[17] *Ibid.*, pp. 4–8.

[18] *Ibid.*, p. 8.

the attractions of the framework, however, four major objections emerged. First, writers like Gard and Lee warned of accepting the objectives approach to course design without criticism. History education, they believed, could be reduced to a collection of skills and behaviours.[19] Despite their warning, Fines noted in 1981 that many teachers had in the previous decade plundered historiographical and psychological works for descriptions of skills and methodological concepts.[20] Second, Moore argued that Coltham and Fines's presentation of skills such as 'comprehension', 'analysis' and 'synthesis' as generic did little to help those educators desperate to secure the place of history in the curriculum.[21] Third, Lee questioned a basic assumption of the framework: that history students could demonstrate the same behaviours and skills as historians. He wrote:

> Historical investigation and specific questions generally have their origins in the current state of the discipline as perceived by its practitioners; history is not just the common sense enquiry of anyone with an antiquarian curiosity.[22]

In so arguing, Lee connected the framework to the increasingly lively debate on whether school history should be organised along the lines that students learn to do what historians do.[23] Fourth, Gard and Lee doubted the adequacy and clarity of Coltham and Fines's description of the nature of history, and called for more attention to be devoted to the task.[24] Hardly a murmur of complaint, though, was heard on whether Coltham and Fines might have ascribed too much to the imagination, thus overstretching the concept. On this point, Fines was her own harshest critic, noting ten years later that 'imagining' and 'empathy' required further thought and clarification.[25]

Schools Council History Projects

Fines was not the only educator to be troubled by 'empathy' and 'imagination' at that time, as the Schools Council History Projects

[19] A. Gard and P.J. Lee, '"Educational Objectives for the Study of History" Reconsidered', in A.K. Dickinson and P.J. Lee (eds), *History Teaching and Historical Understanding* (London, 1978), pp. 21–38.
[20] J. Fines, 'Educational Objectives for the Study of History — Ten Years On', *Teaching History*, no. 30 (1981), pp. 8–10.
[21] R. Moore, 'History and Integrated Studies', p. 110.
[22] P.J. Lee, 'History Teaching and Philosophy of History', *History and Theory*, Vol. 22 (4) (1983), p. 29.
[23] See for example P.J. Rogers, *The New History: Theory into Practice* (London, 1978) and D. Gunning, *The Teaching of History* (London, 1978).
[24] A. Gard and P.J. Lee, '"Educational Objectives for the Study of History" Reconsidered', pp. 24–5.
[25] J. Fines 'Educational Objectives for the Study of History — Ten Years On', p. 8.

show. In the 1960s, much curriculum development was undertaken in Britain. The Nuffield Science and Mathematics Projects offered teachers new activities and resources, the Newsom and Plowden reports questioned whether the needs of all students were being met and studies were undertaken to see if there could be a single system of exams in history for all students aged sixteen and over.[26] By 1972, too, the Schools Council agreed to fund projects in history for primary and secondary students: 'History, Geography and Social Science 8–13'(HGSS8–13) and 'History 13–16'.[27] While these projects differed fundamentally in their location of history in the curriculum — as a part of the social sciences at primary level, as a separate subject at secondary level — they shared the same aims. First, it was assumed that history was a 'form of knowledge', and that courses of study should initiate students into the distinct concepts, logic and methods of that form. For guidance, teachers were to look to the ideas of historiographers and philosophers of history.[28] Second, it was claimed that the skills and concepts acquired through the study of history were valuable for all students, not just those who wanted to go to university. Third, the projects suggested a wider, more inclusive view of the past. Students were to be encouraged to look not only at the experiences of the elite, but also ordinary men and women. Further, they were to be encouraged to test the relevance of what they learned by connecting the past with present-day events and problems. And finally, both projects suggested that students approach the past as professional historians do. That is, students were not just to be receptors for information: they were to be encouraged to acquire concepts and skills that would help them to make sense of that information. In this aim, the projects questioned the prevailing Piagetian assumption that history requires levels of thinking that few students can achieve under the age of sixteen and reinforced Rogers' notion of the student historian.[29] On this point there was continuity with Coltham and Fines' suggestion that students could evidence the skills and behaviours of historians.

[26] Central Advisory Council for Education (England), *Half Our Future* (Newsom Report), (London, 1963); Central Advisory Council for Education (England), *Children and their Primary Schools: A Report* [Plowden Report] (London, 1967).

[27] See R. Wake, 'History as a Separate Discipline: The Case', *Teaching History*, no. 1 (1970), p. 3.

[28] V. Burkitt, J. Campbell and D. Lawton, *Social Studies 8–13*, Schools Council Paper 39 (London, 1971), pp. 1, 4–5; Schools Council, *A New Look at History*, Schools Council History 13–16 Project (Edinburgh, 1976), p. 8.

[29] See for example P.J. Rogers, *The New History: Theory into Practice*.

As part of this final aim, both primary and secondary students were to 're-enact' the past, 'empathise with the people concerned in any past situation' and develop 'imaginative thought'. In HGSS 8–13, 'imaginative' thought is characterised as the ability to:

> Find information through reading, listening, observing; understand and interpret pictures, charts, graphs, maps, etc.; organise information through concepts and generalisations; communicate findings through an appropriate medium, eg. orally, graphically, pictorially, or in writing; evaluate information; and test hypotheses and generalisations and question the adequacy of classification.[30]

On this description, it is clear that imagination has a valuable part to play in history education as a constellation of mental abilities like 'understanding', 'evaluating', 'communicating' and 'interpreting'. In other places, the historical imagination is described as empathy — 'appreciation and understanding of the behaviour of others on the basis of one's own experience and behaviour' — and as a generic social skill. Such an all-encompassing view of 'imaginative' is problematic: the term is stretched to cover so much that it threatens to mean very little. At best, the result is a view in which the imagination is a clearing-house where information is received, organised and distributed. Teachers, however, were offered little practical guidance on how to foster and assess the development of this clearing-house. Nor could this meta-cognitive view of imagination be reconciled with the immediate, affective, motivational view of Coltham and Fines. It is thus hardly surprising that on empathy and imagination at least, HGSS8–13 led to much confusion. Such confusion is evident in the lesson evaluations of Mary Baranowski, whose work was presented by the Schools Council in 1974 as an exemplar of the project.[31] In her evaluation of a unit on medieval towns, for instance, she wrote:

> The main skills were on the intellectual side, this is what I tried to emphasise . . . The children are well 'socialised' and they work well together in pairs or groups but I would doubt if we got far with empathy.[32]

It is clear from this that Baranowski did not see empathy as either a cognitive skill or a generic social skill, as was suggested in the project materials. On this point she differed from other evaluators of the project like Cooper and Blyth, who saw empathy as bringing

---

[30]   V. Burkitt, J. Campbell and D. Lawton, *Social Studies 8–13*, pp. 4–5.

[31]   M. Baranowski, *A Pilgrim's Progress Through the Project*, Schools Council Occasional Paper no. 2 (London, 1974).

[32]   *Ibid.*, p. 8.

together cognitive and affective skills.[33] Baranowski also appeared unsure about how to recognise it for the purpose of assessment. For example, in her evaluation of a unit on the Reformation, she recalled that students:

> ... seem[ed] to be a lot of little Englanders who liked doing the Reformation but saw little purpose in learning about 'foreigners'.

Yet she still concludesd'Yes — empathy most definitely achieved'.[34] Nor did Baranowski have anything to say about the imagination other than in the form of empathy, which is surprising given the wide role attributed to it by the project.

In the 1975 revision of the project, 'Place, Time and Society 8–13' (PTS8–13), the writers declared that one of their aims was to clarify the meaning of imagination and empathy. It is doubtful, however, whether their descriptions offered much of an advance. As with HGSS8–13, the imagination is again cast in the role of a meta-cognitive clearing-house:

> [It] is much more than vague benevolence, for it involves intellectual as well as social skills and also attributes. In fact, it links together a number of the Project's objectives and for this reason the project has given particular emphasis to it.[35]

Nothing more is said on how the imagination draws many of the Project's objectives together, how it develops and how it is to be recognised and thus assessed. Empathy is also defined in a similar fashion to that of HGSS8–13, as the capacity to 'imagine accurately what it would be like to be someone else'.[36] They depart from the suggestion in HGSS8–13 that empathy is a generic social skill, however, as is clear from this excerpt:

> Sometimes, indeed, there is little more than a pious assumption that children who work together will like each other and then come to understand the Tibetans or Sumerians better.[37]

Readers were not enlightened as to the differences between historical empathy and empathy *per se*. Rather, they were offered advice on the distinction between *pseudo* and *genuine* historical empathy: *pseudo* empathy is a 'simple, comfortable level of understanding that

[33] A. Blyth, *Curriculum Planning in History, Geography and Social Science* (Glasgow, 1975), p. 119; K. Cooper, *Evaluation, Assessment and Record Keeping in History, Geography and Social Science* (Glasgow, 1976), p. 36.
[34] *Ibid.*, p. 27.
[35] Schools Council, *Place, Time and Society 8–13: An Introduction* (Bristol, 1975), pp. 21.
[36] *Ibid.*, p. 10.
[37] *Ibid.*

stands as an impediment to genuine empathy', while *genuine* empathy involves 'accurately imagining what it would be like to be someone else'.[38] Nothing more was said about what 'accurately imagining' entails or how it might be fostered in the classroom. Nor were teachers offered advice on how students were to achieve the recommended 'cognitive detachment' when faced with the task of empathising with those thought to be morally indefensible. This was despite the fact that the Schools Council clearly knew that empathy was causing teachers great concern. For example, in the introduction to the project, it was acknowledged that:

> [Empathy requires] a combination of intellectual and attitudinal objectives that many adults find difficult. Such empathy is likely to confront teachers of middle-years children with one of the most demanding challenges.[39]

Teachers might also have found it hard to comprehend the criteria used to divide the particular units of study in the support document *Themes in Outline* into those which promote the study of empathy and those which do not. Casting a critical eye over the list, the connection of some units with empathy appears arbitrary. Why, for instance, does the study of roads promote empathy, but the study of family life does not?

If we look at the three major statements on history education available to primary teachers from 1971 to 1985 — *Educational Objectives for the Study of History*, HGSS 8–13 and PTS 8–13 — it is clear that they all have in common the decision to accord the imagination and empathy a central role. Further, all three describe the imagination as the means by which various skills are brought to work upon evidence of the past. How it does so, how it develops and how it is to be assessed are not specified. It is also worth noting that all three projects follow writers like Gosden and Sylvester in suggesting that empathy is an 'aspect of imagination' but do not articulate the nature of that relationship.[40] Lack of clarification on these issues, coupled with contradictory advice on whether the imagination and empathy were intellectual, affective, social or generic skills must have made practical implementation difficult.

In a number of instances, primary educators sought direction from secondary school projects and articles in professional journals and magazines. What they found, however, was a similar state of

[38] *Ibid.*
[39] *Ibid.*, p. 21.
[40] P. H. Gosden and D. W. Sylvester, *History for the Average Child* (Oxford, 1968), p. 8.

confusion. The first stop for primary educators was the Schools Council history project, 'History 13–16'. In that project, empathy is characterised as a vicarious experience made possible by the interaction between imagination and evidence:

> Analysis and judgement must be illumined by imagination to provide the understanding of people of the past that characterises the historian's perspective. [The student] has to be able to enter into the mind and feelings of all the persons involved in an event and appreciate their differing attitudes without necessarily approving of their motives if he is to understand why, given their situation, they acted as they did. The important point to note here, however, is that the imagination must be disciplined by the evidence available.[41]

Such a description assumes that empathy is part of the tool kit of all historians, and thus that any curriculum interested in the methods and content of history must accord it a role. In the project's aims, this assumption was reinforced through the presentation of empathy as a requirement for all students and as an integral part of all segments of study.[42] As with the primary projects, however, nothing further was said on how this tool is to be developed and assessed, even though there was awareness of the problems that empathy posed, as Denis Shemilt's evaluation of the project shows:

> Such aims as 'appreciation of empathetic reconstruction as a historical method' can only begin to be reduced to even very general objectives once the natural history of adolescent understanding of 'empathy' has been provisionally documented.[43]

Logically, then, in Shemilt's view, it seemed that the way forward to pedagogical clarity with 'empathy' lay with study and research into child and adolescent development, the province of psychology. Philosophical and historiographical works by writers like Collingwood and Burston were seen as having stimulated interest in the concept, but frameworks of cognitive development were needed to flesh it out. Philosophy and historiography were thus cast as preliminary to psychology, something to be consulted before getting onto the business of describing stages of development. Consequently, one finds more reference to psychological research than to philosophy in educational discussions on empathy in the mid-1970s to mid-1980s. Why educators did not pursue philosophical clarifica-

---

[41] Schools Council, *A New Look at History* (Edinburgh, 1976), p. 41.
[42] Schools Council, *Explorations in Teaching Schools Council Projects: History 13–16* (Leeds, 1980), p. 7; D. Shemilt, *History 13–16: Evaluation Study* (Edinburgh, 1980), p. 5.
[43] Schools Council, *Explorations in Teaching Schools Council Projects*, p. 108.

tion in a more sustained fashion is an issue to which we will return at the conclusion of this chapter.

In contemporary psychological research, empathy was characterised generally as the consideration of the experiences of one person by another. Within that research, Davis notes, a distinction was drawn between what are seen as two distinct kinds of consideration: cognitive or intellectual and visceral or emotional. The research of Dymond, Kerr, Speroff and Borke are examples of the former and Stotland, Bryant, Mehrabian and Epstein, Matthews, Sherman, Hansson and Richardson, and Aderman and Berkowitz of the latter.[44] A smaller number of writers, like Davis, Deutsch and Madle, Hoffman, and Feshbach and Roe saw it as containing both components (multidimensional view).[45] There was, however, and still is no consensus on which of these views ought to be adopted by psychologists and thus educators. Nor was there any agreement on how to assess empathy,[46] on whether the development of empathy is a linear, additive process,[47] whether there are gender differences in development[48] and whether empathy correlates with prosocial behaviours

[44]   H. Borke, 'Interpersonal Perception of Young Children: Egocentrism or Empathy?', *Developmental Psychology*, Vol. 5 (2) (1971), pp. 263–9; R.F. Dymond, 'A Scale for Measurement of Empathic Skill', *Journal of Consulting Psychology*, Vol. 14 (1) (1949), pp. 127–33; A. Mehrabian and N. Epstein, 'A Measure of Emotional Empathy', *Journal of Personality*, Vol. 40 (4) (1972), pp. 525–43; D. Aderman and L. Berkowitz, 'Observational Set, Empathy and Helping', *Journal of Personality and Social Psychology*, Vol. 14 (1) (1970), pp. 141–8; E. Stotland, 'Exploratory Investigations of Empathy' in L. Berkowitz (ed.), *Advances in Experimental Psychology*, Vol. 4 (New York, 1969).

[45]   M. Davis, 'Measuring Individual Differences in Empathy: Evidence for a Multidimensional Approach', *Journal of Personality and Social Psychology*, Vol. 44 (1) (1983), pp. 113–26; F. Deutsch and R. Madle, 'Empathy: Historic and Current Conceptualizations, Measurement and a Cognitive Theoretical Perspective', *Human Development*, Vol. 18 (2) (1975), pp. 267–87; M.L. Hoffman, 'Empathy, its Development and Prosocial Implications', in C.B. Kearsey (ed.), *Nebraska Symposium on Motivation*, Vol. 25 (Lincoln, 1977), pp. 169–218; and N. Feshbach and K. Roe, 'Empathy in Six- and Seven-Year Olds', *Child Development*, Vol. 39 (1) (1968), pp. 133–45.

[46]   See for example N. Eisenberg and R. Lennon, 'Sex Differences in Empathy and Related Capacities', *Psychological Bulletin*, Vol. 94 (1) (1983), p. 102.

[47]   See for example, R.F. Marcus, S. Telleen and E. Roke, 'Relation Between Cooperation and Empathy in Young Children', *Developmental Psychology*, Vol. 15 (3) (1979), pp. 346–47; and B.K. Bryant, 'An Index of Empathy for Children and Adolescents', *Child Development*, Vol. 53 (3) (1982), pp. 413–25.

[48]   For reviews of the research, see E.E. Maccoby and C.N. Jacklin, *The Psychology of Sex Differences* (Stanford, 1974); J.H. Block, 'Assessing Sex Differences: Issues, Problems, and Pitfalls', *Merrill-Palmer Quarterly*, Vol. 22 (2) (1976), pp. 283–308; M.L. Hoffman, 'Sex Differences in Empathy and Related Behaviours', *Psychological Bulletin*, Vol. 54 (4) (1977), pp. 712–22; and N. Eisenberg and R. Lennon, 'Sex Differences in Empathy and Related Capacities'.

like altruism.[49] Interestingly, too, none of the psychological papers from this time present empathy as an aspect of imagination.

That psychological scholarship had no clear messages or suggestions of direction regarding empathy is evident from writings on the topic in professional educational publications. Almost all of the papers and book chapters concerning empathy and the historical imagination in education between 1975 and 1985 have in common both the assumption that empathy and the imagination ought to be developed in all students and the argument that multiple and conflicting meanings of these terms make pedagogical design and assessment difficult. Where the differences emerge is in strategies to deal with what Boddington calls this 'portmanteau of meanings'.[50] In *An Experiment in Empathy* (1972), for instance, Natale opted for a multidimensional view and concluded that empathy is best achieved not through direct training but though a programme of 'critical thinking'.[51] Portal also held a multidimensional view, but believed that critical thinking programmes are insufficient for the development of empathy. He argued for the 'dramatization' of history education through improvisation and the use of visual objects like material evidence, pictures and films.[52] Boddington, in turn, argued that the individuality of emotional experiences and the difficulty of reading such experiences in observable behaviour make an affective or multidimensional view of the concept unworkable. He argued in favour of what Gribble and Oliver identify as 'predictive' empathy: understanding experiences from another's point of view.[53] This does not mean 'becoming' that person, involvement, sympathy, identification or portrayal but the reconstruction and consideration of the *reasons* for a person's feeling, thinking and acting as they did.[54] Thompson disagreed with Boddington, suggesting

[49] See for example M.L. Hoffman, 'Developmental Synthesis of Affect and Cognition and its Implications for Altruistic Motivation', *Developmental Psychology*, Vol. 11 (4) (1975), pp. 602–22; and K.H.M. Knudson and S. Kagan, 'Differential Development of Empathy and Prosocial Behaviour', *The Journal of Genetic Psychology*, no. 140 (1982), pp. 249–51.

[50] T. Boddington, 'Empathy and the Teaching of History', *British Journal of Educational Studies*, Vol. 28 (1) (1980) pp. 13–18.

[51] S. Natale, *An Experiment in Empathy* (Slough, 1972), p. 68.

[52] C. Portal, 'Empathy as an Aim for the Curriculum: Lessons from History', *Journal of Curriculum Studies*, Vol. 15 (3) (1983), pp. 303–10. See also J. Fines and R. Verrier, *The Drama of History* (London, 1974).

[53] J. Gribble and G. Oliver, 'Empathy and Education', *Studies in Philosophy in Education*, Vol. 8 (1) (1973), p. 23. See also C. Bailey, 'Knowledge of Others and Concern for Others', in J. Elliott and R. Pring (eds.), *Social Education and Social Understanding* (London, 1975).

[54] T. Boddington, 'Empathy and the Teaching of History', pp. 15–6, 18.

that the key to empathy is identification — 'we become, temporarily, the whole person involved in the situation' — and that it is best developed through drama, role play, films, museum visits and music.[55] Thompson also saw empathy as a transferable social skill, whereas Boddington did not.[56] Portal believed that it is possible to develop empathy for people we abhor, Lee did not.[57] The list of differences goes on and on. Neither could teachers mix and match elements from each of these views, as some cannot be reconciled.

Additionally, relatively little was said on imagination in history or 'the historical imagination' in the professional literature. Three papers stand out: John Fine's 'Imagination and the Historian', Vivienne Little's 'What is Historical Imagination?' and Peter Lee's 'Historical Imagination'.[58] Notably, all three look in the main to philosophical and historiographical works for information, a different approach to that for empathy. For instance, leaning heavily on Collingwood, Little proposed that every historian's account of the past is 'imaginary in every detail' because the past cannot be relived, only constructed in imagination by the drawing together of pieces of evidence into an explanation or interpretation.[59] Looking to Mary Warnock, however, she claimed to extend Collingwood's view in two ways. First, she suggested that the historical imagination is involved in the very act of 'seeing' something as evidence of the past and thus that it is a form of mental imaging; and, second, she claimed that Collingwood's overly rational view of imagination — like that of other contemporary writers — is unconvincing, for excellent history is the result of the 'feeling intellect'. We will return to Little's claim to have extended Collingwood in chapter five. Additionally, she described empathy as an imaginative activity and suggested that the following definition could remedy some of the contemporary confusion about the term:

> It is simply not possible to think another's thoughts or feel another's feel-
> ings. What one does it to imagine or entertain the thoughts and feelings

[55] F. Thompson, 'Empathy: An Aim and a Skill to be Developed', *Teaching History*, no. 37 (1983), pp. 22–6.

[56] *Ibid.*, and T. Boddington, 'Empathy and the Teaching of History', p. 15.

[57] C. Portal, 'Empathy as an Aim for Curriculum', p. 307; P.J. Lee, 'Explanation and Understanding in History', in A.K. Dickinson and P.J. Lee (eds.), *History Teaching and Historical Understanding* (London, 1978), p. 74.

[58] V. Little, 'What is Historical Imagination?', *Teaching History*, no. 36 (1983), p. 27–32; and P.J. Lee, 'Historical Imagination' in A.K. Dickinson, P.J. Rogers and P.J. Lee (eds.), *Learning History* (London, 1984), pp. 85–116.

[59] R.G. Collingwood, *The Idea of History*, p. 245; as quoted in V. Little, 'What is Historical Imagination?', p. 27.

one supposes him to have. The activity is therefore cognitive, though the impulse stirring one to it . . . is affective.[60]

In alignment with both Collingwood and Little, Lee considered the historian's account of the past to be a construction of the imagination in interaction with the evidence. Further, Lee connected empathy with the historical imagination and agreed with Little that it entails entertaining the views of historical agents. He stopped short, however, of endorsing the connection of Collingwood to Warnock on the grounds that mental imaging — even in the wide sense that Warnock employs — is not required in history and that the student's or historian's feelings are not required for successful imagining.[61] Fines, too, looked to Mary Warnock's book, but concluded that it left him 'completely baffled and convinced that somehow I had lost the power to read serious books'.[62] Fines put this down to his own inability — and perhaps that of other history teachers — to follow an argument. Following an argument is one thing; following multiple and contradictory arguments is quite another thing altogether. We will return to Warnock's account of imagination in chapters four and five.

GCSE and the National Criteria for History

By the mid-1980s, history education was perceived by educators as having embraced 'method' as well as 'fact'. Her Majesty's Inspectorate (HMI), for instance, expressed the view in a series of working papers that historical thinking cannot proceed without the identification, nurture and encouragement of specific attitudes such as 'an awareness of evidence; a sense of change and continuity; an interest in cause; and a degree of empathy'.[63] It also expressed doubts, however, about the substantiveness of the rationales and programmes in the Schools Council Projects and warned of the consequent weakness of courses.[64] The deterioration of local government expediture in the 1970s also fuelled calls for greater teacher accountability and a return to the solid ground of 'basics'. James Callaghan, the Labour Prime Minister, capitalised upon this mood in a speech at Ruskin College, Oxford, in 1977. In this he advocated a basic curriculum, accountable to parents and industry. Ministerial proposals and HMI

[60]   V. Little, 'What is Historical Imagination?', p. 30.
[61]   P.J. Lee, 'Historical Imagination', pp. 87, 94, n. 52.
[62]   J. Fines, 'Imagination and the Historian', p. 24.
[63]   Department of Education and Science (England) (hereafter DES), *Curriculum 11–16* (London, 1977), p. 49.
[64]   Her Majesty's Inspectorate (hereafter HMI), *Primary Education in England* (London, 1978), §§3.15.5, 3.17.6.

documents alike called for greater teacher accountability and centralisation.[65] Teacher input into bodies such as the Secondary Examinations Council and the School Curriculum Development
Committee was greatly diminished. Martin Booth sensed that the
'new' approach to history could lose ground, and urged teachers to
work together to clarify the meaning of important historiographical
concepts and the aims of school history.[66]

   The shift to centralisation came soon after, with the replacement of
the General Certificate of Education (GCE) and Certificate of Secondary Education (CSE) by a national system for the assessment of
14–16 year olds in ten subjects: the General Certificate of Secondary
Education (GCSE). Regional policies on history education in previous years often resulted, as we have seen, in piecemeal and contradictory advice. But they also gave teachers a high degree of freedom
to adopt and adapt ideas according to their views, needs and context. Centralisation of policy promised an end to gaps and contradictions and the concentration of resources into larger projects to clarify
the means and ends of history education. But it also meant an end to
the selective use of policies to suit: a 'one size fits all' curriculum had
to cover a disparate body of professionals. Consequently, with the
introduction of the GCSE small-scale disputes erupted into a
national debate and crystallised into a pitched battle between advocates of 'traditional' ('fact-centred') and 'new' ('method-centred')
history. Empathy was at the centre of this dispute.

   In 1985, *GCSE: The National Criteria: History* was published by the
DES. Although the authors of this document claimed that it represented a synthesis of 'traditional' and 'new' approaches, teachers
saw it as inclining to the latter. Much was made, for instance, of the
Examining Group's decision not to stipulate a core of content on the
grounds that it should 'provide a wide range of options to give freedom to innovate and to reflect local interests'.[67] Booth, Culpin and
Macintosh saw this as evidence of 'dissatisfaction with the
Gradgrind approach to teaching history', while Kedourie concluded
that it was one of the 'errors and evils of new history'.[68] Booth,
Culpin and Macintosh also saw the criteria leaning towards 'new'
history on the issue of empathy, even though the term is nowhere
used. They saw it as evident in the expectation that students 'show

---

[65] See for example DES, *A Framework for the School Curriculum* (London, 1980), p. 2;
       HMI, *A View of the Curriculum* (London, 1980), p. 17.
[66] M. Booth, 'Editorial', *Teaching History*, no. 27 (1980), pp. 2–3.
[67] DES, *GCSE: National Criteria: History* (London, 1985), §4.1.
[68] M. Booth, C. Culpin and H. Macintosh, *Teaching GCSE: History* (London, 1987),
       p. 9; H. Kedourie, *Errors and Evils of the New History* (London, 1988).

an ability to look at events and issues from the perspective of people in the past'[69] and concluded that its place in the curriculum was assured:

> There [is] not much point in discussing whether or not it can be done: the national criteria are perfectly plain, and all examinations at GCSE are required to test it.[70]

Nor did Booth, Culpin and Macintosh see it as their job to contribute to the debate on the nature and meaning of empathy. Instead, they referred readers to *Empathy in History: From Definition to Assessment*, published by the Southern Regional Examinations Board (SREB) in 1986. This pamphlet plotted a four-stage model of empathetic development, from 'information gathering' to 'everyday empathy' (present-day motives, feelings and attitudes applied to the past), to 'stereotypical historical empathy' (there is one point of view characteristic of a particular time) and then 'differentiated historical empathy' (different groups and individuals in the past had different points of view).[71] Only stages three and four represented historical empathy, while stages one and two are evidenced both inside and outside the history classroom. It is clear, then, that SREB placed a higher premium on activities to be found only in the curriculum subject of history. Stages two to four clearly represent an advance on the poorly described distinction between pseudo and genuine empathy in PTS8–13 and three and four expanded on the claim in History 13–16 that there is a form of empathy unique to history. Stage one, the active response to and arrangement of information also seemed to echo the account of the historical imagination forwarded by Little and Lee. The term 'imagination', however, was nowhere used, an absence explained by Booth, Culpin and Macintosh in the following way:

> It would be fair to say that the substantial work undertaken on teaching and assessing empathy in recent years has resulted in a slightly more utilitarian view being taken of it as a tool to illuminate motivations . . . This has to some degree downgraded the emphasis placed on imagination, which was once central, since we now recognise that however hard we try we cannot stand in someone else's shoes.[72]

Booth, Culpin and Macintosh evidently saw imagination as the unachievable top of a scale of empathetic contemplation, as actual re-enactment. There is no mention of the 'imaging' or arrangement

[69] DES, *GCSE: National Criteria: History*, §3.3.
[70] M. Booth et al, *Teaching GCSE: History*, p. 12.
[71] SREB, *Empathy in History: From Definition to Assessment* (London, 1986), pp. 1–8.
[72] M. Booth et al, *Teaching GCSE: History*, p. 26.

and understanding of information dimensions envisaged by Little and Lee. This view is also at odds with that presented in a contemporary document by HMI, *History in the Primary and Secondary Years*. There, empathy is 'simply a word used to described the imagination working on evidence, attempting to enter into a past while at the same time remaining outside it'.[73] This, in turn, is quite different from the pejorative 'flight of fancy' connotation given to imagination in *History From 5 to 16*, released by HMI in 1988.[74]

This is the tip of the contemporary debate on empathy in school history. More documents on empathy by educators can be found from the mid- to the late 1980s than earlier. Why? Centralisation of policy fostered belief in an apparent dichotomy between 'traditional' and 'new' history in which empathy was to be a testing ground. Validating or dismissing empathy thus became the key to validating or dismissing 'new' or 'traditional' history. With such a result apparently at stake, it should be of little surprise that the number of contributions to the debate on empathy increased or that they became more heated. In the main, contributions returned to issues raised in earlier discussions. Low-Beer and Ashby and Lee, for instance, disagreed about whether empathy belongs to the affective or cognitive domains.[75] Cairns opted for a multidimensional view but qualified that a 'strong intellect' can hinder empathy.[76] No consensus was achieved on this matter. Nor did writers agree on how empathy was to be clarified: Low-Beer opted for philosophical analysis, Cairns for psychological research. Cairns characterised it as a transferrable skill, Low-Beer as particular to history. No advance was made, either, on clarifying the relationship between the imagination and empathy. In contrast to Booth, Culpin and Macintosh and HMI (1988) Rogers and Simkin saw empathy as involving imagination because only 'a faculty for going beyond' the traces of the past can make historical accounts complete.[77] Cairns agreed that empathy implies imagination but saw the former as 'deeper' than the latter on the grounds that it works from the 'inside out' rather

---

[73] HMI, *History in the Primary and Secondary Years: An HMI View* (London, 1985), p. 2. See also p. 4.

[74] HMI, *History From 5 to 16* (London, 1988), p. 7.

[75] A. Low-Beer, 'Empathy and History', *Teaching History*, no. 55 (1989), pp. 8–12; R. Ashby and P. J. Lee, 'Children's Concepts of Empathy and Understanding', in C. Portal (ed.), *History in the Curriculum* (London, 1987).

[76] J. Cairns, 'Some Reflections on Empathy in History', *Teaching History*, no. 55 (1989), pp. 13–18.

[77] P.J. Rogers, *History: What and Why?* (London, 1987), p. 35; J. Simpkin, *Empathy in GCSE* (London, 1987), esp. p. 5.

than the 'outside in'. No further information was offered on the meaning of 'outside', 'inside', 'beyond' and 'incomplete'.[78]

Readers might have been forgiven for concluding that the discussion on empathy was going nowhere had it not been for two new points. First, Portal and Low-Beer raised the suggestion that empathy might be viewed as a useful part of the learning process, but not as assessable.[79] They thus called for a division between teaching programmes and exams, a division that went against the prevailing tradition of exam-tied policies in British education. Within that tradition, the only perceived ways of solving the 'empathy problem' were either to develop a workable, agreed system of assessment for it, or to remove it from teaching programmes altogether. Shemilt went for the former, outlining four criteria for the assessment of empathy: coherence, consonance, efficiency and parsimony. Coherence is seen in explanations that are internally consistent; consonance in an explanation that slots well into its historical context; efficiency in explanations that account for all the relevant evidence; and parsimony in the simplest explanation that also satisfies the other criteria.[80] While to some extent helpful, a survey of contemporary professional literature suggests that teachers were looking for far more detailed, stage-structured advice. Second, reflecting the linguistic turn of postmodernity, Jenkins and Brickley argued that the achievement of empathy is impossible because of the mediation of historians and history students. The past, they contended, cannot be reached, and the best knowledge we can have of it — history — is a construction by historians and students of history. They thus altered Collingwood's dictum that 'all history is the history of thought' to read 'all history is the history of historian's minds'.[81] Given contemporary concerns raised about the epistemological and ethical implications of the linguistic turn, one doubts whether teachers would have found this a promising line either.

Another feature marks out writings on empathy from the latter half of the 1980s as different: the intensity of negative responses to the concept and the treatment of it as equivalent to 'new' history. Among the critics of empathy, and thus 'new' history, the Centre for

[78] J. Cairns, 'Some Reflections on Empathy in History', p. 14.
[79] A. Low-Beer, 'Empathy and History', p. 11; C. Portal, 'Empathy as an Objective for History Teaching', in C. Portal (ed.), *History in the Curriculum* (London, 1987).
[80] D. Shemilt, 'Beauty and the Philosopher: Empathy in History and the Classroom', in A.K. Dickinson, P.J. Rogers and P.J. Lee (eds.), *Learning History* (London, 1984), pp. 39–84.
[81] K. Jenkins and P. Brickley, 'Reflections on the Empathy Debate', *Teaching History*, no. 55 (1989), pp. 18–23.

Policy Studies occupied a prominent position. Keith Joseph and Margaret Thatcher established this conservative think-tank in 1974. The CPS was one of a number of conservative groups that published papers on education in the 1980s, but when Joseph became Secretary for Education in 1981, it gained a foothold in governmental bodies. As Morris has shown, the role of the CPS in policy formation during the 1980s should not be underestimated.[82] Between 1987 and 1991, the CPS released five papers dedicated solely to the teaching of history. The first, Alan Beattie's *History in Peril: May Parents Preserve It* was advertised as a response to 'new' history. In that work, 'new' history is considered synonymous with declining standards of scholarship, unwarranted concern for relevance and utility in curricula and the 'indulgent promotion of the creative imagination'.[83] Drawing heavily on the writings of Michael Oakeshott, Beattie advanced that history education had shifted away from the study of history for its own sake ('traditional' history) and towards the distortion of the past to fit practical present interests ('new' history).[84] In the quest to make history appealing, historical content had been sacrificed. Any information evidencing bias, racism, sexism, classism and other 'isms' was marginalised. Exams tested the demonstration of skills rather than knowledge and place an unreasonable demand on students.[85] On this point, empathy is paradigmatic. To justify his complaint, Beattie cited a sample examination question on the first Russian Revolution in Tate's *Countdown to GCSE: History* and asked whether God and Booker Prize judges would be examiners:

> How *might* these peasant soldiers have felt when they heard that the Tsar had abdicated? What fears *might* they have had for the future? . . . All the time you are studying history you should be using your imagination *in this way*.[86]

What is asked of candidates is either beyond human knowledge or the boundaries of history. As a remedy, Beattie recommended a shift back to the careful, chronological study of the past for its own sake.[87] This initiative was to be led by parents — as the title of the paper sug-

---

[82] P. Morris, 'Freeing the Spirit of Enterprise' , in R. Keat and N. Abercrombie (eds.), *Enterprise Culture* (London, 1991), pp. 21–37.

[83] A. Beattie, *History in Peril: May Parents Preserve It* (London, 1987), p. 7; CPS, *Catalogue of Publications* (London, 1993).

[84] A. Beattie, *History in Peril*, pp. 6–9. Beattie's claims echo virtually word for word those of Oakeshott in 'The Activity of Being an Historian', in *Rationalism in Politics and Other Essays* (London, 1962), pp. 147, 152–3, 159.

[85] *Ibid.*, p. 37.

[86] N. Tate, *Countdown to GCSE: History* (London, 1986), p. 4.

[87] A. Beattie, *History in Peril*, pp. 22–4.

gests — as teachers had demonstrated their inability to make any progress in clarifying empathy over two decades.

Capitalising on the growing public concern about the description and assessment of empathy, the CPS released Stewart Deuchar's *History — and GCSE History*. In this paper, Beattie's deliberative claim for the study of history for its own sake was replaced by an impassioned plea to save education, and British culture, from 'left-wing forces'.[88] Like Beattie, Deuchar claimed that 'new' history's emphasis on the subjective points of view of historical agents had come at the expense of factual content. As a result, students were deprived of 'their heritage'. As with Beattie, Deuchar located the failings of 'new' history with empathy. To him, the GCSE objective most closely connected with empathy was 'gobbledygook' and evidence of a hijack of the curriculum by the left:

> Empathetic understanding is a desirable quality to develop, but without knowledge, it is nothing more than generalised sentimentality. GCSE is not being very sensible [*sic*] therefore in encouraging empathetic understanding but failing to encourage knowledge. Also GCSE seems to be in a terrible hurry [*sic*] to be sympathetic towards everybody else's predicament before making sure than we have a clear idea of our own standpoint.[89]

Deuchar saw the solution in greater emphasis on a unified, discrete British identity and heritage, an identity and heritage seemingly untouched by post-war immigration and European alignment, among other things.

The concerns raised about empathy by Beattie and Deuchar were made even more acute by the highly publicised conflict between the history department and management at Priory School, Lewes, in the south of England, over the implementation of GCSE history. In 1987, Christopher McGovern, Anthony Freeman and Arthur Franklin's dissatisfaction with the 'unteachable' GCSE history syllabus led them to defy local and national educational authorities and prepare a third of candidates for Scottish examinations. This dispute brought the alleged failings of GCSE history — judged on the basis of empathy — to the attention of the national media, and ultimately cost the dissenters their jobs. Although the relationship between the history department and school management at the Priory school was troubled before the publication of the CPS papers, complaints by the dissenters and CPS rhetoric soon merged to produce a vocal challenge to national educational authorities. In 'How Would You Feel . . . ?',

[88]   S. Deuchar, *History — and GCSE History* (London, 1987), p. 1.
[89]   *Ibid.*, p. 15.

McGovern justified abandoning GCSE history on the grounds that syllabus IV (Britain 1813–1983) was both 'unteachable' and 'unassessable'. At the root of the problem was empathy, a concept easily appropriated by left-wing groups:

> I am sure that the Government will be appalled when it learns that well intentioned ideas for a comprehensive examination have led: in the case of history, to the subject being hijacked by a sectional interest group. The History Committee of the [Secondary Examinations Council], whatever it may claim, is little more in reality than a cabal representing one particular idea and philosophy of history. In its attempt to provide an examination-for-all it has not only perverted parts of history teaching in schools, but it has also betrayed the children.[90]

The idea that empathy was prone to misuse by left wing groups was implicit in CPS rhetoric. It was also picked up by the Social Democrat turned Conservative life peer Robert Skidelsky. Reporting on the Priory case in both the *Times Educational Supplement* and *The Independent*, Skidelsky characterised empathy as an 'indoctrinatory tool of the left' that allowed teachers to 'manipulate students' feelings by depriving them of essential knowledge'. The only protection against such an abuse of power, he contended, was the restoration of the tradition of studying historical facts and heritage.[91] While students believed that in 'new' history they were to be given the opportunity to fashion their own historical narratives, in reality, they were being herded into accepting left wing views of the past. In so portraying empathy, McGovern, the CPS and Skidelsky managed to invert the claim of 'new' history advocates that their approach was to be favoured over 'traditional' history because it fostered critical thinking on the part of students, not just the passive acceptance of information.

This line of attack was also used by Helen Kedourie and Stewart Deuchar in the next CPS paper to be published — *Errors and Evils of the New History* — to describe empathy as 'resting on no basis of knowledge at all' and to locate it 'at the heart of Britain's cultural crisis'.[92] This aligned well with Margaret Thatcher's earlier suggestion that the British public should return to 'Victorian values' and Keith Joseph's judgement that history education should be used to inculcate pride in Britain's past.[93] CPS writings and the Priory case also

---

[90] C. McGovern, 'How Would You Feel . . . ?', *TES*, no. 3745 (1988), p. 3.

[91] R. Skidelsky, 'History as Social Engineering', *The Independent* (1 March 1988), p. 4; 'Mutiny at the Priory', *TES*, no. 3789 (1989), pp. 1–3.

[92] H. Kedourie, *Errors and Evils of the New History*, p. 10, foreword by S. Deuchar.

[93] D. McKeirnan, 'History in a National Curriculum', p. 37; and K. Joseph, *Why Teach History in Schools?* (London, 1984).

raised public awareness about the lack of progress made by teachers and educational researchers in clarifying the developmental stages and assessable features of empathy. Further, in taking empathy as the hallmark of 'new' history, they also managed to cast doubts about the wisdom of shifting from content- to method-centred educational policies. With the possibility that more of the curriculum could be centralised, it seemed that a bitter showdown between advocates of 'new' and 'traditional' history over empathy was inevitable.

History in the National Curriculum

With the publication of *Better Schools* in 1985, it was clear that the British government aimed to establish a national curriculum for ages 5–16. That curriculum was established by law in the Education Act of 1988 and not long afterward a National Curriculum History Working Group was set up, publishing an interim report in 1989 and a final report in 1990. CPS writers like Kedourie and Deuchar believed that it was imperative to lay issues like empathy open to public debate before they became an established part of the national curriculum. As we have seen, to them, the intense interest in empathy had come at the expense of the factual, chronological foundation of history. 'New' history promised few 'oases of learning', and these often turned out to be shallow mirages.[94] Peter Knight, too, saw a problem looming with empathy and the national curriculum, and believed that the stakes were high:

> Empathy is a profoundly unhelpful term, particularly in history. That may not have mattered all the time that school history did not matter, but under the National Curriculum, teachers, governors, parents ... will all be invited to take all subjects seriously and to weigh the evidence of children's historical grasp school by school, and in some cases child by child ... Successful planning, teaching and learning ... will not be served by using ambiguous terms, ... which have no basis in the way children's thinking and learning progress.[95]

Knight, Kedourie and Deuchar were all in agreement that empathy had no place in a national curriculum, and that a national curriculum 'mattered'. Their routes to that conclusion, though, differed. Kedourie and Deuchar objected to empathy because they saw it as easily used by left-wing forces to undermine knowledge and pride in British heritage. Knight, on the other hand, objected on the basis of

[94]   *Ibid.*, p. 18.
[95]   P. Knight, 'Empathy: Concept, Confusion and Consequences in a National Curriculum', *Oxford Review of Education*, Vol. 15 (1) (1989), p. 49.

his experience as an educational researcher. Empathy, he contended, was a vague, elusive, grab bag of terms. Something useful could be done with it, however, if it was broken down into its component elements, many of which had to some extent been successfully tracked in empirical investigations. These elements included recall of salient data, ability to distinguish between one's own and another's perspective(s), skill in re-telling a story from others' perspectives, explanations of actions, predictions of the ways historical situations might develop and judgements (mainly of historical agents).[96]

As with the GCSE Examining Group, the History Working Group aimed to move beyond the 'new' and 'traditional' dichotomy and design programmes of study 'describing the *content, skills* and *processes* which need to be covered during each key stage of compulsory education'.[97] One member of the Group, Henry Hobhouse, considered them to be unified in this aim as a result of the efforts of the chairman, Commander Michael Saunders Watson:

> What united us in the beginning was a determination to gain for history its due place. The sheltered lives of some of the group had not debarred them from engaging in controversies over facts, dates and content or empathy, understanding and skills. Others, including our skilled, empathetic chairman, were convinced that these disputes were sterile. A few were concerned that the group should from the first recognise that we could waste the whole of our allotted year in discussing such problems.[98]

Some members of the Group had indeed contributed to the debate on empathy: Low-Beer and Culpin had been at odds on whether empathy was assessable, and on its connection to the imagination. Interestingly, though, by the time that Culpin — who had previously written on the possibilities of assessment for empathy in the GCSE — was co-opted to the Group (October 1989), it had already opted to follow Knight into apparently dissolving the term into its constituent elements.

The introduction to the *Interim Report* does reflect the effort of the Group to steer between the 'new' and 'traditional' dichotomy and defuse the brewing storm over empathy. For example, the Group transferred from their terms of reference the suggestion that students were to study history for its own sake, to become familiar with the history and 'inheritances' of Britain, to understand chronology, to become aware of their identity, combat anachronism and learn to

---

[96] *Ibid.*, p. 47.
[97] DES, *National Curriculum History Working Group Final Report* (London, 1990), terms of reference, p. 187.
[98] H. Hobhouse, 'Time Steals a March on History', *TES*, no. 3866 (1990), p. 10.

respect the rigours of historical research. In addition, the document lists eighty study topics.[99] Alongside such features stand a number of ideas supported by advocates of 'new' history. First, their talk of history's distinct concepts, ways of using those concepts and distinct methods of research and explanation suggests the influence of Hirst's 'forms of knowledge' theory. Second, the process of education is described in terms adapted from Bruner. This is evident in the illustration of the process of learning by means of a cone and an expanding double helix. To the Working Group, the cone represented the 'broadening accumulation of historical knowledge'. One helix represents increasing understanding and conceptual sophistication and the other represents the development of historical skills. Further, the identification of a middle passage between 'new' and 'traditional' approaches is also demonstrated in the line taken with empathy.

The term 'empathy' is nowhere to be seen in *The Interim Report*. This absence reflects both the weight of public pressure raised by groups like the CPS and the frustration of educational researchers like Knight over progress in clarifying the term. We see the former in the emphasis given to content, chronology and 'inheritances', and the latter in the inclusion of goals and points resembling the fragmented elements of empathy that Knight described. For example, the Working Group wrote of recall of data, predictions of the ways historical situations might develop, judgements and the consideration of events from the perspectives of historical agents. But the group went even further than Knight, in clearly uncoupling 'understanding different points of view' from the idea of students entertaining the experiences of others, as with an 'Imagine you are . . . ' exercise. For example, in Attainment Task Two, awareness of perspective is to be raised simply by the provision of information presenting different points of view and interpretations. No further step of empathy or identification is required.[100] While 'empathy' is notable by its absence in the programme of study, the term 'imagination' appears in the document. History, we are told, is characterised by, among other things, 'the disciplined use of imagination'.[101] It is possible that the group simply transferred the meaning of 'empathy' to that of 'imagination' in line with earlier writers like HMI who used them interchangeably. Given the above description of Attainment Task Two, though, this seems unlikely. More likely, Attainment

[99]   DES, *National Curriculum History Working Group Interim Report* (London, 1989), pp. 3–5, 8, 10, 12–13.
[100] See for example the description of Attainment Task 2 in *Ibid.*, pp. 25–6.
[101] *Ibid.*, §2.1, pp. 10, 26

Task Two points to the arrangement and understanding of information and construction of explanations by the historian, a usage derived from Little and Lee, and in turn, Collingwood and Warnock. As we are not told the meaning of the term explicitly, though, it is hard to offer any firm conclusions.

The *Interim Report* was published in August 1989 with the comments of the new Secretary for Education, John MacGregor. MacGregor thanked the Working Group for its efforts, and asked that three issues be addressed in the preparation for the final report. He recommended, first, that a more explicit chronological framework be adopted; second, that the proportion of British history in the programme of study be increased; and third, that the content be specified in more detail in both the programme and attainment targets. When the report was released, some commentators took MacGregor's comments as overly generous concessions to the advocates of 'traditional' history, conservative politicians and think tanks like the CPS.[102] On the whole, though, the *Interim Report* met with positive reviews in educational circles. John Clare, for instance, was effusive with his praise:

> It must rate alongside Cranmer's Prayer Book as a masterpiece of diplomacy in a minefield of conflicting ideologies. One hesitates to ask them to change anything, just in case they lose the correct balance.[103]

As for empathy, Clare was not sure whether it had been included in the attainment targets, while William Lamont parodied conservative comment:

> 'Empathy' brings them out in spots. There is no particular virtue in this exercise: we tend on the whole to lock up people who think they are Napoleon. But it has its uses *occasionally* as a way of getting children to experience other points of view.[104]

Whilst Clare and Lamont noted that many empathy assessment tasks from the Schools Council Projects and the GCSE were 'uncontrolled', they argued that it could not be used to legitimise the removal of empathy from National Curriculum documents. Rather, more effort on clarification was needed. In response, conservative critics were quick to remind the public of the failings of empathy and thus 'new' history. Kenneth Minogue, for instance, equated empathy with a 'display of megalomania by teachers anxious to gain

---

[102] J.D. Clare, 'Goodbye to all That: History in the National Curriculum', in *TES*, no. 3819 (1989), p. 27; and W. Lamont, 'Forget the Memory Man: "New" History', *TES*, no. 3827 (1989), p. 20.

[103] J.D. Clare, 'Goodbye to all That', p. 27.

[104] W. Lamont, 'Forget the Memory Man', p. 20.

access to the inner lives of students' and concluded that: 'At the age of 11 I was simply told to learn the dates of the kings and queens of England. Nothing, except perhaps the skill of touch-typing, has ever been so useful to me'.[105] And in December 1989, the CPS published Sheila Lawlor's response to the *Report*. Lawlor's work echoed the themes of earlier CPS offerings, but in distinction from them, she had little to say about empathy. Clearly she did not see it as even present, implicitly, in the *Report*. She did, however, pass comment on the inclusion of 'imagination':

> 'The [History Working Group] do not see that history is first and fore-most about the past — [characterised] by particular content, chronologi-cal framework, historical facts. Instead, they allude to "methodology . . . evidence . . . imagination" which could amount to anything.[106]

Though it is unlikely that these concepts could mean *anything*, and that the *Report* was the result of pressure brought to bear by advo-cates of 'new' history, Lawlor was right to highlight the Group's use of the word 'imagination' without offering an account of its meaning.

The History Working Group's *Final Report* was released without government comment in April 1990. The *Final Report* differs from the *Interim Report* in many respects. First, statements on chronology and 'inheritances' are incorporated into the statements on the purpose of school history (§1.7); second, each of the History Study Units is arranged in a broadly chronological sequence; and third, prog-ramme content is specified in detail. All of these appear to be in line with the Secretary of State for Education's requests, and in turn, rep-resent concessions to conservative critics. The Working Group did not comply, however, with the Secretary of State's recommendation that historical content be addressed specifically in the Attainment Targets.[107] Empathy is again absent, but the treatment of imagina-tion is different. The first mention of the imagination comes in §1.4 of 'History in the School Curriculum', and it is employed in a pejorative sense:

> To guarantee that these elements [of history] . . . are inter-related and have proper emphasis, we have placed them in the programmes of study and in the attainment targets . . . By this means we can ensure that

[105] K. Minogue, 'Through the Processor', *TES*, no. 3775 (1989), p. 17.
[106] S. Lawlor, *Proposals for the National Curriculum in History* (London, 1989), p. 2.
[107] DES, *National Curriculum History Working Group: Final Report* (London, 1990), Annex A to chapter 3, §§A2.1–A3.3.

the teaching of history in schools is not characterised by undisciplined use of the imagination.[108]

Gone is the suggestion that school history is characterised in part by the imagination. Confusing, too, is the shift of the imagination from Attainment Target Four ('Organising and Communicating the Results of Historical Study', §7.16) to Attainment Target Three ('Acquiring and Evaluating Historical Imagination', §7.14) even though the former aligns better with Lee and Little's usage of the term. As it is, no elaboration of the meaning of 'imagination' in Attainment Target Three is offered.

The publication of the *Final Report* generated considerable debate that spilled out of educational circles and into parliament, the media, and popular culture. Just prior to the release of the report, for instance, a Conservative MP asked Margaret Thatcher in Question Time:

> Instead of teaching only what are called themes, why cannot we go back to the good old days when we learnt by heart the names of the kings and queens of England, the feats of our warriors and our battles and the glorious deeds of our past?

To which Thatcher replied:

> Most of us are expected to learn from experience of history and we cannot do that unless we know it. Children should know the great landmarks of British history and they should be taught them at school.[109]

The tabloid press picked Thatcher's comment up, and ran the story that the government and the History Working Group were at odds.[110] The debate even moved into popular culture, with Colin Dexter's Inspector Morse weighing in with his opinion (see p. 13). Teacher response was far more positive.[111] It was commonly agreed that despite ideological pressures and a tight schedule, the History Working Group had achieved much in a 'thankless task'.[112] To the majority of teachers, the attainment targets were more clearly defined, and the programme was more interesting, logically sequenced and less prescriptive. Aldrich commented on the continued absence of empathy from the Attainment Targets, but acknowl-

---

[108] *Ibid.*, §1.4.
[109] Hansard 29 March 1990, as quoted in D. McKiernan, 'History in a National Curriculum', p. 42.
[110] *Ibid.*
[111] See, for example, C. Russell, 'Standing the Test of Time', *TES*, no. 3851 (1990), p. 69; M. Roberts, 'Briefing for a Journey to the Past', *TES*, no. 3851 (1990), p. 70; and C. White, 'Doing the Knowledge', *TES*, no. 3851 (1990), p. 72.
[112] M. Roberts, 'Briefing for a Journey to the Past', p. 70.

edged that a lot of work had to be done to clarify the concept.[113] The CPS were also quick to comment, reiterating that historical knowledge, particularly knowledge of British and European history had been undervalued.[114]

In July 1990 the Secretary of State for Education drew together the Working Group's *Final Report*, responses to it collected during statutory consultation by the National Curriculum Council and the recommendations of the School Examination and Assessment Council to produce *History for Ages 5 to 16*.[115] The changes proposed to the *Final Report* appeared very much to teachers to offer further concessions to the Thatcher government and conservative critics like the CPS. First, although the amount of British and European history in the final report could hardly be described, as Lawlor suggested, as 'insufficient', the amount of both was further increased. This was despite the majority of respondents to the National Curriculum Council survey signalling that they wanted to see a reduction in British history.[116] Second, the Secretary of State changed the name of Attainment Target One from 'Understanding History in its Setting' to 'Knowledge and Understanding of History' and increased its weighting to 50%. This was despite the School Examination and Assessment Council and the majority of respondents to the National Curriculum Council survey being against such a change.[117] Third, it was proposed that the four Attainment Targets be collapsed into three by combining Attainment Target Four with the others. In the shift, the Attainment Target most closely approximating Lee and Little's notion of the historical imagination, and the term imagination itself were lost. That rearrangement left only one mention of the imagination in the 'Drama, role-play, simulation and Related Approaches' section of chapter 10: 'Bring History to Life'.[118] With the paring back of policy to Attainment Targets and Historical Study Units in *History in the National Curriculum*, released in March 1991, the result was no mention of either 'imagination' or 'empathy' at all.[119]

[113] *History in the National Curriculum*, ed. R. Aldrich (London, 1991), pp. 26–7.

[114] S. Lawlor, *But What Must Pupils Know?: CPS Response to National Curriculum History Working Group, Final Report* (London, 1990).

[115] DES, *History for Ages 5 to 16: Proposals of the Secretary of State for Education and Science* (London, 1990).

[116] National Curriculum Council (hereafter NCC), *National Curriculum Council Consultation Report: History* (York, 1990), §2.15, p. 11.

[117] *Ibid.*, §2.2, p. 9; SEAC, letter in DES, *History for Ages 5 to 16: Proposals of the Secretary of State for Education and Science*.

[118] DES, *History for Ages 5 to 16: Proposals of the Secretary of State for Education and Science*, §10.4.

[119] DES, *History in the National Curriculum (England)* (London, 1991).

Afterglow

It is of course possible to argue — as Knight and Farmer and Lee have done — that empathy is present in *History in the National Curriculum* in substance but not in name.[120] This conclusion, however, presupposes a level of agreement on what 'empathy' is, to the point that it will clearly suggest itself to readers. Looking at the extent of the disagreements about the meaning of empathy up to 1991, this assumption seems optimistic. It also seems curious to argue that empathy is one of the central organising concepts of history, but that it makes no difference if we operate simply with its elements and dispense with the label. Indeed Knight, Farmer and Lee seemed to want to make connections between the elements of 'empathy' and to use a label to signal those connections, even if it is something like 'the elements formerly known as empathy'. Further, the absence of the terms 'imagination' and 'empathy' from *History in the National Curriculum* and subsequent policies has had a marked impact on educational research and writing, reducing the number of publications on these concepts. If you take away the terms, then it seems that you take away the imperative to address the issues of clarification and implementation. It is no longer urgent, and perhaps no longer 'matters'. In *Learning to Teach History in the Secondary School* (1997), for instance, Hayden, Arthur and Hunt told their readers that they avoid using the word 'empathy' because it does not appear in GCSE or National Curriculum documentation and that it is up to teacher trainees to decide whether to use it in the classroom.[121] Similarly, Cooper summarised psychological research into empathy and the imagination, but offered readers no advice on how or whether it ought be implemented in the classroom.[122]

For a small number of writers, though, 'empathy' and, to a lesser extent, 'imagination' matter in both label and substance. For instance, echoing the sentiments of Brooks, Aris and Perry, Slater and Husbands, Clements wrote:

> In the world of the National Curriculum, we can say goodbye to empathy and concentrate on skills which may be easier to quantify. One cannot help thinking, however, that unless students are encouraged to

[120] A. Farmer and P. Knight, *Active History in Key Stages 3 and 4* (London, 1994), pp. 11–12; P.J. Lee, 'History and the National Curriculum in England', in P.J. Lee, A.K. Dickinson, P. Gordon and J. Slater (eds.), *International Yearbook of History Education* (London, 1997), pp. 73–123.

[121] T. Hayden, J. Arthur and M. Hunt, *Learning to Teach History in the Secondary School* (London, 1997), p. 98.

[122] H. Cooper, 'Historical Thinking and Cognitive Development in the Teaching of History', in H. Bourdillon (ed.), *Teaching History* (London, 1994), pp. 101–11.

consider what may have gone on in the minds of people in the past, something very valuable and interesting is being lost in our teaching of history.[123]

For them, empathy is central to historical understanding, and thus to history. When it comes down to meaning, though, these writers are no closer to agreement than earlier writers. The same confusions and disagreements remain. Clements saw empathy as affective, for instance, while Brooks, Aris and Perry and Slater saw it as multidimensional. Clements saw it best developed through oral interviews, Slater through creative writing exercises and Brooks, Aris and Perry through the careful study of documents. There is also the ever present variety of views on the relationship between empathy and imagination: Slater saw imagination as a part of empathy, Husbands vice versa and Clements, Brooks, Aris and Perry did not mention the imagination at all. Working in the shadow of the linguistic turn in philosophy, Husbands extended the constructive notion of imagination offered by Little and Lee to incorporate Hayden White's suggestion that histories, like novels, are built upon creative imagination, literary conventions and styles.[124] Apart from Husband's extension, the points raised in writings after the National Curriculum have about them the air of eternal return; indeed we could argue that with empathy and imagination, we have the educational equivalent of the labours of Sisyphus.

After more than twenty years of intense scrutiny, educational writers made little headway in clarifying the meaning and conceptual form of the terms 'empathy' and 'imagination'. Nor did they manage to articulate the nature of the relations between these concepts, let alone that between the historical imagination and imagination *per se*. Further, their role in historical understanding, historical education and the life of the mind still remains far from clear. Surveys of the period commonly cite ideological factors or interference as an explanation for the lack of progress.[125] Ideological issues form only a proximate or multiplying factor at best, though, for conservative critics merely magnified and brought to public attention doubts about empathy that teachers already held. A more satisfactory explanation suggests itself if we consider the *ways* that clarification

[123] P. Clements, 'Historical Empathy — R.I.P.?', *Teaching History*, no. 85 (1996), pp. 6–8; R. Brooks, M. Aris, and I. Perry, *The Effective Teaching of History* (London, 1993), p. 108; J. Slater, *Teaching History in the New Europe* (London, 1995), pp. 128–30; and C. Husbands, *What is History Teaching?* (Buckingham, 1996), ch. 5.

[124] C. Husbands, *What is History Teaching?*, pp. 57–8.

[125] See for example D. Sylvester, 'Change and Continuity in History Teaching 1900–93', and D. McKiernan, 'History in a National Curriculum'.

was approached. Tasks of clarification and meaning are philosophical tasks; yet philosophers of education are notable by their almost total absence from the debate on empathy and imagination in history. Why?

The answer, I believe, lies with the approach that dominated Anglo-American philosophy of education after the second-world war: analytic or 'ordinary language' philosophy. Ordinary language philosophy suggests that if language is taken to be an expression of thought, then the study of language ought to be central to philosophy. For example, in order to understand what teaching or indoctrination are, we should analyse how people use the words 'teaching' and 'indoctrination'.[126] This entails looking at the ways in which terms are used and when they are not, in order to track the features of the concepts they convey. This helps to explain why in 'Historical Imagination' (1984), for instance, Lee placed great importance in distinguishing between *in* imagination and *with* imagination and empathy as a power, an achievement, a process and a disposition or propensity.[127] Lee's aim was to make teachers aware of subtle but important differences between these usages in order to help them write study programmes with a better understanding of what their students were doing.

Few works of ordinary language philosophy of education, however, actually helped to clear up confusions and to direct policy. Why did postwar philosophy of education achieve so little? First, I believe that educators did not value or support it — and bypassed it in favour of psychology — because it gave the impression of being trite or mere semantics. Analyses of how many ways there were to spill ink, or the meaning of 'to sit on a chair', or the contexts in which 'to teach' made sense seemed far away from and perhaps pointless to teachers. Second, ordinary language philosophy of language seemed to talk only of words, and not things, practices or even the ethical implications of those words. For example, philosophers of education described uses of 'indoctrination' but offered teachers no guidance on the ethics involved. It was as if, by clearing up the meaning of the words, ethical problems would magically also be addressed. Third, teachers complained that the topics philosophers selected for ordinary language analysis were of little practical interest to them. Philosophers of education favoured the analysis of larger terms like 'aims', 'teaching', 'knowledge' and 'initiation', leaving few to work on concepts like 'empathy' and 'historical imag-

[126] I. Sheffler, *The Language of Education* (Springfield, IL, 1960); and I.A. Snook, *Indoctrination and Education* (London, 1972).
[127] P.J. Lee, 'Historical Imagination', pp. 85–90.

ination'. Of the writings surveyed in this chapter, only three were substantially philosophical in focus.[128] These are all well-known criticisms of postwar philosophy of education. There are two more problems with the approach, however, that have been overlooked.

First, there is its ahistorical methodology. Although ordinary language philosophy claims to analyse terms *as they are used*, these uses are removed from any historical context, as if that had no bearing on their meaning. Nowhere is this problem clearer, or perhaps more ironic, than in the case of 'empathy' and the 'historical imagination'. It seems reasonable to expect in a discussion on history education by history educators and philosophers of education, that acknowledgment be made of possible differences in meaning across space and time. After all, with 'empathy', many educators hoped that students would become better attuned to different ways of seeing the world. That an historical dimension is present in the debate is suggested by the frequent references to writers like W.H. Burston, Mary Warnock and above all, R.G. Collingwood. In almost all the writings described in this chapter, Collingwood's name is cited, or quotes used from his well-known works, *An Autobiography* and *The Idea of History*. He is clearly an important name in this debate; but the way in which he is referred to leaves him as a name. Collingwood is readily conjoined with particular terms from policies — like 'pseudo empathy' — leaving readers with the impression that he was a live participant in the debate: no allowance is made for the possibility that he might have viewed the historian's mind differently or that he might have chosen different terms deliberately. No attempt is made to see the way in which Collingwood's views were shaped by the times in which he lived. Finally, all of his writings on the historian's mind are collapsed into a single point, as if phrases or quotes like 'the historical imagination' or 'All history is the history of thought'[129] are transparent out of context and he never changed his mind. While British policy offers an extreme case, Collingwood's name features in educational discourse around the world. This is the first work to offer a sustained analysis of his views of history education, and education *per se*.

Second, very little thought was given by philosophers of education to the form of concepts to be clarified. For example, can 'imagination' and 'empathy' be reduced to a single meaning? If not, how

[128] J. Gribble and G. Oliver, 'Empathy and Education'; C. Bailey, 'Knowledge of Others and Concern for Others' and D. Shemilt, 'Beauty and the Philosopher: Empathy in History and the Classroom'

[129] R.G. Collingwood, *An Autobiography* (Oxford, 1939), p. 110.

are the various instances of these concepts related to one another? Finally, how might we accommodate changes in usage over time?

R.G. Collingwood's writings, I believe, speak to these issues. We will need to, though, delve deeper than educators have to date. As Collingwood himself argued in *An Autobiography*, we should not be content with what others say about a thinker: we should read that thinker for ourselves.[130]

---

[130] *Ibid.*, p. 27.

Chapter II

Sympathy, Empathy or Re-enactment?

To embody thought is to express it. To express thought is to be language.[1]

Despite the many changes of view on the nature and role of imagination and empathy in twentieth-century British educational discourse, two things remained constant. Educators persistently made a connection between empathy — and what were often taken to be its cognates, 'sympathy' and 're-enactment' — and the imagination, and further associated R.G. Collingwood with those connected concepts. Any attempt to clarify those concepts should therefore begin by looking to the writings of Collingwood himself. In this chapter, we do just that by posing two relatively straightforward questions. First, did Collingwood actually employ the terms 'empathy', 'sympathy' or 're-enactment' in his historiographical writings, and if so, did he view them as synonymous? Second, did Collingwood make any explicit connection between those concepts and that of 'imagination'? In addressing these questions, we will look first to writings on empathy, sympathy and re-enactment that predate Collingwood, and then to his published and unpublished works from his commentary on Aristotle's *De Anima* (1913–14) to *The New Leviathan* (1942). Along the way, we will discover that while Collingwood eschewed the use of jargon or technical terms in his philosophical writings, this did not mean that he was careless about the words that he used. Moreover, we will discover that they are embedded in views of language and mind not unlike those of the later Wittgenstein.

[1]   R.G. Collingwood, 'The Principles of History' (1939), p. 50.

Sympathy

The identification of sympathy as a power of imagination that allows people to identify with one another first appeared in James Arbuckle's *Hibernicus's Letters* (1722, republished as *Collection of Letters and Essays*, 1729). To Arbuckle, the imagination was a 'divinely implanted' guide to moral action, without which benevolence and the Golden Rule would not be possible.[2] Arbuckle, as well as other writers such as Campbell and Cooper were satisfied with having established the connection; they did not much dwell on the nature of it.[3] A consideration of that connection was not to come until the publication of Hume's *Treatise on Human Nature* (1739) and *Enquiry Concerning the Principles of Morals* (1772). In those works, Hume shows the complexity of the connection through a range of examples. He remarks, for instance, that people who most resemble us in desires and passions operate more readily on our imagination than those who are different from us.[4] And there must be some overlap between the two persons, for, he writes, '[v]iews and sentiments, so opposite to known truth and to each other, could never have place, at the same time, in the same person'.[5] Even when there are similarities, however, envy and selfish tendencies permit identification only for a short time. This is particularly the case when others are 'better' than us. We can look to the experiences of others via the sympathetic imagination, but only, it seems, out of concern for what we can learn about ourselves. Burke, too, noted the delight we take in contemplating the distress and misfortune of others when it does not press too close to us. He was more willing than Hume, though, to believe in the possibility of real sympathetic identification with others via the imagination. Burke characterised the sympathetic imagination as functioning prior to reasoning 'by an instinct that works us to its purposes without our concurrence', but we are nevertheless aware of its operation. It is brought into action 'easily' by the looks and gestures of others or by words which, because they suggest imperfect and obscure ideas, raise strong emotions. It does not work through

[2]   J. Arbuckle, *A Collection of Letters and Essays on Several Subjects* [1729], ed. D. Berman and P.O'Riordan (Bristol, 2002).

[3]   A. Campbell, *Enquiry into the Original of Moral Virtue* [1773 edition, first published in 1734] (Bristol, 2000); and J.G. Cooper, *Letters Concerning Taste* [1755 edition] (Bristol, 1998), p. 17.

[4]   D. Hume, *A Treatise on Human Nature* [1739], ed. D. and M. Norton (Oxford, 2000), §§3.2.2, 2.2.5.

[5]   D. Hume, *Enquiry Concerning the Principles of Morals* [1772], ed. L.A. Selby-Bigge (Oxford, 1975), §6.1.

images — mental or physical — because the clear ideas they give of things in themselves offer little opportunity to spark off emotions.[6]

   While Burke focused on the possibility of sympathetic identification, Adam Smith argued in *Theory of Moral Sentiments* (1759) that it is indispensable to moral and social activities. People, he claims, habitually and instinctively form an idea of what they themselves would feel in the situation of another, past or present. For example, we automatically flinch at the thought of a blow about to hit another person. This is made possible via the imagination, which works instantaneously and prior to knowledge via the reading of looks and gestures. Imagination works most easily when we consider feelings that we approve of, look to the experiences of people we know well or consider pain caused by external sources like a blow. As a corollary, we may need to know the causes of and even tone down the feelings of others — as with anger that initially repels us — or work harder to contemplate the experiences of strangers. Pain caused by internal causes, like toothache, generates little possibility for sympathy, because it is private to the sufferer. The imagination may also allow us to contemplate feelings that others are unaware of, such as fear for madmen or babies who put themselves unknowingly in danger. He even notes that we commonly impute feelings of sadness and terror to the dead.[7] Despite Smith having offered little clue of exactly how imagination works upon looks and gestures, his views were enormously influential. They suggested, for instance, an association between the poet or playwright's powers of sympathy and the imagination to literary critics up to the mid-nineteenth century. In his *Essay on Taste* (1759), for example, Gerard characterised sympathy as a 'happy structure of imagination' that guides poets to the production of characters that are convincing and complete.[8] Morgann thought this well demonstrated through Shakespeare, whose imagination created characters that were so convincing that it would be proper to consider them 'rather as Historic than Dramatic beings'.[9]

   Smith can also perhaps be credited for stirring up the rather curious discussion on the possibility of sympathy with animals and inanimate objects. In Smith's view, identification of one person with another — alive or dead — works because humans share common

[6]   E. Burke, *A Philosophical Inquiry into the Origin of Our Ideas of the Sublime and Beautiful* [1756], in *The Works of Edmund Burke* (Oxford, 1907), §§1.8, 1.9, 2.4, 4.4, 5.5, 5.7.

[7]   A. Smith, *The Theory of Moral Sentiments* [1759] (Indianapolis, IN, 1969), §§1.1.1, 1.1.2, 1.1.3, 1.1.4, 1.2.1, 1.2.3, 1.3.1, 7.3.1.

[8]   A. Gerard, *Essay on Taste* [1759] (Menston, 1971), §3.2.

[9]   M. Morgann, *An Essay on the Dramatic Character of Sir John Falstaff* [1777] (New York, NY, 1970), p. 61n.

intellectual and emotional traits. What interested other contemporary writers was whether true identification with animals and even inanimate objects was possible, or whether it was no more than projection onto those organisms or objects. Noting Smith's discussion on sympathy and the dead, for instance, Beattie claimed that inanimate objects with which we have a personal association might arouse feelings, such as sadness at the loss of a much-used walking stick or the sight of a house in ruins.[10] This is clearly a case of projection, as are others cited in the literature, including Priestley's observation that it was common for people playing bowls to 'lean their own bodies, and writhe them in every possible attitude, according to the course they would have their bowl to take'.[11] That there was agreement on such activities amounting to projection or 'humanisation' suggests an important characteristic of sympathy: it is only genuinely possible among humans. We will return to the idea of humans contemplating the experiences of non-human animals in the next chapter.

Early in the twentieth century, the association between sympathy and imagination crossed over into works on the fledgling profession of history. Hart, for instance, used his 1909 presidential address to the American Historical Association to declare that 'a little imagination helps one to sympathise with the great men of the past'.[12] As we shall see in chapter four, connections between the historical imagination and sympathy continued to be made into the latter half of the twentieth century by writers like Butterfield and Ritter. More often, though, the term 'empathy' was opted for.[13]

Empathy

Eighteenth- and nineteenth-century English philosophers and literary critics organised their discussions on the identification of one individual with another, or 'fellow feeling' under the concept of 'sympathy'. In distinction, German writers generally opted for the term 'empathy' — derived from the Greek *empátheia* — in the form of *Einfühlen*, *Einfühlung*, or *Mitfühlen*, meaning literally 'in-feeling' or

[10]   J. Beattie, *Elements of Moral Science* [1790–3], Vol. 1 (New York, NY, 1977), §1.1.10.
[11]   J. Priestley, *Course of Lectures on Oratory and Criticism* [1762] (Carbondale, IL, 1965), p. 127.
[12]   A.B. Hart, 'Imagination in History', in *American Historical Review*, Vol. 15 (1910), p. 240.
[13]   H. Butterfield, *History and Human Relations* (London, 1951); H. Ritter, 'Imagination', *Dictionary of Concepts in History* (Westport, CN, 1986), p. 216.

'with feeling'.[14] In *Yet Another Philosophy of History* (1774), for example, Herder exhorted his readers to 'enter the century, the region, the entire history — empathise with or 'feel onself into' [*sich einfühlen*] every part of it'.[15] That he connected *Einfühlen* with imagination, though, was purely the interpretation of one of his most influential commentators in English, Isaiah Berlin.[16] There is no direct connection between empathy and imagination to be found in the writings of Dilthey either, nor was he the uncritical promoter of *Einfühlung* that many commentators have taken him to be. Dilthey used *Einfühlen* to describe Herder's ideas but seldom used it in a positive manner himself. In *The Rise of Hermeneutics*, he declared his preference rather for the terms *Nachfühlen* and *Nacherleben*, meaning 're-feel' and 're-experience' respectively. The use of the prefix *Nach* is important here, suggesting critical distance on the part of the person contemplating the experience of others. *Einfühlen*, on the other hand, implies emotional and ethical engagement. As Scheler describes it:

> *Nachfühlen* remains still in the sphere of cognitive behaviour . . . Intellectual historians, novelists and dramatists must possess the gift of *Nacherleben* to a high degree; but they need not in the slightest have 'sympathy' [*Mitgefühl*] for their objects and persons. *Nachfühlen* and *Nacherleben* must therefore be strictly distinguished from *Mitfühlen*. Certainly they involve a feeling of others' feelings, not mere knowledge of them, or mere judgement that the others have these feelings; but they do not involve experience of the actual feelings as states in us. In *Nachfühlen* we grasp experientially the quality of the other's feelings — but without these feelings migrating into us or stimulating actual feelings in us.[17]

Clearly, the prefixes *Ein*, *Mit* and *Nach* signalled some important conceptual distinctions in German writing from the late nineteenth century, namely the distancing of the critical efforts of historians from the approval implied in *Mitfühlen*. Those distinctions are important in Dilthey's writing. The same could not be said of English language scholarship, however. Not only were the technical differences between *Nachfühlen* and *Nacherleben* and *Einfühlen* or

---

[14] The connection of 'sympathy' with a sensitivity for the feelings of another becomes obvious in the second aorist *páschio* meaning 'I suffer', the infinitive of which is *páschien* meaning 'suffering'. This is associated with the affective pathos.

[15] J.G. Herder, 'Yet Another Philosophy of History' [1774], *Against Pure Reason: Writings on Religion, Language and History*, trans. and ed. M. Bunge (Minneapolis,1993), p. 39, slight modification of translation to recall the sense that readers might have got before Lee's coining of the English term 'empathy' in 1904.

[16] See for example I. Berlin, *Vico and Herder* (London, 1976), p. xxii.

[17] M. Scheler, *Wesen und Formen der Sympathie* (Bonn, 1985), p. 20; as translated in A. Harrington, 'Dilthey, Empathy and Verstehen: A Contemporary Reappraisal', *European Journal of Social Theory*, Vol. 4 (3) (2001), pp. 311–29.

Mitfühlen not carried over into English, after Vernon Lee's coining of the term 'empathy' in 1904 a number of writers even dissolved the boundaries between 'sympathy' and 'empathy' by using them interchangeably.[18] And it was via the conflation of empathy with sympathy that the former came to be associated with imagination in English scholarship.

It is this process of translation and conflation that produced the association of Dilthey's view of *Verstehen* (understanding) with empathy, sympathy and imagination in English and later, German language scholarship, an association that only began to be questioned in the mid-1970s.[19] This view is to be found in various forms in the writings of Gadamer, Habermas, Harrington and Wisner,[20] but is typified in Ritter's entry on 'Understanding' in the *Dictionary of Concepts in History* (1986):

> Unlike *explanation*, *understanding* is not a *logical* process but a largely emotional and intuitive experience through which the practitioner of the human sciences establishes a 'psychological rapport' with the object of his study . . . Through this process he 'internalises' the past by 'imagining what emotions may have been aroused by the impact of a given situation or event' . . . By steeping himself in the records of the past, the historian may intuitively enter into a sympathetic relationship with the past and can to some degree reexperience the past and 'rethink' the thoughts of historical personalities.[21]

It is also in this context of conflation and association that R.G. Collingwood's writings on 're-enactment' appear.

Collingwood and 'Re-enactment'

As Dray has noted, Collingwood's first venture into the area of scholarship we are concerned with is to be found in his first book, *Religion and Philosophy* (1916). In that work, he talks of 'sympathetic understanding' and the need for entering 'with some degree of sym-

[18] V. Lee and C. Anstruther Thomson, *Beauty and Ugliness and Other Studies in Psychological Aesthetics* (1904).

[19] See R. Makkreel, *Wilhelm Dilthey: Philosopher of the Human Sciences* (Princeton, NJ, 1975); M. Ermath, *Wilhelm Dilthey: The Critique of Historical Reason* (Chicago, IL, 1978), esp. pp. 252–3n.5; and I. Oliver, 'The "Old" and the "New" Hermeneutic in Sociological Theory', *British Journal of Sociology*, Vol. 34 (4) (1983), pp. 519–53.

[20] H.- G. Gadamer, *Truth and Method*, trans. W. Glen-Doepel (London, 1979), pp. 153–214; J. Habermas, *Knowledge and Human Interests*, trans. J. Shapiro (London, 1973), p. 337 n.2; A. Harrington, 'Dilthey, Empathy and Verstehen', p. 313; and D.A. Wisner, 'Modes of Visualisation in Neo-Idealist Theories of the Historical Imagination (Cassirer, Collingwood, Huizinga)', *Collingwood Studies*, Vol. 6 (1999), pp. 54–6.

[21] H. Ritter, 'Understanding', *Dictionary of Concepts in History*, p. 436.

pathy into the problems which men wished to solve' when writing about the history of Christian heresies. This is because, in his view, the 'merely external history of dogma killeth; it is the internal history — the entering into the development of thought — that maketh alive'.[22] This, however, is an unusual case, for in his more explicit reflections on historical method throughout his life he opts exclusively instead for the terms 're-enactment' and the cognates 're-discover', 'revive', 'recover', 're-live', 're-create' and 'reconstruct'.[23] Now it is clear from looking at Collingwood's free exchange of 're-enactment' and its cognates throughout his writings that he did not employ it to mark out a tightly defined technical concept. That indeed would not have been in keeping with his statement in *An Essay on Philosophical Method* (1933) that it was the duty of philosophers to 'avoid the technical vocabulary proper to science' and to choose rather 'words according to the rules of literature'.[24] But this does not mean that Collingwood was not careful in his choice of words, for he does not consider 'empathy' and 'sympathy' to be cognates of 're-enactment', as many historians and history educators do. In *The Idea of History*, for example, he aligns sympathy with the 'outside' of history and 're-enactment' with the 'inside' of history.[25] And in 'The Principles of History', his portrayal of biography as a web woven of sympathy and malice is clearly not a compliment: biographers use sympathy simply to arouse the feelings of their readers.[26] Importantly, too, nowhere does he use the English term 'empathy' to support his historiographical claims, despite the fact that commentators persistently connect him with it. Given the wide circulation and conflation of the terms 'sympathy' and 'empathy' in English scholarship at the time that he wrote, decisions of non-usage might be just as important as those of usage. Put simply, a term may be defined in part or whole *via negativa* or by what it is not. So why did Collingwood avoid 'sympathy' and 'empathy'? It is contended here that he did so because he wanted to delineate space between

[22] W.H. Dray, *History as Re-enactment: R.G. Collingwood's Idea of History* (Oxford, 1995), p. 33; R.G. Collingwood, *Religion and Philosophy* [1916] (Bristol, 1994), pp. 42, 43.

[23] M. H. Nielsen, 'Re-enactment and Reconstruction in Collingwood's Philosophy of History', *History and Theory*, Vol. 20 (1) (1981), pp. 1–31. See also R.G. Collingwood, *The Idea of History*, pp. 58, 65, 69–70, 115, 117, 138, 163, 170, 202–3, 283, 284, 286, 289, 293, 296–7, 300–1, 303–4, 308, 312–3, 326–7, 334, 441–50, 463.

[24] R.G. Collingwood, *An Essay on Philosophical Method* (Oxford, 1933), p. 207.

[25] R.G. Collingwood, *The Idea of History* [1946], rev. edn., ed. W.J. van der Dussen (Oxford, 1993), pp. 302–3.

[26] R.G. Collingwood, 'The Principles of History', *The Principles of History and Other Writings*, ed. W.H. Dray and W.J. van der Dussen (Oxford, 1999), p. 70.

contemporary English usages of those terms and his own view of historical scholarship. First, the identification of the historian with the historical agent in 'sympathy' does not, as we shall see, sit with his characterisation of history as a critical and even 'autonomous' discipline. And second, Collingwood probably opted for 're-enact-ment' to distance himself from the immediate, intuitive psychologism associated with the English term 'empathy'. This is supported by Collingwood's common complaints about the expla-nations of human action provided by psychology[27] and his criticism of Dilthey in *The Idea of History* for connecting psychological analysis with historical understanding.[28] The clear distance between his views and the intuitive psychologism of 'empathy' will also become apparent when we look in more detail to his explanation of the workings of re-enactment. Collingwood was evidently influenced by English language scholarship on Dilthey. He was, however, not tied to the terms employed in English language scholarship, for he was able to read historiographical works in a number of other lan-guages, including German and Italian. In his analysis of Croce's *Teoria e Storia della Storiografia* from 1921, for instance, he writes that history 'goes on in the mind of the historian: he thinks it, he *enacts* it within himself'.[29] In translating for himself, Collingwood was thus able to access and question concepts and conceptual distinctions ignored in English language scholarship. Given his attempts to distance himself from contemporary English language views, his looking to foreign scholarship for terms made a great deal of sense.

The earliest extant statement that Collingwood makes about 're-enactment' in connection with his own historiographical views is to be found in his 'Outlines of a Philosophy of History', a series of lectures from April 1928. In a discussion on music history, he sug-gests that past music must be 're-enacted in the present' and signals

[27] See for example R.G. Collingwood, 'Reality as History' [1935], *The Principles of History and Other Writings*, pp. 174–6, 195–7; 'Human Nature as Human History: March 1936, First Draft', Ms Collingwood Dep. 12 (11), pp. 8, 9a, 24–5; 'Draft of Opening Chapters of a "Prolegomena to Logic" (or the Like)' [1920–1], Ms Collingwood Dep. 16 (5), pp. 41–56; 'Principles of History' [1939], esp. 'Psychol-ogy in Lagado', *The Principles of History and Other Writings*, pp. 89–91; *Religion and Philosophy*, pp. 41–4; *An Autobiography* (Oxford, 1939), pp. 92–5; *An Essay on Metaphysics* [1940], rev. edn., ed. R. Martin (Oxford, 1998), pp. 122–32; and *The Idea of History*, esp. pp. 172–5.

[28] R.G. Collingwood, *The Idea of History*, pp. 172–5.

[29] R.G. Collingwood, 'Croce's Philosophy of History' [1921], in *Essays in the Philos-ophy of History*, ed. W. Debbins (New York, 1966), p. 6, my emphasis.

the importance of this phrase by circling it.[30] To this he later added another historiographical example, which reads:

> To write the history of a battle, we must re-think the thoughts which determined its various tactical phases: we must see the ground of the battlefield as the opposing commanders saw it, and draw from the topography the conclusions that they drew: and so forth. The past event, ideal though it is, must be actual *in the historian's re-enactment* of it.[31]

Collingwood returned to the idea of re-enactment in a number of lectures and essays from 1936: 'Notes on the History of Historiography and Philosophy of History', 'Can Historians Be Impartial?', 'Human Nature and Human History', 'History as Re-enactment of Past Experience' and 'The Subject-matter of History', which were reprinted in *The Idea of History*.[32] Re-enactment is also mentioned in *An Autobiography* (1939),[33] though only the cognate 'reconstruct' is present in the manuscript 'The Principles of History' (also 1939), despite both Collingwood and Knox's indication that the latter would largely be about re-enactment.[34]

Despite this range of references — all available in published form since 1999 or earlier — historians, history educators and some historiographers repeatedly turn to two passages from Collingwood's writings as if they were the quintessential statements of his doctrine: page 218 from 'Human Nature and Human History' in *The Idea of History* and page 111 from *An Autobiography*. They read:

> Historical knowledge is the knowledge of what mind has done in the past, and at the same time is the redoing of this, the perpetuation of past acts in the present. Its object is therefore not a mere object, something outside the mind which knows it; it is an activity of thought, which can

---

[30] R.G. Collingwood, 'Outlines of a Philosophy of History, April 1928', Ms Collingwood Dep. 12 (4), p. 14.

[31] *Ibid.*, as reprinted in R.G. Collingwood, *The Idea of History*, p. 441, Collingwood's emphasis.

[32] R.G. Collingwood, 'Can Historians Be Impartial? — Paper Read to the Stubbs Historical Society, 27 January 1936' and 'Notes on the History of Historiography and Philosophy of History 1936', *The Principles of History and Other Writings*, pp. 211, 223; and *The Idea of History*, pp. 39, 65, 97, 115, 138, 158, 163, 177–8, 202, 204, 215–19, 226, 228, 282–304, 308, 312–13, 326–7. 'Human Nature and Human History' was published as an essay in 1936, but 'History as Re-enactment' and 'The Subject-matter of History' were originally part of Collingwood's lectures from 1936, which make up the first four sections of *The Idea of History*. See van der Dussen's introduction to the revised edition of *The Idea of History*, pp. ix–xix.

[33] R.G. Collingwood, *An Autobiography*, pp. 112, 114.

[34] R.G. Collingwood, 'Notes on Historiography Written on a Voyage to the East Indies 1938–9', *The Principles of History and Other Writings*, p. 245; on Knox's comment, see M. Nielsen, 'Re-enactment and Reconstruction in Collingwood's Philosophy of History', pp. 2–3.

be known only in so far as the knowing mind re-enacts it and knows itself as so doing.[35]

And:

> [T]he historian must be able to think over again for himself the thought whose expression he is trying to interpret. If for any reason he is such a kind of man that he cannot do this, he had better leave that problem alone. The important point here is that the historian of a certain thought must think for himself that very same thought, not another like it.[36]

Why they were chosen as representative is beyond my ken, for neither on their own nor in combination would they be sufficient to explain the breadth of what Collingwood is trying to achieve. Using ordinary language, he visits and revisits ideas, allowing his readers to build up understanding from different angles. He is not an analytic philosopher who proceeds by definition. Even if a reader had access only to *The Idea of History*, many other statements on re-enactment would be available. It is as if these passages were selected by one early commentator and subsequent commentators read them as representative perhaps without looking to the primary sources themselves.

Given this restricted range of materials used in commentaries, it is hardly surprising that error and confusion abounds over Collingwood's view of 're-enactment'. And this confusion, I believe, emanates more particularly from four words he uses which in combination appear to jar: 'inside', 'outside' and 'same thought'.

'Inside', 'Outside' and 'Same Thought'

In the passage from 'Human Nature and Human History' cited above, Collingwood asserts that the object of history is 'not a mere object, something outside the mind'. This is just one of a host of cases where he uses the words 'inside' and 'outside' and the near-synonyms 'internal' and 'external' to distinguish the efforts of historians from those who he saw as furnishing lesser explanations such as psychologists and natural scientists. Put simply, the 'outside' of history refers to that 'which can be described in terms of bodies and their movements', like portraying Caesar's death as the spilling of blood on the floor and the time at which his bodily organs ceased to function. The 'inside' of an event, on the other hand, refers to that 'which can only be described in terms of thought', as with seeing

---

[35] R.G. Collingwood, *The Idea of History*, p. 218.
[36] R.G. Collingwood, *An Autobiography*, p. 111.

Caesar's death in terms of his defiance of Republican law.[37] Collingwood's distinction here is not too dissimilar from Gilbert Ryle's account of 'thin' and 'thick' description, where the former considers the contraction of the eyelids of two boys as the same and the latter identifies one as an involuntary twitch and the other as a conspiratorial wink.[38] Both Collingwood and Ryle are expressing a preference for the description of the social meaning of actions. Collingwood's terminology, however, is problematic because the stronger spatial connotation of 'outside' and 'inside' lead to them being easily confused with 'public' and 'private', prompting in turn the erroneous conclusion that he is presenting not a view of *description* but a view of *mind*.

Dualism assumes that the mental world is private and therefore inaccessible to public observation. This view of mind leads to scepticism about other minds and thus about the very possibility of historical understanding. It also calls into question Collingwood's claim in *An Autobiography* that historians must think the *same* thoughts as the historical agents they study. Though not stated directly, most commentators who are not closely acquainted with Collingwood's writings — here I would place most history educators, most historians and a smaller number of historiographers — assume that he was a dualist and let that view infuse their understanding of re-enactment. Where they diverge is on whether the identity of thought sought in re-enactment is achieved indirectly via analogy, directly via special penetrative powers or is not possible at all. We will now look at the analogical and intuitive explanations for the possibility of re-enactment and explain why they do not match Collingwood's understanding of the concept.

The first interpretation of Collingwood's re-enactment doctrine suggests that the historian can achieve identity of thought with historical agents via analogy. Such a view of re-enactment is clearly conveyed by Griffith, who writes:

> one knows about the present by reasoning about the 'whys' and 'whats' of one's actions. By analogy, one can reason that others act the way they do for similar reasons. Likewise, we can re-think the past and come to some conclusions about the reasons people acted as they did.[39]

Thus, for example, if a behaviour such as raising one's hand, palm extended, in front of another person has been associated with a

[37] R.G. Collingwood, 'Can Historians Be Impartial?', *The Principles of History and Other Writings*, p. 217; and *The Idea of History*, p. 213.
[38] G. Ryle, *Collected Works*, Vol. 2 (London, 1971), pp. 480–96.
[39] B. Griffith, 'Historical Thinking as a Mode of Experience', *Becoming a Canadian Teacher* (Toronto, 1993), pp. 32–3.

request for that person to stop, then any instances where we find historical agents doing the same or similar will lead us to conclude that they are probably requesting the same thing. As van der Dussen and Dray have identified, Collingwood sometimes uses analogical reasoning, but only for setting forth exploratory hypotheses. For example, in 'Roman Signals on the Cumberland Coast' (1929), he wonders whether the construction of frontier works on the Danube in response to raids might also explain the construction of Hadrian's Wall.[40] Analogical reasoning, however, is absent from his discussions on re-enactment and with good reason, for a number of problems are evident. First, any argument from analogy is nondeductive. That is, there is no way of establishing with absolute certainty what is going on in the mind of the other person. For example, the historical agent who has their hand raised may not be requesting that another person stop, but may be signalling compliance with the Nazi regime. Second, the analogical approach provides very weak inductive reasoning, for its conclusions are drawn from one case only, that of the historian. As Wittgenstein asks, 'How can I generalise the *one case* so irresponsibly?'[41] Third, the argument from analogy implies that historians must learn from their own cases alone what it means to have a mental attribute, say joy. But this is absurd. If 'joy' is given meaning solely by a procedure in which the historian is the only participant, then there is really no sense to the idea that others can have joy too. Indeed, on this view, the historian's joy and joy *per se* would have exactly the same meaning. But surely this is wrong. To have a concept of an experience like joy is not to have the concept of one's experience alone. Otherwise, the distinctions between 'my joy', 'her joy' and 'your joy' would make no sense at all. As Strawson puts it:

> It is a necessary condition of one's ascribing states of consciousness, experiences to oneself . . . that one should also ascribe them or be prepared to ascribe them, to others . . . The main point here is purely a logical one: the idea of a predicate as correlative with that of a *range* of distinguishable individuals of which the predicate can be significantly, though not necessarily truly, affirmed.[42]

Moreover, if each of us had to name a sensation such as joy from our own case, then no public use of the word 'joy' would be possible.

---

[40] R.G. Collingwood, 'Roman Signal-Stations on the Cumberland Coast', *Transactions of the Cumberland and Westmorland Antiquarian and Archaeological Society*, 1920, ns no. 29, p. 143; as cited in W.H. Dray, *History as Re-enactment*, p. 101.

[41] L. Wittgenstein, *Philosophical Investigations*, ed. G.E.M. Anscombe, R. Rhees and G.H. von Wright (Oxford, 1953), §293.

[42] P.F. Strawson, *Individuals* (London, 1959), p. 99.

While this point will receive further examination when we look to Collingwood's view of how re-enactment works, the foregoing discussion suggests that the argument from analogy rests on shaky ground.

The second and far more popular explanation of how identity of thought is achieved in re-enactment bestows upon the historian special penetrative powers of intuitive insight. This view of Collingwood's work is present in the judgements of Cohen, Hayden White, Walsh and Marwick[43] but is most strongly expressed by Gardiner. In *The Nature of Historical Explanation* and a paper for *Philosophy*, Gardiner ascribes the view to Collingwood that minds are private and thus that re-enactment requires an 'additional power of knowing' possessed by historians, 'which allows them to penetrate into the minds of their study and take, as it were, psychological X-ray photographs'.[44] No deliberative process connects the historian with the historical agent: the historian knows the agent's thoughts in an immediate and unmediated fashion.[45] And this view is also evident beyond the academy: it is worth noting that since the publication of *The Idea of History*, 're-enactment' has come to denote in common usage the staged recreation of events, where participants dress up and talk of becoming historical agents. This idea of re-enactment has been richly parodied, for example, in Monty Python's 'Batley Townswomens' Guild Presents the Battle of Pearl Harbour' and in conservative attacks on empathy in the British press during the 1980s and 1990s as promoting the behaviour of the mad (i.e. 'He thinks he is Napoleon').[46] Such views, of course, make it difficult for readers to take Collingwood's ideas seriously. That this is the most popular view of Collingwood is unsurprising, though, for the combination of the spatial connotations of 'inside' and 'outside' and the prevailing view of 'empathy' in English language scholarship as an intuitive power would have made it difficult to read his ideas any other way. As with the analogical view, however, the intuitive view of re-enactment fails because 'same thought' cannot be given meaning entirely by a procedure in which the historian is the only partici-

[43] L.J. Cohen, 'A Survey of Work in the Philosophy of History 1946–50', *Philosophical Quarterly*, Vol. 2 (7) (1957), p. 177; H. White, 'Collingwood and Toynbee: Transitions in English Historical Work', *English Miscellany*, Vol.8 (1957), p. 166; W.H. Walsh, *An Introduction to the Philosophy of History* (London, 1964), pp. 44, 48; and A. Marwick, *The Nature of History* (London, 1970), p. 23.

[44] P. Gardiner, 'The "Objects" of Historical Knowledge', *Philosophy*, Vol. 27 (1952), pp. 211–20; and *The Nature of Historical Explanation* (Oxford, 1952), pp. 117, 128, 130, 135.

[45] P. Gardiner, *The Nature of Historical Explanation*, p. 130.

[46] *Monty Python's Flying Circus*, series 1, show 11, first aired 28 December 1969.

pant. To have a concept of 'same thought' is not to have the concept of one's experience alone because the rules binding its use are established in social practices.[47]

Criticisms of this intuitive view of re-enactment have been expressed since the 1950s in the writings of Grant, Donagan, Dray and Goldstein,[48] but they have gained force since Nielsen's mashalling of unpublished materials. As she points out, Collingwood tends in both his published and unpublished works to use the concept of 'intuition' in connection with 'immediate experience' or art, not with history, and does not endorse it. This is clear from multiple comments in his 'Lectures on the Philosophy of History' from Trinity Term 1929. He writes, for instance:

> History is now no longer the mere irrational intuition with which the nineteenth-century Germans had identified it; it is no longer simply the aesthetic intuition with which Croce had identified it in his first essay. It is not intuition but judgement. It does not merely apprehend the individuals, it makes judgements about it, attaches predicates to it. These predicates are universals; and hence the universality, the *a priori* character, of thought, is present in history in the form of the predicates which historical thought attaches to agents and acts, events and movements.[49]

As this quote shows us, the various forms of dualism do not exhaust the possibilities open to the interpreter of Collingwood's re-enactment doctrine. Nor must we resort to behaviourism. Rather, Collingwood's position is a middle stance between dualism and behaviourism. Mental events and states, he explicitly argues in 'Human Nature and Human History' and *The New Leviathan* (1942), are neither reducible to bodily expressions (as behaviourists argue) nor totally separable from them (as dualists argue): historians investigate actions, which are the unity of both.[50] For him, it is public language that provides us with the means of achieving identity of thought between the historian and the historical agent. The strength of this public, conceptual view of re-enactment derives from the rec-

[47] H. Saari, 'R.G. Collingwood on the Identity of Thoughts', *Dialogue*, Vol. 28 (1) (1989), p. 83.

[48] C.K. Grant, 'Collingwood's Theory of Historical Knowledge', *Renaissance and Modern Studies*, Vol. 1 (1) (1951), pp. 65–86; A. Donagan, 'The Verification of Historical Theses', *Philosophical Quarterly*, Vol. 6 (1956), pp. 197, 198; W.H. Dray, 'R.G. Collingwood and the Acquaintance Theory of Knowledge', *Revue Internationale de Philosophie*, Vol. 2 (1957), pp. 420–32; and L.J. Goldstein, 'Collingwood's Theory of Historical Knowing', *History and Theory*, Vol. 9 (1) (1970), pp. 13–36.

[49] R. G. Collingwood, 'Lectures on the Philosophy of History — II C. T[rinity] T[erm] 1929', Ms Collingwood Dep. 12 (6), p. 35, see also pp. 27, 28, 29, 33 and 36.

[50] R.G. Collingwood, *The Idea of History*, p. 213; *The New Leviathan* [1942], rev. edn., ed. D. Boucher (Oxford, 1992), §2.41–2.43.

ognition of commonalities in Collingwood's and Wittgenstein's writings on the nature of mind and language. A few writers — von Leyden, Walsh, J. Martin, Saari, Llewelyn, Boucher, Vanheeswijck, Lewis and Blackburn — have identified similarities between various aspects of Collingwood's and Wittgenstein's views, but none have yet done so in more than an exploratory fashion nor included 'The Principles of History' in their comparisons.[51] Many more writers, though, see Collingwood's declared hostility towards contemporary analytical philosophy in *An Autobiography* as a signal that he and Wittgenstein are poles apart or even that Wittgenstein's 'unhistorical' views had 'deleterious' consequences for Collingwood's theories.[52] In contrast, here and in the chapters that follow, we will see that Collingwood and Wittgenstein are not so far apart as is supposed.

Collingwood and Wittgenstein on Mind and Language

For Collingwood as for Wittgenstein, mind is not to be defined as a thing but as an activity.[53] Nor is the relationship between mental activities and their manifestations denied (as with dualism) or viewed as a causal connection to be discovered by the regular concurrence between two types of events (behaviourism). Rather, the physical expression of a mental activity in verbal and non-verbal forms (including material evidence) is a *criterion* for that activity.

[51] W. von Leyden, 'Philosophy of Mind: An Appraisal of Collingwood's Theories of Consciousness, Language and Imagination', in M. Krausz (ed.), *Critical Essays on the Philosophy of R. G. Collingwood* (Oxford, 1972), pp. 23ff; W.H. Walsh, 'Collingwood and Metaphysical Neutralism', in M. Krausz (ed.), *Critical Essays on the Philosophy of R. G. Collingwood*, p. 149; J.A. Martin Jnr, 'Collingwood and Wittgenstein on the Task of Philosophy: An Interesting Convergence', *Philosophy Today*, Vol. 25 (Spring) (1981), pp. 12–23; H. Saari, 'R.G. Collingwood and the Identity of Thoughts', esp. pp. 83–4; J.E. Llewelyn, 'On Not Speaking the Same Language — II', *Australasian Journal of Philosophy* (1962), pp. 127–45; D. Boucher, 'Editor's Introduction', *The New Leviathan*, p. xvii; G. Vanheeswijck, 'Collingwood en Wittgenstein: hervormde versus deiktische metafysica', Vol. 84 (3) (Algemeen, Nederlands, 1992), pp. 165–81; P. Lewis, 'Collingwood and Wittgenstein: Struggling with Darkness', *Collingwood Studies*, Vol. 5 (1998), pp. 28–42; and S. Blackburn, 'Reenactment as Critique of Logical Analysis: Wittgensteinian Themes in Collingwood', in H.H. Kögler, and K.R. Stueber (eds.), *Empathy and Agency: The Problem of Understanding in the Human Sciences* (Boulder, CO, 2000), pp. 270–87.

[52] G.P. Ramachandra, 'Re-Experiencing Past Thoughts: Some Reflections on Collingwood's Theory of History', *Journal of Indian Council of Philosophical Research* (1996), pp. 67–82. See also P. Johnson, *R.G. Collingwood: An Introduction* (Bristol, 1998).

[53] R.G. Collingwood, *Religion and Philosophy*, p. 100; L. Wittgenstein, *Zettel*, ed. G.E.M. Anscombe and G.H. von Wright (Oxford, 1967), §608–10.

That is, it is part of the concept of a mental activity of a particular kind that it should have a characteristic manifestation. Fundamental to this view of mind is the distinction between criteria for and symptoms of mental activities. We recall that, where the connection between physical expression and the conclusions drawn from it is a matter of analogy, the evidence is a symptom of the mental activity. Where the relation between physical expression and the conclusions drawn from it is something that is grasped by anyone who possesses that concept of the relevant activity, then the physical expression is a criterion of the mental activity. For example, a raised hand may be a symptom of support for Nazism, but Nazi beliefs and ideas are criteria for support for Nazism. This view of mind, I believe, clearly underpins Collingwood's writings on 'criteriological sciences'.[54] For Collingwood, 'criteriological' signals not only a particular relationship between expressions and conclusions made about them but also the passing of judgement on other people as 'having succeeded or failed' in their purposes.[55] If 'judgement' here meant simply the critical study of the rules for applications of concepts, then he would be in agreement with Wittgenstein's view of mind. His use of ethics as an example in his discussions on criteriological sciences, though, indicates an interest also in judgements of 'good'. The match between Collingwood's and Wittgenstein's criterial views of mind is therefore not exact. But the way in which he handles his favourite example of a non-criteriological science — psychology — does suggest a link between 'inside' and 'criteriological' and 'outside' and 'non-criteriological'. Nowhere is this clearer than in his interesting extension of *Gulliver's Travels* in 'The Principles of History', where psychologists try to study enjoyment of music solely by measuring bodily changes in listeners.[56] Put simply, in order to be critical about events, you must first go 'inside' them, and to go inside them is to consider criteria.

When we acknowledge, evaluate and respond to peoples' actions — past and present — we use mentalistic concepts. And with regard to mentalistic concepts, common concepts and the criteriological rules that bind them provide the intersubjective ground on which we base our judgements about actions. Wittgenstein expresses this

[54] See for example R.G. Collingwood, 'The Principles of History', *The Principles of History and Other Writings*, pp. 84–8.

[55] R.G. Collingwood, *The Principles of Art* (Oxford, 1938), p. 171n; *An Essay on Metaphysics*, pp. 109–11; 'The Principles of History', *The Principles of History and Other Writings*, pp. 84–9.

[56] R.G. Collingwood, 'The Principles of History', *The Principles of History and Other Writings*, pp. 89–91.

idea clearly by saying that 'if language is to be a means of communication there must be agreement not only in definitions but also (queer as this may sound) in judgements'.[57] Clearly, the cornerstone of Wittgenstein's view of mind is the idea that language is public and shared. This view may also be found in Collingwood's writings, particularly *The New Leviathan*, where he describes a word as 'a linguistic habit of the community using it' and argues that the word 'good':

> or any equivalent in any language, is used in common by numbers of men; and if every man used it in a sense peculiar to himself, to signify the object of his own desire and nobody else's, there would be (so far as that word is concerned) not a language but a babel.[58]

Hence his recommendation in the same work that to understand the meaning of 'civilisation' we should ask how people have used the word and what they meant by it.[59] This view of language as public and shared, though, is more explicitly laid out in Wittgenstein's well known demolition of the dualist claim that minds are private and that each one of us gives meaning to our experiences via a 'private language', which we recapitulate here.

Language is public if it refers to what is shared amongst people; language is private if it refers to the experiences of which only the speaker is aware and that only they can understand. As Wittgenstein writes of the latter:

> Imagine a language in which a person could write down or give vocal expression to his inner experiences — his feelings, moods and the rest — for his private use? — Well, we can't do so in our ordinary language? — But that is not what I mean. The individual words of this language are to refer to what can only be known to the person speaking; to his immediate private sensations. So another person cannot understand the language.[60]

Wittgenstein distinguishes two senses of the word 'private'. The first sense of privacy refers to knowledge. In this sense, something is private to me if I alone know about it. The second sense of privacy refers to possession. In this sense, something is private to me if I alone own it. The second sense is most relevant to us in our pursuit of re-enactment, for it is commonly assumed by critics that thoughts are the private property of the individuals that contemplate them. What can be said of this 'inalienable'[61] sense of privacy, according to which only I

[57] L. Wittgenstein, *Philosophical Investigations*, §242.

[58] R.G. Collingwood, *The New Leviathan*, §§34. 12 and 11.45; see also *The Principles of Art*, p. 225.

[59] Ibid., §34.13; see also 'What Civilisation Means', *The New Leviathan*, p. 480.

[60] L. Wittgenstein, *Philosophical Investigations*, §243, see also §256.

[61] A. Kenny, *Wittgenstein* (Harmondsworth, 1975), p. 183.

can have sensations? Here, Wittgenstein asks two questions: 'Which
are my pains?' and 'What counts as the criterion of identity here?'
Wittgenstein addresses the first by suggesting that the possessor of
pain is the person who gives it expression. Thus my pains are the
pains that I express. Now one person's pain can be in another's body.
For example, if I see a friend with a black eye, I say 'Ouch!' How
painful'. And when I am asked to identify the location of the pain, I
touch my friend's eye. So, my pain is not necessarily the pain felt in
my body.[62]
    Furthermore, it is a mistake to assume that the possessive in 'my
pain' is the same as that used to refer to material objects. In order to
use a possessive in the case of material objects, such as 'my pen' or
'your pen', one must correctly identify the owner of the article.
When referring to sensations on the other hand, in order to employ a
possessive such as 'her pain' it is sufficient to know who is in pain.
There is no further step requiring correct identification of owner-
ship: to ask 'Are you sure that it is *you* who have the pain?' would be
nonsensical.[63] The question 'Which are my pains?' implies the further question about how we distinguish particular types of pain,
such as toothache, headache and so on from one another. One can
respond that we can establish that identity by phenomenal characteristics such as intensity and location. If these phenomenal characteristics are the same, it is possible for us to have the *same* pain. For
example, if we both thump our fingers with a hammer then it is perfectly reasonable for us to say that we have the same pain. One may
object that this is not quite correct, since the pains are only in corresponding places in two bodies. In his response, Wittgenstein notes
quite rightly that we count pain in a different way from objects. In
counting objects one can take into account the owner as an identifying mark: for example, 'my pen' and 'your pen' refer to two pens. In
the case of pains, the owner cannot be regarded as an identifying
mark: for example, 'my toothache' and 'your toothache' are not two
toothaches.
    At base, the question of identity can convey the mistaken notion
that 'the same' is always governed by the same fixed rule irrespec-
tive of context. This error is seen, for instance, in Ayer's account of
mental images:

> Physical objects are public because it makes sense to say of different peo-
> ple that they are perceiving the same physical object; mental images are
> private because it does not make sense to say of different people that

[62]   L. Wittgenstein, *The Blue and Brown Books* (Oxford, 1958), p. 49.
[63]   *Ibid.*, p. 67.

they are having the same mental image, they can be imagining the same thing but it is impossible that their respective images should be literally the same.[64]

His talk of mental images not being 'literally the same' makes use of the word 'same' as if it had one and the same meaning in all contexts. This is not the case. When we talk of the identity of physical objects, such as pens, we use 'same' and 'exactly like' interchangeably, as in 'This pen is identical with that'. Here we are talking of two pens. That is, when we talk of the identity of physical objects we talk of two or more things: they are numerically distinct. But in the case of mental activities or colours, they are numerically indistinct.[65]

These mistakes concern private language as knowledge. The second error that the supporter of the idea of private language makes is to believe that concepts acquire meaning and can be used by private definition. Wittgenstein objects to this view on two grounds. First, a great deal of 'stage setting' is involved in the formation of a concept: what is presupposed is the grammar of the word that shows us 'the post where the word . . . is to be stationed'.[66] A word without grammar is like a pawn without a chess set, as Wittgenstein demonstrates with his 'beetle in a box' analogy:

> Suppose everyone had a box with something in it: we call it a 'beetle'. No one can look into anyone else's box and everyone says he knows what a beetle is only by looking at *his* beetle — Here it would be quite possible for everyone to have something different in his box. One might even imagine such a thing constantly changing — But suppose that word 'beetle' had a use in these people's language? — If so, it would not be used as the name of a thing. The thing in the box has no place in the language game at all; not even as *something*: for the box might even be empty. — No one can 'divide through' by the thing in the box; it cancels out whatever it is. That is to say: if we construe the grammar of the expression of sensations on the model of object and designation the object drops out of consideration as irrelevant.[67]

What matters is the grammar — the intersubjective criteriological rules of use — of the word 'pain'. Private definition would also make nonsense of common statements like 'Are you in pain?' or even 'That looks painful'. Part of my thinking that another person experiences the same private sensation that I feel when I have pain is that I imagine that person having a private sensation. But how can I do this?[68] Furthermore, if one learns the meaning of the concept of pain from

[64]   A.J. Ayer, *The Problem of Knowledge* (Harmondsworth, 1956), p. 36.
[65]   L. Wittgenstein, *Philosophical Investigations*, §253.
[66]   *Ibid.*, §257.
[67]   *Ibid.*, §293.
[68]   *Ibid.*, §§350, 302.

one's own experience, then a person who has never experienced pain would not be able to use the concept, and a blind person would never be able to use the words 'see' or 'I have an image of'. All of this tells us that 'pain' is not a private sensation; it is a word in language, the use of which requires us to know its grammar. Thus a concept is not formed by merely experiencing a sensation. To have a concept means to know how a word is used, to be able to follow the rules that govern the use of the word. That requires shared or public language.

Even if we did grant that a private linguist can acquire a concept, could it be retained? On the private linguist's account, possessing a concept is like having a mental filing cabinet in which sensations are matched with labels. Being able to use a concept in future means being able to detect a resemblance between the current and the 'filed' sensation. The private linguist's justification for using a concept, then, is a subjective justification. But our linguist forgets that appealing for the justification of something is to ask for an objective criterion; otherwise, whatever I think is right on any one occasion will be right. And that is no guarantee for consistent usage even by the private linguist alone over time.[69]

In his refutation of private language, Wittgenstein repeatedly affirms the social dimension of language. A language is a set of activities or practices defined by certain rules which govern the various usages of words. On his account, then, understanding others is made possible by virtue of the training we receive in the language rules of our community. Though not as explicitly stated, that same view of language underpins Collingwood's view of re-enactment.

Re-enactment: A Conceptual View

Let us assume that historians try to identify the thoughts they have re-enacted as those of historical agents by applying inner, subjective or 'private' criteria of identity. As a result, only historians can know whether their acts of thought are those of historical agents. We recall that such a view underpins most commentaries on Collingwood's re-enactment doctrine by history educators, historians and some historiographers. For example, as Jenkins argues in *Rethinking History*:

> What is effectively ignored in empathy is that in every act of communication there is an act of translation going on; that every act of speech (speech-act) is an interpretation between privacies.[70]

[69]   *Ibid.*, §§265, 258.
[70]   K. Jenkins, *Rethinking History* (London, 1992), p. 39.

Recalling Wittgenstein's views on language, we now see that this interpretation makes no sense, because historians cannot establish private rules of identity outside of the linguistic communities of which they are a part. Our usage of the concept of 'rules' involves the idea that they are public because they are rooted in social practices. If historians want to communicate with each other, they must use concepts like 'same thought' in socially recognisable ways. As Saari first demonstrated in *Re-enactment: A Study in R.G. Collingwood's Philosophy of History* (1984), the view of re-enactment as functioning by means of public conceptual criteria infuses Collingwood's published and unpublished writings.[71] To this we can add further evidence from unpublished manuscripts that Saari had not seen, particularly 'The Principles of History'.

Evidence of Collingwood's alignment with Wittgenstein may be found in his rejection of 'copy' theories of sense and thought identity. It is first hinted at in his distancing of Aristotle, Berkeley and Reid from 'medieval' theories of representative perception in his commentary on book three of *De Anima* (1913–14). In that unpublished commentary, he argues that the notion that we do not perceive objects but private copies that resemble them can be refuted on the grounds that we cannot escape perception to judge resemblance. Thus he concludes that we do not perceive copies, but 'precisely' the objects.[72] In 1935 he revisits this idea through the example of the sound of a piano wire, though this time he uses the word 'identity' explicitly and hints at this identity being numerically indistinct. He writes:

> the relation of this rhythm to the rhythm in the air and in the piano wire is not one of resemblance; it is one of identity. It is the very same rhythm which vibrates in the string, in the air, and in our heads.

And:

> The vibration-rhythm which rings in the ear is not another vibration-rhythm somehow copying that which vibrates in the instrument; it is the very same rhythm, for this rhythm is a form, and therefore immaterial, and therefore capable of being embodied in a multiplicity of different things without itself undergoing multiplication.[73]

In between the composition of those two documents, Collingwood evidently realised that the same argument could be transferred to

---

[71] H. Saari, *Re-Enactment: A Study in R.G. Collingwood's Philosophy of History* (Åbo, 1984).

[72] R.G. Collingwood, '*Aristotelis De Anima Libri Tres* — Translation and Commentary' [1913–14], Ms Collingwood Dep. 11, p. 105.

[73] R.G. Collingwood, 'Central Problems in Metaphysics — Lectures Written April 1935, for Delivery in T[rinity] T[erm] 1935', Ms Collingwood 20 (1), pp. 36, 57.

thought identity. That he could so easily transfer from perception to thought will be explained when we examine his writings on imagination in chapter five. Like Wittgenstein, he holds that our usage of the concepts 'same thought' signals identity in conceptual content alone, not identity in content *plus* spatial and numerical identity. That is, the same thought can be contemplated by two different individuals who do not even have to be in the same place. But more radically than Wittgenstein, Collingwood also explicitly notes that *temporal* identity is not required. As a result, re-enactment is possible because 'same thought' denotes identity in conceptual content, not identity in conceptual content plus numerical, spatial *and* temporal identity. Collingwood's first extant expression of this point may be found in 'Outlines of a Philosophy of History' (1928):

> The re-enactment of the past in the present *is the past itself* so far as that is knowable to the historian. We understood what Newton thought by thinking — not *copies* of his thoughts — a silly and meaningless phrase — but his thoughts themselves over again. When we have done that, we know what Newton thought, not mediately, but immediately. The historian's thought, then, neither is nor contains nor involves any copy of its object. The historian's thought is, or rather contains as one of its elements, that object itself, namely, the act of thought which the historian is trying to understand, re-thought in the present by himself. A person who failed to realise that thoughts are not private property might say that it is not Newton's thought that I understand, but only my own. That would be silly because, whatever subjective idealism may pretend, thought is always and everywhere *de jure* common property, and is *de facto* common property wherever people at large have the intelligence to think in common.[74]

Further evidence that Collingwood holds a conceptual view of re-enactment may be found in 'History as Re-enactment of Past Experience' in *The Idea of History*. In this section of the epilegomena, he argues that the intervening time interval is no grounds for denying that Euclid's thinking 'the angles are equal' and my thinking 'the angles are equal' are the same thought, because we are mistaken if we believe that 'acts of thought are numerically distinct and therefore numerable'.[75] He demonstrates this by citing the examples of a person who thinks 'the angles are equal' for five seconds and a person who thinks 'the angles are equal', wanders off that thought and returns to it after three seconds. Do we not talk of these two individ-

---

[74] R.G. Collingwood, 'Outlines of a Philosophy of History' [1928], *The Idea of History*, p. 450. In the manuscript, the words 'neither is nor contains nor involves any copy of its object' are underlined in blue pencil. See 'Outlines of a Philosophy of History', Ms Collingwood Dep. 12 (4), p. 24.

[75] R.G. Collingwood, *The Idea of History*, p. 286.

uals thinking the same thought, even though there was a break and revival in the second case and there may be two or more 'numerically different but specifically identical' thoughts in the first case? Given this, why not talk of the same thought held by different people in different times?[76] Collingwood reinforces this point when he asks in 'Outline of a Philosophy of History':

> If the objector says that *no* kind of re-enactment is possible, merely because nothing can happen twice, we shall treat his objection with less courtesy: pointing out that he would himself not hesitate to speak of dining twice in the same inn, or bathing twice in the same river, or reading twice out of the same book, or hearing the same symphony twice. Is the binomial theorem as known to him, we should ask, the same theorem that Newton invented, or not? If he says yes, he has admitted all we want. If he says no, we can easily convict him of self-contradiction: for he is assuming that in our mutual discourse we have ideas in common, and this is inconsistent with his thesis.[77]

Common language furnishes us with the criteria by which to judge the identity of sense data and even thought in re-enactment. But common language also provides us with the means to make re-enactment possible. This explanation of re-enactment is explicitly present in Collingwood's 'The Principles of History'.

Historians, Collingwood argues in that document, study actions expressing thoughts. And to express thought, he continues, 'is to be language'.[78] That is, whenever a trace of thought is evident, it can be 'read'. Traces include verbal and non-verbal communication and notations of language, whether in writing or material evidence. These thoughts can be 'read' and 'reconstructed' with precision. To explain more particularly what is involved in this 'reading' Collingwood works through the example of a charter reputedly issued by Henry I. First, he tells us, the historian must establish that, if the document is a copy, it is a true one. Here the historian might consider errors of transcription or even mechanical reproduction, like the omission of a word due to human error or even a mark on a photographic negative. Second, the historian must establish that it is not a forgery. Third, the historian then reads the charter, as you are

---

[76] *Ibid.*, p. 286; see also *Religion and Philosophy*, p. 116. On Collingwood's notion of thoughts and acts of thought standing outside time, see G. D'Oro, 'Collingwood on Re-enactment and the Identity of Thought', *Journal of the History of Philosophy*, Vol. 38 (1) (2000), pp. 87–101.

[77] R.G. Collingwood, 'Outlines of a Philosophy of History', *The Idea of History*, p. 446.

[78] Interestingly, the title of this section was originally 'Evidence as Language'. This was changed to 'Evidence and Language'. See *The Principles of History and Other Writings*, p. 48n. This corresponds to p. 40 of the ms.

reading the words on this page. Finally — and most importantly — the historian must determine what it means, by considering for instance how the king saw the situation he faced and what he was trying to achieve through the issue of the charter. The first three steps are an accepted part of scholarship but do not correspond to historical thinking. At best, they are non-essential (processes one and two) and essential (process three) preliminaries to it. It is only when the historian 'reads' historically that historical thinking is achieved.[79] Later on in the same chapter, Collingwood also considers an example of material evidence, suggesting that archaeologists treat triangular slabs of clay historically when they 'read' them as a piece of language and then seek to know something about the thoughts of the people that made them.[80] 'Reading' is therefore not an activity confined to documents.

In that same work, Collingwood notes that two other things characterise historical thinking: autonomy and imagination. In describing historical thinking as 'autonomous', Collingwood here means not only that historians have critical control over the evidence they use, but that they 'make it in their heads' via historical 'reading'. To explain the idea of 'making evidence in their heads', Collingwood cites the analogy that an animal's food is not what it ingests, but what nourishes it; and nourishment is only produced after internal processes like digestion. Fascinating though this is, it does not really enlighten the reader as to the nature of those mental processes. It is enough, however, to suggest distance between Collingwood's views and contemporary uses of 'sympathy'. Similarly intriguing is Collingwood's suggestion that the 'reconstruction' of a thought from the traces left by it is at least partly a reconstruction in the historian's imagination. This is the only explicit connection between imagination and 're-enactment' or its cognates (in this case 'reconstruction') to be found in Collingwood's writings. It is worth asking why that is so, for Collingwood's implication of imagination in historical 'reading' clearly bestows upon it some importance. Unfortunately, however, Collingwood offers only the implication, not an explanation for it. In their analysis of that manuscript, Dray and van der Dussen thus understandably express the wish that Collingwood had gone on to link his comment on the imagination to the analysis he offers of it in both the rough notes for and final copy of his inaugural lecture as Waynflete Professor of Metaphysical Philosophy — 'The Historical Imagination' (1935) — and *The Principles of Art*

[79] *Ibid.*, pp. 48–53.
[80] *Ibid.*, pp. 66–7.

(1938).[81] In chapter five of this work, an attempt at such a link is made.

Mere Semantics?

At the start of this chapter, two relatively straightforward aims were adopted: first, to establish to what extent Collingwood actually employed the terms 'empathy', 'sympathy' and 're-enactment' in his historiographical writings; and second, to examine whether he made any explicit link between any of these and the concept of 'imagination'. We have discovered in the course of this chapter that answers to these questions can be easily offered. We now know that while Collingwood met his aim to avoid the use of technical terms in his philosophical writings, he did not use 'empathy', 'sympathy' and 're-enactment' interchangeably, as many history educators and historians do today. Rather, he employed the term 'sympathy' rarely, and never in the context of his historiographical writings. He preferred instead to use the term 're-enact' and cognates such as 're-think', 're-create' and 're-construct'. Importantly, too, we have noted that nowhere did he use the term 'empathy'. And, to round things off, we have noted that there is only one place in Collingwood's writings in which a direct link between imagination and 're-enactment' or one of its cognates can be found, namely in 'The Principles of History'.

Collingwood would no doubt acknowledge that I have demonstrated a grasp of both the non-essential (processes one and two) and essential (process three) preliminaries of historical thinking, as set out in 'The Principles of History'. But have I demonstrated historical thinking? That is, have I 'read' historically? In response, I believe that in describing Collingwood's historiographical vocabulary, we have begun to gain some idea of both how he viewed his historiographical situation and what he was trying to achieve in writing of 're-enactment'. Collingwood, it has been pointed out, had the language skills to avoid the use of the English term 'empathy' and had good reason to avoid it, given its characterisation as a special penetrative power of intuitive insight in English language scholarship. This is because for Collingwood, the operation of 're-enactment' and the judgement of identity of thoughts are made possible by shared, public language. Similarly, the association of 'sympathy' in English language and German scholarship with the

[81] R.G. Collingwood, 'The Historical Imagination', in *The Idea of History*, 231–48; and 'Inaugural: Rough Notes' [1935], *The Principles of History and Other Writings*, pp. 143–69.

identification of historian with historical agent clearly conflicted with his aim to characterise historical thought as critical and even autonomous. But such statements are only tentative beginnings, however, for much of what Collingwood took to be 'historical thinking' still lies in shadow. We do not yet, for instance, understand what role the imagination plays in it, or what he understood the terms 'autonomous' or 'reading historically' to be. Nor, moreover, have we even established what historians can gain access to via re-enactment: that is, what Collingwood meant by 'thought'. In the chapters that follow, I hope to bring some light to the shadow.

Chapter III

The Subject-matter of History

The idealist fallacy consists in interpretations of human conduct which rest upon a conception of man as Homo sapiens in a narrow and exclusive sense. To isolate merely the rational component of human existence is to falsify both humanity and rationality. Collingwood's [neo-idealism] is antihistorical, antiempirical, and absurd.[1]

One of the most significant changes to historical research and writing in the twentieth century was the dramatic broadening of the subjects considered. Whereas history prior to that time had been conceived largely as an account of the political activities of great European or North American men, historians began to recover the experiences of those marginalised by that focus. First social historians drew upon Marxist approaches to track the strategies and resources 'ordinary' or 'everyday' people used to adapt to changes and even to bring about changes themselves. Other insights followed from alliances with other disciplines such as economics, demographics, geography, psychology, sociology and anthropology. As the range of methodologies grew, race and gender came to be considered alongside class as shapers of both experiences and policy. The expansion of methods meant that the range of items considered as evidence also broadened and that familiar pieces of evidence were looked at in new ways. For example, a number of cultural historians have used inquisition records to build up accounts of the life experiences of non-elites, and women's historians have examined how women used the writing of biography to

[1]   D.H. Fischer, *Historian's Fallacies*, 1971, p. 195.

both affirm and challenge gender mores and historiographical assumptions.[2] And finally historians also began to explore social features previously thought to be immune to change or too trivial to be worthy of study: for example, death, childhood, madness, sexuality and smell.[3]

Located in this context, Collingwood's declaration that 'all history is the history of thought' seems curiously old fashioned and deserving of the criticism that has been heaped upon it.[4] Walsh, for instance, has written of Collingwood's 'narrow, rational view' of history, Gardiner of his 'neglect of social contexts' and Toynbee of a history that 'squeezes out the emotions'.[5] Mink sees Collingwood as offering a form of 'epistemological individualism' in which history is no more than the 'sum of innumerable biographies', and Evans sees the resulting methodology as too limiting.[6] Marwick, in *The Nature of History*, simply declares Collingwood's idea to be 'absolute rubbish'.[7] In this chapter, our aim is assess the validity of these challenges through a careful examination of Collingwood's writings, particularly the manuscript 'The Principles of History' (1939). Such an examination will show us, I contend, that there is little to support the common conception of him as writer who saw history as exclusively concerned with the rational activities of individuals.

Most criticisms of Collingwood's views on the subject-matter of history are formulated in response to section five of the Epilegomena in *The Idea of History* ('The Subject-Matter of History'), which was originally part of his lectures on the philosophy of history from 1936. In this, Collingwood addresses the question 'Of what can there be historical knowledge?' His answer is quite blunt: only that which can be re-enacted by historians, and that is 'reflective

[2]   E. Le Roy Ladurie, *Montaillou: The Promised Land of Error*, trans. B. Bray (New York, NY, 1979); C. Ginzburg, *The Cheese and the Worms: The Cosmos of a Sixteenth-Century Miller*, trans. J. and A. Tedeschi (Harmondsworth, 1980); and M. Spongberg, *Writing Women's History Since the Renaissance* (London, 2002), ch. 4.

[3]   P. Ariès, *Centuries of Childhood*, trans. R. Baldick (London, 1973); id., *Hour of Our Death*, trans. H. Weaver (London, 1981); M. Foucault, *Madness and Civilization: A History of Insanity in the Age of Reason*, trans. R. Howard (New York, NY, 1988); *The History of Sexuality*, trans. R. Hurley and R. McDougall (3 vols., Harmondsworth, 1978–86); and A. Corbin, *The Foul and the Fragrant: Odour and the Social Imagination*, trans. anon (London, 1986).

[4]   R.G. Collingwood, *An Autobiography* (Oxford, 1939), p. 110.

[5]   W.H. Walsh, *An Introduction to Philosophy of History* (London, 1964), pp. 52–6; P. Gardiner, *The Nature of Historical Explanation* (Oxford, 1952), p. 117; and A. Toynbee, *A Study of History*, Vol. 9 (London, 1954), pp. 718–37.

[6]   L. Mink, *Mind, History, and Dialectic* (Bloomington, IN, 1969), p. 159; and R. Evans, *In Defence of History* (London, 1997), pp. 91–2.

[7]   A. Marwick, *The Nature of History* (London, 1970), p. 83.

thought'. Reflective thought implies awareness of what one is doing and of what one has achieved. Excluded from re-enactment is everything else, including the 'mere flow of consciousness consisting of sensations, feelings and the like' because they are not activities of thinking. As a consequence, research that claims to speak of sensations and feelings is 'at its best, poetry, at its worst, an obstructive egoism; but history it can never be'.[8] Here, then, Collingwood makes a clear distinction between self-conscious thought and other mental activities, and excludes the latter from the purview of historians. Reading these comments in conjunction with the examples he uses elsewhere in the *Idea of History* concerning the actions of Julius Caesar and Napoleon it is easy to conclude that Collingwood is as his critics portray him.[9] As with our treatment of re-enactment in the previous chapter, though, it is important not to rely on any single statement as a sufficient presentation of Collingwood's views.

Fortunately, we have more sources to consider in building up an account of Collingwood's views, most notably 'The Principles of History'. In the second chapter of that manuscript, Collingwood restates the familiar argument that historians concern themselves with the study of 'actions done by reasonable agents in pursuit of ends determined by their reason' and thus that 'all history is the history of thought'.[10] In a departure from his previous writings, though, he explicitly broadens the reach of re-enactment to accommodate acts done by unreasonable agents, 'essential' emotions and the activities of non-specified historical agents. We will look to these three areas in turn.

Unreasonable Activities

Perhaps one of the most striking features of Collingwood's account of the range of re-enactment in 'The Principles of History' is his inclusion of unreasonable activities. This will come as a surprise to those who see him as a rationalist, as will his use of the rhetorical question 'is it necessary to add?' to suggest that the point is perhaps too obvious to labour. Why is it surprising? Some of Collingwood's other writings suggest a possible space for the unreasonable in historical research. For example, in his lectures from 1928 he states that

[8]   R.G. Collingwood, *The Idea of History* [1946], rev. edn., ed. W.J. van der Dussen (Oxford, 1993), pp. 302, 304, 305, 308.
[9]   *Ibid.*, pp. 213–5, 240–1, 223.
[10] R.G. Collingwood, 'The Principles of History' [1939], *The Principles of History and Other Writings*, ed. W.H. Dray and W.J. van der Dussen (Oxford, 1999), pp. 46, 67.

historians look to 'all conscious activities of the human spirit', in 'Human Nature and Human History' (1936) he declares that it is only in a 'flickering and dubious manner' that humans are rational at all and in the lectures from 1936 he criticises Graeco-Roman historians for looking at peoples' actions and experiences exclusively through the lens of rationality.[11] It will be surprising to commentators, I believe, because it is — thanks to Knox's editing — easy to conflate what Collingwood says about 'reflective thought' in section five of the epilegomena of *The Idea of History* with his comments on 'rational thought' in the section that follows ('History and Freedom').[12] Reflective thought and rational thought are not necessarily the same thing. To Collingwood, a reflective activity is simply one in which we are aware of what we are trying to do. He spells out no explicit requirement that what is done is reasonable or rational.

Having said that, though — and as odd as it sounds — we might nevertheless still be able to talk of some acts of 'unreasonable' agents as being 'rational'. To do so, we need to acknowledge more than just the historian's point of view in re-enactment: we need to look to that of the historical agent. Collingwood does not describe in detail how the re-enactment of unreasonable acts proceeds, but he does give us an important clue: 'unreason' 'is not the absence of reasons but the presence of bad ones'.[13] It is the presence of reasons that gives the historian something to work with. For Collingwood, as for Davidson, a rational action is one that stands in a certain relation to the historical agent's reasons for acting.[14] Those reasons do not have to be what we would consider good ones. For example, if an historical agent desires to acquire a larger house, and believes that the most effective means to achieve that goal is to notify the local authorities that the occupants of such a house are Jewish, then that person acts rationally if they notify the authorities to bring about their goal. That the historian views such actions as morally deplorable does not undermine their standing as rational, and therefore open to re-enactment.

In order to make judgements about the rationality or irrationality of the actions of historical agents, the historian must first be able to 'read' them historically. Could there be cases, though, where the actions of historical agents are so different from our own experiences

[11] R.G. Collingwood, *The Idea of History*, pp. 445, 227, 41.
[12] *Ibid.*, pp. 302–320. 'The Subject-matter of History' is from his lectures on the philosophy of history from 1936 and 'History and Freedom' is a part of chapter four of 'The Principles of History' [1939].
[13] R.G. Collingwood, 'The Principles of History', *The Principles of History and Other Writings*, p. 47.
[14] D. Davidson, *Truth and Interpretation* (Oxford, 1984).

that they are incommensurable?[15] A useful example here is Wittgenstein's account of a group of wood pilers. In *Remarks on the Foundations of Mathematics*, he asks us to imagine a group of people who pile wood into heaps of arbitrary height and sell it at a price proportionate to the area covered by the piles. We could, he tells us, take one of the piles they classify as 'a little wood' and by taking some of the logs off the top and laying them around the bottom of the pile, show that their 'a little wood' and 'a lot of wood' are really the same in this case. But perhaps, he continues, they might respond by saying that there is now 'a lot of wood' and it would cost more. By way of conclusion, he states that the wood pilers clearly do not understand 'a little wood' and 'a lot of wood' as we do, and have quite a different system of payment.[16] Here, Wittgenstein suggests that understanding can proceed on the basis of the assumption that most of the beliefs and practices of the wood pilers are in principle intelligible because they are rational. This approach would not rule out the attribution of irrationality to some of the actions of the wood pilers. What it would rule out is 'reading' the actions of others where a radically different system of rationality is involved, that is, with different notions of the concept of truth or consistency in reasons. Attributing to an agent such different basic cultural norms would make their beliefs and practices appear incredibly irrational to us. While Collingwood notes that the fundamental presuppositions that people hold may vary across cultures and time, I do not believe that he considered the possibility that they may be so different as to be beyond interpretation via overlaps in concepts or 'distinct' concepts. More will be said on 'distinct' concepts in chapter five. For Collingwood, as for his father, W.G. Collingwood, 'all history is a history of overlaps'.[17] In line with van der Dussen and Saari, I therefore believe that Collingwood's view of re-enactment begins with the assumption of intelligibility and rationality.[18] This is not to say that the historian cannot conclude that an action is irrational: what is

[15] R. Martin, 'Review of Re-enactment: A Study in R.G. Collingwood's Philosophy of History (Saari)', *Theoria*, Vol. 51 (2) (1985), pp. 121–3.

[16] L. Wittgenstein, *Remarks on the Foundations of Mathematics*, trans. G.E.M. Anscombe (Oxford, 1964), §§148–9.

[17] W.G. Collingwood, *Lake District History* (Kendal, 1925), p.4; as cited in D.H. Johnson, 'W.G. Collingwood and the Beginnings of the Idea of History', *Collingwood Studies*, Vol. 1 (1994), p. 14. See R.G. Collingwood, *The Idea of History*, p. 225. See also H. Saari, 'R.G. Collingwood on the Identity of Thoughts', pp. 86–7.

[18] W.J. van der Dussen, *History as a Science: The Philosophy of R.G. Collingwood* (The Hague, 1981), p. 273; and H. Saari, *Re-enactment: A Study in R.G. Collingwood's Philosophy of History* (Åbo, 1984), p. 19.

simply described here is a starting point. As he writes in *An Essay on Philosophical Method*:

> If the scientist is obliged to assume that nature is rational, and that any failure to make sense of it is a failure to understand it, the corresponding assumption is obligatory for the historian, and this is not least when he is the historian of thought.[19]

We have so far considered acts that entail what Dray calls 'subjective rationality', that is, acts that are rational from the historical agent's point of view. These need not be rational from the historian's point of view, or 'objectively' rational.[20] We reach the limits of re-enactment, though, when we consider activities that are neither objectively *nor* subjectively rational.[21] Here, an historical agent would be described as acting irrationally if they chose an action that was not a means to the goal that they wished to achieve: for example, the agent who seeks a bigger house hopes to secure it by putting their fingers in their ears. Hence Derrida's contention that a rational historian cannot write a history of madness.[22] What I believe Collingwood is driving at here — but does not express clearly — is that while failure to act rationally might occur for a number of complicated reasons such as frustration or 'foolishness', they all entail some sort of failure in critical thinking or consistency. Without some kind of culturally accepted bond between goal and action, the historian cannot 'read' historically.

Emotions

Collingwood's explicit exclusion of the emotions from 'The Subject-matter of History' has been convenient for many commentators, for it has been taken as support for his reputedly dualist view of mind. According to the dualist view, an emotion is a private mental event and thus can only be accessed in re-enactment if it entails the use of special intuitive insight or analogy. As was suggested in the last chapter, though, the idea of concepts — including emotions — acquiring and retaining meaning by a purely private act makes no sense. Support for this public view of emotions comes from *The Principles of Art*, where Collingwood states that they are expressed by

[19]   R.G. Collingwood, *An Essay on Philosophical Method* (Oxford, 1933), p. 226.
[20]   W.H. Dray, *History as Re-enactment: R. G. Collingwood's Idea of History* (Oxford, 1995), pp. 116–18.
[21]   R.G. Collingwood, 'The Principles of History', *The Principles of History and Other Writings*, p. 47.
[22]   J. Derrida, 'Cogito and the History of Madness', *Writing and Difference* (London, 1978), pp. 31–63.

'the controlled activity of language'.[23] Uncoupled from the dualist view of mind, Collingwood's comments on the re-enactment of emotions in 'The Principles of History' are not so hard to account for. In that manuscript, Collingwood makes it clear that the subject-matter of history includes:

> the history of emotions so far as these emotions are essentially related to the thoughts in question: not of any emotions that may happen to accompany them; nor, for that matter, of other thoughts that may happen to accompany them.[24]

So for example, in considering the case of a military officer who built a fort, the historian will discount as inessential the officer's unhappiness at leaving his newly married wife because this unhappiness is neither the direct cause nor result of him building the fort.[25] Unfortunately, as Dray notes, we are offered no example of an 'essential' emotion in the example, and the likely candidate, fear, is explicitly ruled out in the manuscript. I do not, however, agree with Dray's assessment that Collingwood's admission of the emotions is less than generous because he does not allow that they may be the focus of study in their own right.[26] Here, Dray neglects an important feature of the emotions: their intentionality.

Emotions, as Wilson and Kenny have argued, have objects: for example, we are afraid *of* a spider, angry *with* a parking officer, or embarrassed *that* we forgot an appointment. Further, emotions involve concepts, judgements and beliefs: for example, an awareness of a threat can lead to fear or the belief that one has been insulted to anger. Emotions are intentional because they must be about something or directed to an object.[27] That is, intentionality furnishes the 'content' of emotions. That content may not be connected with any physiological state or behavioural expression: for example, there is no characteristic behavioural expression of hope as there is for joy. An emotion, on this cognitive view, is a particular way of viewing and responding to the world and may or may not be expressed in certain forms of behaviour. Now because emotions are intentional and involve cognition, the explanation of emotions requires reference to the beliefs and attitudes of the person experiencing them.

[23] R.G. Collingwood, *The Principles of Art* (Oxford, 1938), p. 266.
[24] R.G. Collingwood, 'The Principles of History', *The Principles of History and Other Writings*, p. 77.
[25] *Ibid.*, p. 68.
[26] W.H. Dray, 'Broadening the Historian's Subject-Matter in The Principles of History', *Collingwood Studies*, Vol. 4 (1998), pp. 9–10.
[27] A. Kenny, *The Metaphysics of Mind* (Oxford, 1989), p. 52. See also A. Kenny, *Action, Emotion and Will* (London, 1963), ch. 9, and J.R.S. Wilson, *Emotion and Object* (Cambridge, 1972), ch. 15.

Collingwood's military officer might be angry because a previous engagement with the enemy went badly. This cognitive view of emotions would offer us an explanation as to why Collingwood does not consider emotions independently of thought. Furthermore, because emotions consist in part of cognition they can be evaluated in terms of the same criteria that the historian uses to evaluate the rationality of other mental activities.[28] Thus it is the intentionality of emotions that opens them up to explanation via re-enactment.[29]

Non-specified Historical Agents

A number of commentators, most notably Mink, view Collingwood as peddling a form of 'epistemological individualism' in which history is no more than 'the sum of innumerable biographies'.[30] This again serves as a convenient prop for shoring up the view of Collingwood as a dualist, for in epistemological as well as methodological individualism, thoughts are the private possessions of individual agents and cannot be re-enacted except via them. Again, the public and shared nature of mental concepts suggested in the last chapter kicks away this prop, for both historians and historical agents and more than one historical agent can share the same thought. Thus it is possible to talk of the beliefs and practices of a particular historical agent as representative of a wider group, or even to talk of the beliefs and practices of a group without identifying particular individuals. In 'The Principles of History', Collingwood approaches his discussion of the reach of re-enactment to non-specified historical agents through a rather acerbic attack on biography. In Collingwood's view, biographies are built out of sympathy, malice and materials chosen for gossip and snobbery value. While such a claim is clearly contentious, it is not out of keeping with

---

[28] R. de Sousa, *The Rationality of Emotions* (Cambridge, MA, 1987), ch. 7; P. Greenspan, *Emotions and Reasons* (New York, 1988); and R.C. Solomon, *The Passions: Emotions and the Meaning of Life* (Indianaopolis, IN, 1993).

[29] While I note Collingwood's claims on the use of analogy, projection and intuition to understand emotions in *The Principles of Art*, it is important to remember that he is discussing understanding in art, not history. See R.G. Collingwood, *The Principles of Art*, pp. 118, 250.

[30] L. Mink, *Mind, History, and Dialectic*, p. 159. See also, for example, J. Balazova, 'Methodological Individualism in R.G. Collingwood's Philosophy of History', *Filozofia*, Vol. 47 (1992), pp. 450–73; E.H. Carr, *What is History?* (London, 1961), p. 46; L. Code, 'Collingwood's Epistemological Individualism', *Monist*, Vol. 72 (1989), pp. 542–67; and D.H. Fischer, *Historian's Fallacies* (London, 1971), p. 197.

contemporary attacks on biography as amateurish and a 'gendered diminutive of history'.[31]

Embedded in his criticisms are some claims, though, that can further enhance our understanding of re-enactment. A good case in point is his treatment of sympathy, which we first touched upon in chapter two. Sympathy, Collingwood instructs us in 'The Principles of History', refers to the alignment of feelings between the reader of biography and the historical agent and thus entails no more than the recognition of an historical agent as an individual. What matters is whether the reader, for example, feels the same anger as the historical agent: no wider awareness of the possibility of such is required. That is, sympathy entails no awareness that public language makes this alignment possible.[32] Clearly, sympathy falls short of re-enactment because it entails no acknowledgement of conceptual identity, hence Collingwood's conclusion that the contemporary discredit into which biography had fallen was of great service to history. Similarly, his alignment of 'scissors-and-paste' history with biography will be illuminating when we look to his idea of the historical imagination in chapter five. More puzzling though is Collingwood's conclusion that 'the history of a thought has nothing to do with the names of the people who think it'.[33] This might be read as a radical deconstruction of self in historical research, where the expressors of thought are incidental to the thoughts themselves. Such a view of the subject-matter of history is to be found in a range of present-day historiographical approaches, from Foucauldians to memeticists.[34] This reading of Collingwood's writings is highly implausible though, for as we shall see in chapter six, his social and political writings reveal a strong interest in the self.[35] It might also be read in a less radical fashion, however, as a refutation of the view of thoughts as only the private possessions of particular individuals. The social nature of thoughts means that they can never just be tied to individuals, and thus history is never just about individuals. This is not to say that individuals cannot present original or innovative ideas, just that those ideas can never be detached from the public language through which they are expressed. While Collingwood's presentation of the

[31]   M. Spongberg, *Writing Women's History Since the Renaissance*, p. 121.
[32]   R.G. Collingwood, 'The Principles of History', *The Principles of History and Other Writings*, p. 71.
[33]   *Ibid.*, p. 75.
[34]   For a memetic view of imagination, see M. Pollan, *The Botany of Desire* (New York, NY, 2001), pp. 145–9.
[35]   See for example R.G. Collingwood, *The New Leviathan*, rev. edn., ed. D. Boucher (Oxford, 1992), pp. 55.

point is perhaps a little overstated (ie. 'nothing to do'), it is not unintelligible.[36]

Non-Human Animals

By noting the expansion of re-enactment in 'The Principles of History' to include unreasonable actions, essential emotions and the experiences of non-specified historical agents, we have to some extent followed in the tracks laid down by van der Dussen, Boucher and Dray.[37] Neglected in their, and all other, commentaries on Collingwood, though, are his views on the possibility of re-enacting the experiences of non-human animals. Collingwood, as is clear from 'Human Nature and Human History' and 'The Principles of History', was not an advocate of human exceptionalism: no gulf separates human thought and communication from that of other animals. Rather, the differences between them are a matter of degree. He writes:

> The idea that man, apart from his self-conscious historical life, is different from the rest of creation in being a rational animal is a mere superstition. It is only by fits and starts, in a flickering and dubious manner, that human beings are rational at all. In quality, as well as in amount, their rationality is a matter of degree: some are oftener rational than others, some rational in a more intense way. But a flickering and dubious rationality can certainly not be denied to animals other than men. Their minds may be inferior in range and power to those of the lowest savages, but by the same standards the lowest savages are inferior to civilized men, and those whom we call civilized differ among themselves hardly less. There are even among non-human animals the beginnings of historical life: for example, among cats, which do not wash by instinct but are taught by their mothers.[38]

This last sentence is particularly interesting, for it not only adds an historiographical angle to current research on cultural evolution in animals, it also challenges the anthropocentrism of historiography. In Collingwood's view, we may talk of rationality and minds at least

---

[36] D. Boucher notes quite rightly that at times, Collingwood can be a 'master of overstatement'. See 'The Significance of R.G. Collingwood's Principles of History', *Journal of the History of Ideas*, Vol. 58 (2) (1998), p. 320.

[37] J. van der Dussen, 'Collingwood's "Lost" Manuscript of The Principles of History', *History and Theory*, Vol. 36 (1) (1997), pp. 32–62; D. Boucher, 'The Significance of R.G. Collingwood's Principles of History', pp. 309–30; and W.H. Dray, 'Broadening the Historian's Subject-Matter in The Principles of History', pp. 2–33.

[38] R.G. Collingwood, *The Idea of History*, p. 227. See also 'Human Nature and Human History, March 1936 — First draft of a paper rewritten May 1936 and sent up for publication by the British Academy', Ms Collingwood Dep. 12 (11).

in animals with brains, and perhaps even in animals with nervous systems but not brains.[39] And that animals may be rational, even if in a 'dubious and flickering manner', suggests that their experiences may be open to re-enactment.[40] That possibility is clearly acknowledged by Collingwood in 'The Principles of History':

> The old belief that man is the only 'rational animal' may well be mistaken, not so much because it implied too much rationality in man; it never did that, for it never implied that man was more than feebly, intermittently, and precariously rational; as because it implied too little in non-human animals. And yet it may be true enough for the purposes of history, if the rationality of non-human animals is so much feebler, more intermittent, and more precarious than our own, or so concealed from us by defective powers of communication, that we can never lay a finger on any action of a non-human animal and say with confidence 'here reason is at work; here the animal is not obeying its instincts but acting on its thoughts'.[41]

Importantly, Collingwood does not rule out the re-enactment of non-human animal experiences by humans on philosophical grounds, he simply points to the pragmatic difficulties of doing so, particularly given the comparatively poor powers of communication among non-human animals.

Collingwood's views on animal rationality and re-enactment distinguish him from the majority of philosophers and historians. For example, Quine assumes that because animals do not have language the ascription of thoughts to them is an 'essentially dramatic idiom', and Davidson argues that animals cannot have thoughts because thoughts must occur in a network of beliefs held together by the concept of belief.[42] Even those who, like Kenny, do not deny that animals may have simple thoughts conclude that they cannot be rational because, without language, they do not have the capacity to give reasons for their actions.[43] Historians are similarly sceptical about the possibility of animals as historical agents: most writers tend to look to animals only when they impinge on human activities. We recall, too, from the previous chapter Smith's and Priestley's characterisations of sympathy with animals as a form of projection. Notably, what is assumed in all these arguments, as in Colling-

[39]   R.G. Collingwood, 'Human Nature and Human History, March 1936', p. 21; 'Notes Towards a Metaphysic: A' [1933], Ms Collingwood Dep. 18 (3), p. 1 (c).

[40]   Collingwood also presents animals as being capable of sympathy: see 'The Principles of History', *The Principles of History and Other Writings*, p. 71.

[41]   *Ibid.*, p. 47.

[42]   W.V. Quine, *Word and Object* (Cambridge, MA, 1960); and D. Davidson, 'Thought and Talk', in *Truth and Interpretation*, pp. 155–70.

[43]   A. Kenny, *The Metaphysics of Mind*, pp. 38–40.

wood's writings on re-enactment, is the close connection of rational thought and language.

Recent ethological research has shown that even under natural conditions, many animals participate in sophisticated communicative activities. Cheney and Seyfarth, for instance, have shown that the vervet monkeys of Amboseli utilise at least ten 'words'.[44] Commentators hesitate to apply the terms 'words' and 'language' to such vocalisations without inverted commas, though, because no trace has been found of syntactical or grammatical rules that determine the meaning of combinations of vocalisations. Most animal vocalisations are single utterances. Few ethologists expect that any animal has evolved a grammar as complex as that of humans, but combinations of vocalisations among capuchin monkeys, gibbons, and various species of dolphins and whales have not been deciphered and extensive studies of the vocalisations of wild common and bonobo chimpanzees are yet to be done.[45]

Given the lack of information explicitly ruling out animal grammar, might re-enactment of non-human animal activities proceed — as with Wittgenstein's wood pilers — after the adoption of the assumption that they are in principle intelligible because they are rational? Yes it might, provided there is at least some overlap in the system of rationality of the historian and the non-human animal and thus overlap in concepts of truth and consistency. It is also possible, though, that the activities of non-human animals entail a system of rationality that is so different from that of humans that attributing our concepts of truth and consistency may render their activities irrational or nonsensical. As with his treatment of human rationality, Collingwood does not acknowledge the possibility of the latter, for he assumes that human and non-human systems of rationality differ in degree, not kind. In support of this view of continuity across species, for example, Savage-Rumbaugh and Pepperberg have demonstrated that some captive apes and African grey parrots can acquire human linguistic capacities to some degree.[46] There is, though, no unequivocal evidence for apes or parrots having mastered to any degree the syntactic or grammatical aspects of human language. Without that evidence, and any identification of non-human animal grammar under natural conditions, we must

---

[44]   D. Cheney and R. Seyfarth, *How Monkeys See the World* (Chicago, IL, 1990). See also C. Ristau (ed.), *Cognitive Ethology* (Hillsdale, MI, 1991).

[45]   J. Diamond, *The Rise and Fall of the Third Chimpanzee* (London, 1991), pp. 135–6.

[46]   E.S. Savage-Rumbaugh and R. Lewin, *Kanzi: The Ape at the Brink of the Human Mind* (New York, NY, 1994); and I.M. Pepperberg, *The Alex Studies: Cognitive and Communicative Abilities of Grey Parrots* (Cambridge, MA, 2000).

conclude that to date, Collingwood's claims about the re-enactment of the activities of non-human animals are possible but improbable.

Presuppositions and Philosophy

Public language provides us with the means to share the same thoughts — reasonable and unreasonable — and emotions of specified and non-specified human historical agents. Thoughts and emotions are not private, isolated possessions but concepts that entail grammatical or syntactical signposting or rules of usage. And as the rules of usage for concepts are not apart from concepts,[47] it therefore makes sense to claim, as Boucher has, that re-enactment can allow historians to gain access to the 'presuppositions' that give shape to the thoughts and emotions of historical agents.[48] Indeed, if historians were to go about their research in the critical and autonomous manner Collingwood favoured, one would expect them to seek out presuppositions.

In Collingwood's view, all fields of knowledge are shaped by fundamental presuppositions. These presuppositions reside neither in the unconscious nor in an ideal Platonic realm but are a part of all conceptual claims and practices.[49] This does not mean, however, that the historian or the historical agent must be able to enunciate the presuppositions that give shape to their activities. What it means, at least, is that the historian and historical agent must be able to distinguish between correct and incorrect applications of these presuppositions. This is because presuppositions are fundamental rules of practice, and both the historian and the historical agent must understand the difference between following and breaking a rule if they can be said to be following a rule at all. As with the rules for games, presuppositions are not exhaustive: some possibilities are left open. In cricket, for instance, there is no rule specifying how fast a ball is to be bowled yet cricket is a game laden with rules.[50] Nor must presuppositions be conditional imperatives: for example, 'Before starting the match, toss a coin to see who will bat'. They may play varied roles in practices, a point that Wittgenstein — an extensive commentator on concepts — puts well:

[47]   R.G. Collingwood, *The New Leviathan*, §§34.12, 11.45.

[48]   D. Boucher, 'Editor's Introduction', *The New Leviathan*, pp. xxviii–xxix.

[49]   R. Martin, 'Editor's Introduction', *An Essay on Metaphysics* [1940], rev. edn. (Oxford, 1998), p. xxvi. See also R.G. Collingwood, *An Essay on Metaphysics*, pp. 102–3, 194, 196–7.

[50]   L. Wittgenstein, *Philosophical Investigations*, trans. G.E.M. Anscombe, ed. G.E.M. Anscombe, R. Rhees and G.H. von Wright (Oxford, 1953), §68.

The rule may be an aid in teaching the game. The learner is told it and given practice in applying it. — Or it is an instrument of the game itself. — Or a rule is employed neither in the teaching nor in the game itself; nor is it set down in a list of rules. One learns the game by watching how others play. But we say that it is played according to such-and-such rules because an observer can read these rules off from the practice of the game — like a law of nature governing the play.[51]

Further, for a rule to be a rule, it must be applied more than once.[52] Thus following a rule is a practice or custom: it is not something that a single individual does on one occasion.[53] This does not imply, though, that our presuppositions are simply the result of abiding by, or having adopted, more or less arbitrary conventions or even fashions to which there are clear and intelligible alternatives. Again Wittgenstein puts this point well:

So much is clear: when someone says: 'If you follow the rule, it *must* be like this', he has not any clear concept of what experience would correspond to the opposite. Or again: he has not any clear concept of what it would be like for it to be the opposite.[54]

Here, Wittgenstein echoes Collingwood's suggestion in *An Essay on Metaphysics* that on the whole we are ignorant of the 'absolute presuppositions' that we hold.[55] That means that they cannot be changed directly or formulated prior to adoption. As Collingwood writes:

How can we ever satisfy ourselves that the principles on which we think are true, except by going on thinking according to those principles, and seeing whether unanswerable criticisms emerge as we work? To criticise the conceptions of science is the work of science itself as it proceeds; to demand that such criticisms should be anticipated by the theory of knowledge is to demand that such a theory should anticipate the history of thought.[56]

As with Hegel's Owl of Minerva taking its flight at dusk, Collingwood sees philosophers as identifying past presuppositions

---

[51] *Ibid.*, §54.
[52] R.G. Collingwood, 'Rule Making and Rule Breaking: Sermon Preached in St. Mary the Virgin's Church, Oxford, 5 May 1935', Ms Collingwood Dep. 1 (9), pp. 2-3, 8.
[53] R.G. Collingwood, *An Essay on Metaphysics*, p. 48n. See also L. Wittgenstein, *The Blue and Brown Books* (Oxford, 1958), p. 96; *Philosophical Investigations*, §199.
[54] L. Wittgenstein, *Remarks on the Foundations of Mathematics*, III, §29.
[55] R.G. Collingwood, *An Essay on Metaphysics*, p. 48n.
[56] R.G. Collingwood, *The Idea of History*, p. 230.

and illuminating 'unanswerable criticisms' 'as we work'.[57] This means that, in the main, philosophy is a retrospective, historical activity.

The crucial notions in Collingwood's writings on absolute presuppositions are those of understanding the meaning of a word, rule or presupposition and that it makes no sense to ask questions concerning the truth or falsity of such.[58] Indeed, the idea of asking questions about the truth or falsity of an absolute presupposition does not apply for such questions are only meaningful with relative presuppositions. A relative presupposition is an assumption or rule that stands in relation to both a prior and a successive assumption or rule.[59] Whereas relative presuppositions have logical links in two directions, absolute presuppositions form the starting point in a chain of presuppositions.[60] Absolute presuppositions are the fundamental rules that bind our activities and allow the formation of subsequent relative presuppositions. They are not propositions, so the question of their correctness or otherwise does not arise. This clearly accords with Wittgenstein's suggestion that 'The danger, here, I believe, is one of giving a justification of our procedure when there is no such thing as a justification and we ought simply to have said: that's how we do it'.[61] Because these presuppositions cannot be given a justification it does not follow that they are shaky or unreliable or that we are foolish if we act according to them. We do not decide to reject or accept them at all, any more than we decide to be human beings as opposed to chimpanzees. To ask whether our human practices or 'forms of life' are correct or justified is to ask whether we are correct or justified in being the sorts of things we are.

A complex or 'constellation' of absolute presuppositions forms the foundation upon which all our intellectual activities, and indeed the very possibility of intellectual activity, rests. As noted previously in our discussion of Wittgenstein's wood pilers, Collingwood acknowledges that constellations of absolute presuppositions may vary across cultures.[62] But, importantly, they may also vary across time: any constellation is perpetually subject to strains and conflicts,

[57] G.W.F. Hegel, *Elements of the Philosophy of Right*, trans. H.B. Nisbet, ed. A. Wood (Cambridge, 1991), pp. 12–13. See also R.G. Collingwood, *An Autobiography*, p. 66.

[58] *Ibid.*, p. 31; 'Function of Metaphysics in Civilization', *An Essay on Metaphysics*, p. 412.

[59] R.G. Collingwood, *An Essay on Metaphysics*, p. 29.

[60] D. Boucher, *The Social and Political Thought of R.G. Collingwood* (Cambridge, 1989), pp. 227–8.

[61] L. Wittgenstein, *Remarks on the Foundations of Mathematics*, II, §74.

[62] R.G. Collingwood, *An Essay on Metaphysics*, p. 60.

the intensity of which varies, but when the strains become too great the structure collapses and is replaced by another.[63] As Martin notes, this is an important departure from the Kantian account of the universal categories of human reasoning and judgement.[64] And more radically, it sees the departure of philosophy from the search for timeless knowledge.

It has long been assumed that without a firm foundation all philosophical inquiry is rendered precarious. Traditionally, philosophers have sought to secure such a firm foundation by arguing that human thought mirrors or corresponds to an objective, independent Reality or Truth. Consequently, the possibility of a rational understanding rests on a correspondence between thought and Reality or Truth. As Dewey writes of the traditional view:

> Because ultimate . . . reality is fixed, permanent, admitting of no change or variation, it may be grasped by rational intuition and set forth in rational, that is, unreal and necessary demonstration . . . The predisposition of philosophy towards the universal, invariant, eternal was fixed. It remains the common possession of the entire classic philosophical tradition.[65]

In current day philosophy, though, a consideration of grounds or foundations has come to be seen as hankering after the myths of an earlier, less advanced period. The traditional problem of finding the conditions and limits of thought, and hence of knowledge, has become the problem of determining the conditions and limits of language. Meaning is immanent in language in a way that denies a meaningful pre-linguistic world. The traditional view, in which language and the world are separate, each having a character of its own and capable of being correlated, is rejected. A number of commentators, of whom Rorty seems to be the most celebrated, have equated the rejection of the search for timeless foundations with an anti-foundationalist stance. In *Philosophy and the Mirror of Nature*, for instance, he characterises Wittgenstein, Heidegger and Dewey as radically breaking from tradition and abrogating all that went before them: 'Each of the three, in his later work, broke free of the Kantian conception of philosophy as foundational, and spent his time warning us against those very temptations to which he himself had once succumbed'.[66]

---

[63] *Ibid.*, p. 48n.
[64] R. Martin, 'Editor's Introduction', *An Essay on Metaphysics*, p. xxix. See also R.G. Collingwood, *An Essay on Metaphysics*, pp. 179–80.
[65] J. Dewey, *The Quest for Certainty* (New York, 1929), p. 15.
[66] R. Rorty, *Philosophy and the Mirror of Nature* (Oxford, 1980), p. 5.

While it would be unlikely to see Collingwood's name figure in Rorty's postmodern commentary, clearly much of the criticism of Collingwood's views similarly equates the rejection of timeless foundations with anti-foundationalism. This assumption has also generated a dichotomous rivalry between historicist and metaphysical readings of Hegel. It is clear that Collingwood did not hold to the claim that philosophy involves the search for atemporal knowledge.[67] That does not mean, however, that he was an 'anti-foundationalist'. And, more radically, the same can be said about Wittgenstein, despite the fact that his views on philosophy have been used as a foil for those of Collingwood.[68] Rather than dealing a deathblow to the idea of foundations, it appears that Collingwood and Wittgenstein continue the discussion — no matter how radically they transform the understanding of the term 'foundation'.

For Collingwood, constellations of presuppositions provide the foundations for human activities. They are neither subject to rapid change due to whim or fashion nor permanent. The imagery of Wittgenstein's later works suggests a similar, though more nuanced view. In *Philosophical Investigations*, for instance, he speaks of a given which must be accepted: 'forms of life'.[69] The 'forms of life' ground language and meaning. As he argues in *On Certainty*, though, the ground is not bedrock, but a riverbed. Having meaning only in the stream of life, language is not longer static but dynamic, changing with time as the flow of a river.

These 'river-bed' presuppositions are implied in conversation and form the framework of everyday behaviour.[70] They are a firm background on which all of our intellectual activity depends. They are a part of our intellectual behaviour, and are presupposed by it. They do not, however, form the invariant foundations of knowledge that philosophers such as Kant sought to expose:

> It might be imagined that some propositions, of the form of empirical propositions, were hardened and functioned as channels for such empirical propositions as were not hardened but fluid; and that this relation altered with time, in that fluid propositions hardened, and hard ones became fluid.
>
> The mythology may change back into a state of flux, the river-bed of thoughts may shift. But I distinguish between the movement of the

---

[67] G. Vanheeswijck, 'Robin George Collingwood on Eternal Philosophical Problems', *Dialogue*, Vol. 40 (3) (2001), pp. 555–70.

[68] P. Johnson, *R.G. Collingwood: An Introduction* (Bristol, 1998), esp. ch. 3.

[69] L. Wittgenstein, *Philosophical Investigations*, §§19, 23, 241, II, pp. 174, 226.

[70] L. Wittgenstein, *On Certainty*, ed. G.E.M. Anscombe and G.H. von Wright (Oxford, 1969), §95.

waters and the shift of the bed itself; though there is not a sharp distinction of the one from the other.[71]

The bed of the river consists partly of hard rock, which appears as unalterable or as subject only to minor imperceptible alterations, and partly of sand, which does shift, washing away, being redeposited or carried in the river flow. Some concepts and presuppositions are obviously subject to great historical and cultural variation. The river currents are seen as the historical outcome of successive responses to the human situation and world.[72]

There is a particular open-endedness herein that is not characteristic of the traditional approach to philosophy. Plato, Kant and Frege, for instance, assumed that whatever the ultimate foundation and source of objectivity, principles and concepts must be historically invariant. For Plato, rationality is rendered possible through the existence of the atemporal objectivity of ideas distinct from the knowing mind. With Kant, for there to be knowledge, the ultimate foundation must be a temporally invariant structure of understanding. Without atemporal, absolute invariants, everything would be reduced to the arbitrary and chaotic. As Frege argues, 'If everything were in constant flux, there would no longer be any possibility of getting to know the world and everything would be plunged into confusion'.[73] In response, I think that Collingwood's and Wittgenstein's writings point to an objectivism rather than absolutism or extreme relativism. Absolutism posits absolute or permanent, unchanging standards, principles, presuppositions and concepts. Objectivism, on the other hand, allows for objective principles of judgement, standards, and concepts that are not decided solely by personal preference or the whim of individuals. They are, nevertheless, subject to change. Collingwood and Wittgenstein are therefore not the agents of chaos that Frege so feared.

Constellations, Paradigms, Epistêmês and Archives

In this and the previous chapter, we have noted some deep-seated similarities between the views of Collingwood and Wittgenstein. Looking more specifically to Collingwood's writings on presuppositions and philosophy, commentators such as Lord have also noted 'remarkable similarities' to Kuhn's views of paradigms in the his-

[71]   *Ibid.*, §§96–7.
[72]   L. Wittgenstein, *Zettel*, ed. G.E.M. Anscombe and G.H. von Wright (Oxford, 1991), §§63, 65.
[73]   G. Frege, *The Laws of Arithmetic*, trans. and ed. M. Furth (Berkeley, CA, 1964), p. vii.

tory of science and Foucault's idea of the *archive*.[74] On the face of it, the similarities between Collingwood's writings on constellations of presuppositions and the pattern of 'paradigm' shifts Kuhn identifies in the history of science are striking.[75] For Kuhn, the term 'paradigm' denotes the 'rules of play' that constrain and provide guides for scientific practice. These 'rules of play' are not all explicit; much of the scientist's knowledge is tacit.[76] In 'normal science', discoveries accord with the 'rules of play', hence Kuhn's account of normal science as the elucidation of 'topographical detail on a map whose main outlines are available in advance'.[77] Sometimes, though, discoveries go against expectations, and may spark off a period of 'extraordinary science' or 'science in the crisis state' in which the 'rules of play' are subjected to critical scrutiny and new ones are adopted. After this 'paradigm shift', 'normal science' is resumed under new rules of play. These new rules are incommensurable with those of the old paradigm because the structure of their 'lexicons' is different. That is, the meaning and scope of their concepts cannot be matched. This is not to say that they are incomparable or that there is no continuity in the history of science because some of the achievements of the previous paradigm are carried over: for example, use of the same experimental apparatus.[78]

As with Collingwood's constellations of absolute presuppositions, Kuhn's 'rules of play' in ordinary science do their work 'in darkness' and are subject to strain, collapse and replacement.[79] And as with Collingwood, Kuhn notes the resistance ordinary scientists show towards analysing or questioning their fundamental assumptions: Collingwood calls this being 'ticklish in one's absolute presuppositions'.[80] All the same, there are at least two differences in their views that should not be neglected. First, despite popular interpretation to the contrary, Kuhn saw his ideas as specific to the natural sciences. Indeed in *The Structure of Scientific Revolutions* he suggests that fields like history are in a 'preconsensus' phase because there is a lack of consensus in ideas and activities.[81] No such restriction is to be

[74] T.C. Lord, 'R.G. Collingwood: A Continental Philosopher?', *Clio*, Vol. 29 (3) (2000), pp. 325–36.

[75] T.S. Kuhn, *The Structure of Scientific Revolutions*, 3/e (Chicago, 1996).

[76] T.S. Kuhn, 'Logic of Discovery or Psychology of Research' and 'Second Thoughts on Paradigms', *The Essential Tension: Selected Studies in Scientific Tradition and Change* (Chicago, 1977), pp. 285, 307.

[77] T.S. Kuhn, 'The Essential Tension', *The Essential Tension*, p. 235.

[78] T.S. Kuhn, *The Structure of Scientific Revolutions*, pp. 6, 82, 86, 87, 91, 101, 130, 154.

[79] R.G. Collingwood, *An Essay On Metaphysics*, p. 43.

[80] *Ibid.*, p. 44.

[81] T.S. Kuhn, *The Structure of Scientific Revolutions*, ch. 2.

found in Collingwood's writings: presuppositions shape all fields of knowledge, even those where there is little apparent agreement. Second, in distinction from Kuhn's view of extraordinary or crisis-state science, Collingwood does not consider it possible for us to identify new presuppositions and then apply them. For him, new presuppositions arise within activities, and like the ones they replace, do their work 'in darkness'. This is why he characterises metaphysics in *An Essay on Metaphysics* as the historical study of how presuppositions have changed.

Foucault also recognises the retrospective and historical nature of the analysis of what he calls the *archive*; a system of 'rules' that are not consciously held that shape and constrain both linguistic and material practices such as concepts and the movement of bodies.[82] He writes: 'It is not possible for us to describe our own *archive*, since it is from within these rules that we speak . . . [it] emerges in fragments, regions, and levels, more fully, no doubt, and with greater sharpness, the greater the time that separates us from it'.[83] Again, there are some important differences between Collingwood and Foucault that should be noted. First, Foucault holds that linguistic and material practices are related to issues of power. Discourse, he writes:

> appears as an asset — finite, limited, desirable, useful — that has its own rules of appearance, but also its own conditions of appropriation and operation; an asset that consequently, from the moment of its existence poses the question of power; an asset that is, by nature, the object of a struggle, a political struggle.[84]

While such an echo of Nietzsche's will to truth and power may, as Hinz has shown, be drawn up against Collingwood's response to the contemporary corruption of thought in 'barbarism', presuppositions do not necessarily have to be considered through the lens of power relations.[85] Second, Foucault questions the traditional obsession among historians with linking *archives* (and the related notion of *epistêmês*) in continuous chronological chains. For him, *archives* and *epistêmês* can be discrete and discontinuous, a point promoted in all of his historical writings.[86] Even though, as Skagestad and Dray

---

[82] M. Foucault, *The Archaeology of Knowledge*, trans. A.M. Sheridan-Smith (London, 1972), pp. 48–9.

[83] *Ibid.*, p. 130.

[84] *Ibid.*, p. 120.

[85] M. Hinz, *Self-Creation and History: Collingwood and Nietzsche on Conceptual Change* (Lanham, MD, 1993).

[86] M. Foucault, *The Order of Things: An Archaeology of the Human Sciences*, trans. anon (London, 1970), p. 251.

have noted, Collingwood failed to produce continuous narratives of presupposition shifts in *The Idea of Nature* and *The Idea of History*, he certainly held to it as an aim for historians and metaphysicians.[87]

Collingwood's views do not match those of Kuhn and Foucault. We have seen, though, that there are sufficient similarities to perhaps shake off the portrayal of his views as 'sterile', 'dull' and even old-fashioned.[88]

Reconsiderations of Philosophy

It has been suggested that Collingwood's, Wittgenstein's and Foucault's views entail a humbling of philosophy. In the end our search for meaning must conclude with the idea that this is what we do and are. One cannot give further grounds or reasons. Continued inquiry regarding the ground of our form of life is unproductive idling, or to Foucault, simply the demonstration of a desire for comfortable, solid ground.[89] Yet Wittgenstein recognises the difficulty of limiting inquiry and the dynamism of curiosity that leads us into explanatory considerations. As he writes in *On Certainty*: 'It is so difficult to find the *beginning*. Or better: it is difficult to begin at the beginning. And try not to go further back'.[90] I think that Wittgenstein's account is unduly restrictive in that it prematurely limits the scope of inquiry. Further, as will be demonstrated in chapter six, the fundamentally educative purpose of Collingwood's social and political writings suggests that he was unwilling to restrict philosophy to retrospective analysis.

We could throw up our hands and simply conclude that Collingwood was inconsistent. More positively, though, we can work towards articulating an account of philosophical inquiry in the light of the multi-temporal image of the riverbed. What emerges from the combination of Collingwood's and Wittgenstein's ideas outlined earlier in this chapter is a multi-temporal view of philosophy. Some presuppositions are so long lived as to appear permanent; others change more rapidly. Plotting out the various durations possible for presuppositions and the consequences for philosophy is impossible. As with Braudel's view of time, then, I have opted instead to identify two broad groupings, though it is important to

[87] P. Skagestad, *Making Sense of History: The Philosophies of Popper and Collingwood* (Oslo, 1975), p. 82; W.H. Dray, *History as Re-enactment: R.G. Collingwood's Idea of History* (Oxford, 1995), p. 143.
[88] K. Jenkins, *Rethinking History* (London, 1992), pp. 2–3.
[89] L. Wittgenstein, *Zettel*, §314; M. Foucault, *The Order of Things*, p. 387.
[90] L. Wittgenstein, *On Certainty*, §471.

recall Wittgenstein's advice that there will be no sharp distinction between them.[91] First, philosophy would entail the illumination, consideration, and clarification of the human form of life and thereby human forms of understanding. The philosopher's task would be to reveal and explore the kind of being the human person is. According to Wittgenstein, the final philosophic task would be simply to state that this is the way persons are. In light of the fact that he and Collingwood hold to a conditional necessity rooted in existing human conditions rather than in necessarily invariant features of reality, it would seem that one philosophic task would be the exploration and explication of such conditional necessities. Here, philosophy would serve a descriptive clarifying role, much like that ascribed to metaphysics by Collingwood in *An Essay on Metaphysics* and *An Autobiography*.[92] Philosophy would thus allow a metaview, a perspective whereby a better understanding, appreciation and acceptance of this shared form of life could be attained. What we do and say does have a certain form; there is a structure to our activities. We can attempt, at least, to describe this and render more explicit the most significant, fundamental and inescapable features of ourselves and our world. We may not bring to light our entire assembly of absolute presuppositions, but this does not mean that we cannot articulate those held by others. And it is through others that we may catch a glimpse of ourselves. More will be said on this task for philosophy in chapters five and six.

And a second task for the philosopher may also be proposed. Within the fundamental unity of the human form of life, there nevertheless arise various forms of human life. Within the same riverbed, varied currents can be seen to flow. People do dwell in particular perspectives and may come to render them at least partly explicit through the study of others' perspectives. This (at least) twofold but interwoven view of philosophy accords well with Collingwood's comments in 'The Historical Imagination':

> In part, the problems of philosophy are unchanging; in part, they vary from age to age, according to the special characteristics of human life and thought at the time; and in the best philosophers of every age these two parts are so interwoven that the permanent problems appear *sub specie saeculi*, and the special problems of the age *sub specie aeternitatis*.[93]

---

[91] F. Braudel, 'The Situation of History in 1950', *On History*, trans. S. Matthews (Chicago, 1980), p. 11. See also *The Mediterranean and the Mediterranean World in the Age of Philip II*, trans. S. Reynolds (2 vols., Glasgow, 1972–3).

[92] See for example, R.G. Collingwood, *An Autobiography* (Oxford, 1939), p. 66.

[93] R.G. Collingwood, *The Idea of History*, pp. 231–2.

In *Zettel*, Wittgenstein tells us that 'the philosopher is not a citizen of any community of ideas'.[94] The distinctive character of philosophers is that while dwelling, like everyone else, in a particular constellation of presuppositions, they are keenly aware of doing such and of the possibility of alternative constellations. Herein, the philosopher becomes a voice in what Oakeshott calls 'the conversation of mankind'.[95] Rorty characterises this as hermeneutic conversation:

> Hermeneutics sees the relation between various discourses as those of strands in a possible conversation; a conversation which presupposes no disciplinary matrix which unites the speakers, but where the hope of agreement is never lost as long as the conversation lasts.[96]

The participants in Rorty's conversation are political liberals and philosophical ironists who have doubts about the finality and realism of the vocabularies they use.[97] Thus Rorty views this hermeneutical conversation as abandoning the traditional philosophical preoccupation with securing the foundations of knowledge and meaning. For Rorty, abandoning our search for foundations is supposed to free us to engage in a conversation that seeks agreement. What constitutes agreement is not laid down prior to the conversation. Rather, he means by 'agreement' no more than the dominance of some point of view or other in the discussion. Civility is what really allows the conversation to happen, for Rorty believes that it is the virtue that makes strangers acquaintances and allows us to learn of new points of view. Rorty further characterises hermeneutic discourse as 'abnormal discourse' because, unlike normal discourse, it has no established methods for settling disputes. Consequently, there is no room in such a conversation for absolute values or commitments. Even dominant or agreed points of view must not be considered as absolute.[98]

Such an edifying conversation simply provides useful 'kibitzing', or novel ways of speaking and thinking.[99] One moves from the search for an atemporal, ahistorical foundation to a totally groundless conversation that can promise nothing but novel possibilities. Seeing no other alternatives, and recognising the difficulties of a nostalgic return to a pre-Kantian search, philosophy becomes but a voice, and no longer a privileged voice, in a conversation that

---

[94]   L. Wittgenstein, *Zettel*, §455.
[95]   M. Oakeshott, 'The Voice of Poetry in the Conversation of Mankind', *Rationalism in Politics and Other Essays* (Indianapolis, 1991), pp. 488–542.
[96]   R. Rorty, *Philosophy and the Mirror of Nature*, p. 318.
[97]   R. Rorty, *Contingency, Irony, and Solidarity* (Cambridge, 1989), pp. xv, 73.
[98]   R. Rorty, *Philosophy and the Mirror of Nature*, pp. 315–22.
[99]   *Ibid.*, p. 393.

weaves together different conversationalists and areas of discourse. Continuing his reference to Oakeshott, Rorty writes of persons united in a *societas*, 'persons whose paths through life have fallen together, united by civility, rather than by a common goal, much less by a common ground.[100] Oakeshott and Rorty agree that in conversation 'different universes of discourse meet, acknowledge each other and enjoy an oblique relationship which neither requires nor forecasts their being assimilated to one another'.[101] There is, though, the danger that Rorty's hermeneutic conversation is the conversation of the *dilettante;* someone who cannot commit themself to anything. Oakeshott avoids such a danger by insisting that the excellence of conversation:

> springs from a tension between seriousness and playfulness. Each voice represents a serious engagement (though it is serious not merely in respect of its being pursued for the conclusion it promises); and without this seriousness the conversation would lack impetus. But in its participation in the conversation each voice learns to be playful, learns to understand itself conversationally and learns to regulate itself as a voice among voices.[102]

Unless we allow people to bring their commitments to the conversation, and help them to recognise themselves as a 'voice among voices', then tolerance can degenerate into easy acquiescence. Furthermore, is genuine conversing — as distinct from talking past each other — possible without common ground? Without a shared basis, what possibility is there for dialogue, let along agreement or disagreement? If there is at present no common ground and philosophy gives up searching for one, what possible reasons could be advanced to convince people not to drift into indifferent monologues or silence rather than striving to continue the 'conversation of mankind'? Doesn't Rorty's own assumption that there is no common ground or foundation overlook the very obvious fact that conversationalists participate in a common ground by virtue of their being human?

Herein lies the weakness of Rorty's vision of the future of philosophy as reducible to the weaving of new discourse among different strands of conversation. Conversation is sustained by the search for common ground, and when the hope for such ground is silenced, all subsequent talk is threatened. It is proposed that philosophy can only study that which renders such conversation possible: our shared form of life. Thus, in the end, the philosopher tells us about what we already implicitly know, what we continually reveal in our

---

[100] *Ibid.*, p. 318.
[101] *Ibid.*, pp. 315–22.
[102] M. Oakeshott, 'The Voice of Poetry in the Conversation of Mankind'.

activities. Collingwood's description of philosophy in *An Essay on Philosophical Method* sums up this point well:

> What we are trying to do is not to disclose something of which until now we have been ignorant, but to know better something which in some sense we know already; not to know it better in the sense of coming to know more about it, but to know it better in the sense of coming to know it in a different and better way — actually instead of potentially, or explicitly instead of implicitly.[103]

This is no small task, and it is not one to be taken lightly. In chapters five and six, we will discover that Collingwood framed it as a duty to be undertaken by all of us to the best of our abilities for the sake of civilisation.

The Widening Lens

We seem to have traversed a lot of ground, moving from the popular presentation of Collingwood's doctrine of re-enactment as overly rational and individualistic to seeing it as reaching unreasonable thoughts and essential emotions of both specified and non-specified historical agents. Along the way, we have discovered that Collingwood considered history and philosophy to be connected via the study of the absolute and relative presuppositions that give shape to human activities. Collingwood's writings on presuppositions bear some similarities to Kuhn's and Foucault's writings on science and history, but more importantly, he is not as out of step with Wittgenstein's view of philosophy as is commonly supposed. In particular, in this chapter we have discerned that they both support a form of temporal foundationalism. Thus the more we look to Collingwood's writings on history the wider we discover his ideas to be. Yet we have seen only a fragment of what he has to offer, for we still have not looked at how, if at all, his views on re-enactment connect with those on the historical imagination and what roles these concepts play in the lives of individuals and civilisations. Nor do we yet have any idea of what 'reading' historically entails. In the next chapter, we will sketch the context in which Collingwood's views on the imagination and historical imagination appear, and then proceed in chapter five to reveal how original the content and form of his views are.

---

[103] R.G. Collingwood, *An Essay on Philosophical Method*, p. 11. See also L. Wittgenstein, *Philosophical Investigations*, §§127–31.

Chapter IV

Theories of Imagination and Historical Imagination

When the imagination sleeps, words are emptied of their meaning... [1]

The diversity of ways in which 'historical imagination', 'imagination' and their cognates have been employed can make the task of discovering any shape or coherence in their usage appear impossible. This is even more difficult if we restrict ourselves — in analytical style — to current usages employed. If there is one thing that is clear about the 'historical imagination' and the 'imagination', it is that they are colourful compounds of meanings from different times and places. In order to gain any understanding of their shapes and boundaries, then, we must look to the ways in which they were used in the past and see which of those usages survive today. And, on a smaller scale, this historical approach to conceptual analysis will help us to see the extent to which Collingwood's 'historical imagination' is an interesting and original amalgam of Western philosophical theories. In line with Kearney, I offer not an all-inclusive catalogue of every usage of 'historical imagination' and 'imagination in Western culture, but instead have selected views that represent the dominant ways in which they were used in various

[1]   Albert Camus, *Resistance, Rebellion, and Death*, 1961, p. 177.

historical periods.[2] As will become apparent, this methodological decision is itself an example of Hayden White's notion of the 'historical imagination' at work.

Imagination as 'Appearances'

Early Greek formulations of imagination cover a broad range of 'appearances' or *phantasmata*. For Plato the objects of imagination (*eikasia*) are physical and mental images, shadows, semblances, reflections and dream images of the works of God, nature and human hands.[3] At best imagination is a passive state of mind[4] — receiving appearances without rational awareness or judgement of reality or truth — and at worst it seeks to arouse dangerous desires and promote the uncritical acceptance of sense experience, ideas and conduct through an apparent resemblance to truth.[5] In the human journey from the acceptance of shadowy appearances to the rational apprehension of the transcendent forms, the objects of imagination, including art, can act as an obstacle to the achievement of morally enlightened rationality.[6] This is because imagination can mesmerise us with mental likenesses of the earthly manifestations of the transcendent forms: it is thus at three removes from reality. Aristotle's use of *phantasia* covers a similarly broad range of phenomena, from ordinary perception, illusions, hallucinations, 'after-images',[7] hypnopompic and hypnagogic images,[8] dreams, metaphors that set things 'before the eyes' of the reader to memories and perceptual traces of smells, sounds and flavours.[9] In distinction from Plato, though, *phantasia* plays a positive mediating role between percep-

[2]   R. Kearney, *The Wake of Imagination: Toward a Postmodern Culture* (Minneapolis, 1988), p. 17.

[3]   Plato, *Republic*, trans. D. Lee (Harmondsworth, 1987), 510a; id., *Sophist*, trans. F.M. Cornford (London, 1935), 266c; id., *Parmenides*, trans. L. Tarán (Princeton, NJ, 1965), 164b–165e; *Philebus*, trans. S. Benardete (Chicago, 1993), 24a–25; id., *Timaeus*, trans. D. Lee (Harmondsworth, 1977), 52b–c.

[4]   See for example H.J. Paton, 'Plato's Theory of Eikasia', *Proceedings of the Aristotelian Society*, no. 22 (1921–2), pp. 69–104.

[5]   See for example H.S. Thayer, 'Plato on the Morality of Imagination', *Review of Metaphysics*, Vol. 30 (3) (1977), pp. 594–618; and I. Murdoch, *The Fire and the Sun: Why Plato Banished the Artists* (London, 1977). See also R.G. Collingwood, 'Aristotelis De Anima Libri Tres: Translation and Commentary' [1913–14], Ms Collingwood Dep. 11, pp. 57, 123.

[6]   This is best seen in the allegory of the cave: Plato, *Republic*, 514–21.

[7]   For example, the bright light that persists after we have stopped looking at the sun.

[8]   Images that occur just before we go to sleep and just after we wake up.

[9]   See Aristotle, *De Anima*, trans. H. Lawson-Tancred (Harmondsworth, 1986), III.3, 9–11.

tion and thought.[10] *Phantasia* allows us to perceive an object *as* an object of a certain type and retain, manipulate, combine and interpret traces of perceptions, whether they are of actual or possible phenomena.[11] While all animals share the capacity to perceive objects *as* objects of a certain type, ants or bees or grubs are not able to retain such perceptions, and only animals with intellect can retain, manipulate, combine and interpret traces of perceptions.[12]

Later Greek and Roman writers preserve the broad view of mental 'appearances' and, like Aristotle, work to turn 'this form of hallucination to some profit'.[13] In Quintilian's *Institutio Oratio* and the treatise on excellence of expression attributed to Longinus, for instance, it is argued that the orator and poet who wish to move their audience must themselves be moved by feelings visualised courtesy of the imagination.[14] Quintilian sees this as a power that all people may develop; Longinus goes even further, using *phantasia* to designate any visualisation that prompts speech.[15] With each subsequent writer, the 'profit' of imagination increases. Cicero and Plotinus hold that the imagination can help us to conceive the ideal of perfect oratory or sculpture, and then pursue their realisation.[16] Flavius Philostratus is insistent that imagination can make orators, poets and artists aware not only of the sensible world, but also of the spiritual world. To him, imagination is:

> A wiser and subtler artist by far than imitation; for imitation can only create its handiwork from what it has seen; for it will conceive of its ideal with reference to the reality, and imitation is often baffled by terror, but imagination by nothing; for it marches undismayed to the goal which it has itself laid down.[17]

[10] *Ibid.*, III.3, 427b. On this, see R.G. Collingwood, '*Aristotelis De Anima Libri Tres*', p. 117.

[11] M. Nussbaum, *Aristotle's 'De Motu Animalium'* (Princeton, NJ, 1978), pp. 255–61; see also Aristotle, *De Anima*. III.3; id., *De Memoria*, trans. G.R.T. Ross (New York, 1973), 441b, 450a.

[12] Aristotle, *De Anima*, III, 3, 428a, 11. See also II.2.9–11 and R.G. Collingwood's commentary on such in 'Aristotle's *De Anima* Libri Tres', p. 11.

[13] Quintilian, *Institutio Oratoria*, trans. H.E. Butler (London, 1921), VI.2.30.

[14] *Ibid.*; and Longinus, *On the Sublime*, in *Classical Literary Criticism*, trans. T.S. Dorsch (Harmondsworth, 1965), p. 121.

[15] *Ibid.*, Longinus writes: 'In a general way, the term "image" is used of any mental conception, from whatever source it presents itself, which gives rise to speech. . .'.

[16] Cicero, *Orator*, trans. G.L. Hendrickson (London, 1962), II.7–III.10; Plotinus, *Enneads*, trans. S. MacKenna (London, 1969), V.8.1. See also *Enneads* V.9 on musicians.

[17] Flavius Philostratus, *The Life of Apollonius of Tyana*, trans. F.C. Conybeare (London, 1912), VI.19; II.22.

Here, the Platonic restriction of imagination to perceptible appearances is overturned, as it becomes the vehicle of transcendent knowledge. In the works of other Neoplatonists, Aristotle's notion that *phantasia* is the intermediary between perception and mind is further extended to the divine mind: it creates perceptible appearances from transcendent reality through imagination.[18] Consequently, there is much interest in images and other appearances as possible sources of divine knowledge.[19] Further, writers like Proclus link the imagination to self-knowledge.[20] Imagination thus becomes a means to *nous* or mind or 'vehicle of the soul', and *nous* itself, Cocking notes, becomes less abstract than in Classical Greek thought.[21]

The 'Jabbering' Servant

But the shift in favour of imagination was not unanimous. While many medieval writers echo the Aristotelian notion of imagination as a mediating faculty between the senses and abstract reason, they also frame it as highly problematic. Augustine, for instance, places abstract reason above the products of imagination, that 'power innate in the mind'.[22] And while he recognises the positive power of the imagination 'to alter the data brought in by the senses, and by subtraction . . . or addition, to produce things which in their totality have been experienced by none of the senses', he also expresses concern that these kinds of images are much more subject to error than those coupled with sense impressions.[23] Such errors are dangerous because if we desire something strongly, we can be deluded into thinking that self-created images of what we desire correspond to experience. Richard of Victor, too, sees the imagination as a necessary but problematic part of the transition from apprehension of earthly pleasures to the ecstasy of divine contemplation. In the alle-

[18] J.M. Cocking, *Imagination: A Study in the History of Ideas* (London, 1991), p. 53.
[19] See for example Plotinus, *Enneads*, V.8.1; Synesius of Cyrene, *The Essays and Hymns of Synesius of Cyrene*, trans. A. Fitzgerald (London, 1930), II.349; and Hugh of St. Victor and Richard of St. Victor, in M.W. Bundy, *The Theory of Imagination in Classical and Medieval Thought* (Chicago, 1927), p. 201–3.
[20] Proclus, *Proclus: A Commentary on the First Book of Euclid's Elements*, trans. G.R. Morrow (Princeton, NJ, 1970), pp. 112–3.
[21] See Iamblichus, Plutarch of Athens and Synesius of Cyrene in M.W. Bundy, *The Theory of Imagination in Classical and Medieval Thought*, pp. 150–1; and J.M. Cocking, *Imagination*, p. 61.
[22] Augustine, letter 7 (to Nebridius, 389 CE), in *Letters*, trans. W. Parsons, Vol. 1 (New York, NY, 1951), p. 18.
[23] See also Moses Maimonides, *The Guide for the Perplexed*, trans. M. Friedlander (New York, 1956), I.73 and II.36 (pp. 130–1 and 225–6).

gorical work *De Unione Corporis et Spiritus* he advances that it is only when the incessant 'jabbering of imagination, which is to say the inrunning of idle thoughts' is calmed that one may gain an inkling of the pleasures and pains resulting from divine judgement, self-knowledge and thus some knowledge of God, of whom 'man is the image and likeness'.[24] Richard's likening of the discovery of self-knowledge to the cleaning of the soul's mirror is further developed by St. Bonaventure. Just as all images — mental and physical — are reflections of the divine image of Christ, so too human imagining mirrors the divine act of creation. Again, though, it is stressed that knowledge is required to judge images for their veracity as evil can result from their unbridled use.[25] Imagination, as Pico Della Mirandola echoes, can 'damn man', because:

> Neglecting reason, she gives precedence to injustice rather than to justice, to lust rather than to continence, to savagery rather than to clemency, to avarice rather than to generosity, to discord rather than to peace.[26]

Imagination is the nurse of ambition and the root of cruelty, wrath, lust, greed, heresy and discord among scholars because it is prior to rational judgement.[27] Aquinas further restricts the role of imagination in the journey to knowledge of God by arguing that it is intellect that makes the understanding, combination and alteration of sense impressions possible.[28] To his view, the imagination is best viewed as a 'storehouse of forms received through the senses'.[29] These writers thus all have in common both the endorsement of Greek views of imagination as mimetic and mediatory and an acute awareness that without the supervision of reason, it might lead us to illusions and even evil ideas because it possesses no power to judge the real from the unreal.[30]

---

[24]   Richard of St. Victor, *Treatise on the Study of Wisdom that Men Call Benjamin*, trans. D. Barnes (Lewiston, ME, 1990), pp. 30, 39, 45, 46.

[25]   St. Bonaventure, as quoted in R. Kearney, *The Wake of Imagination*, pp. 123–8.

[26]   G. Pico Della Mirandola, *On the Imagination*, trans. H. Caplan (Westport, CT, 1930), pp. 43, 47.

[27]   *Ibid.*, pp. 45, 47, 49.

[28]   St. Thomas Aquinas, *Summa Theologica*, trans. Fathers of the English Dominican Province (New York, 1947), 1a.84.3.

[29]   *Ibid.*, 1a.78.4. On this, see also A. Kenny, *Aquinas: A Collection of Critical Essays* (London, 1969), pp. 273–96 and A. Lisska, 'Aquinas on "Phantasia"', *Thomist*, Vol. 40 (1976), pp. 294–302.

[30]   Jacques Le Goff has documented the existence of what he calls the 'profane imagination', but he is interested not so much in usages of the concept, but in products that he ascribes to it. See J. Le Goff, *The Medieval Imagination*, trans. A. Goldhammer (Chicago, 1988).

The Particulars and Pleasures of the Imagination

Early in the seventeenth century, Aristotle's ideas on the imagination were replayed in the writings of Thomas Hobbes. Imagination is for Hobbes primarily a passive image-receiving and image-retaining faculty, where 'image' covers sensory perceptions, illusions, after-images, hypnopompic and hypnagogic images, dreams and emotions.[31] Such images are constructed out of sensations and indeed classified by Hobbes as 'decaying sense'. This is because sensations recalled by the mind are obscured by later ones in the same way that the light of the sun obscures the light from a star.[32] Images are thus usually old and fading, 'as if they were worn out with time'.[33] As with earlier writers inspired by Aristotle, Hobbes notes both the inventive power of the imagination and its need to be guided by reason. Moreover, the imagination can only apprehend the particular, not the general or the infinite. In a bold departure from his predecessors, though, he argues that the novelty of imagination is not just restricted to mental images, for mental images can inspire many products:

> All that is beautiful or defensible in building; or marvellous in engines or instruments of motion; whatsoever commodity men receive from the observations of the heavens, from the description of the earth, from the account of time, from walking on the seas; and whatsoever distinguisheth the civility of Europe, from the barbarity of the American savages; is the workmanship of fancy, but guided by the precepts of true philosophy.[34]

Here, Hobbes transforms the imagination from a rudimentary faculty to the wellspring of creativity and even civility.[35] Unfortunately, there are many points in his claim which he does not explore or expand, leaving us to wonder about just how this creative power operates.

No answer was forthcoming in the rationalist writings of contemporaries like René Descartes. Descartes, who located the source of meaning in human understanding rather than in the world or a transcendent realm, recast the imagination as an intermediary between

---

[31] Thomas Hobbes, *Leviathan*, ed. R. Tuck (Cambridge, 1996), chs. 1 and 2.

[32] *Ibid.*, ch. 2.2–3; id., *De Corpore*, in *The English Works of Thomas Hobbes*, Vol. 1 (London,1839), §4.25.7.

[33] Thomas Hobbes, *De Corpore*, in *The English Works of Thomas Hobbes*, §4.25.8.

[34] Thomas Hobbes, 'The Answer of Mr. Hobbes to Sir William Davenant's Preface Before Gondibert', in *The English Works of Thomas Hobbes*, Vol. 4 (London, 1839), pp. 449–50.

[35] J. Engell, *The Creative Imagination: Enlightenment to Romanticism* (Cambridge, MA, 1981), p. 17.

mind and body. Indeed the imagination is 'in no wise a necessary element in my nature, or in the essence of my mind' but only exists by virtue of the mind's location in a body.[36] Imagination is below understanding because it operates prior to judgement and we cannot use it to comprehend the infinite or anything beyond a particular range, such as the idea of God or the human soul.[37] This is because the imagination operates only through images. Images are considered by Descartes to be residues of sensory experiences and always of particulars rather than universals.[38] For example, the imagination sees a thousand-sided figure as the same as a ten-thousand sided figure.[39] In cases like this, the imagination can hinder understanding.[40] Descartes acknowledges the power of the imagination to combine sensory experiences into novel appearances, but notes that these kinds of images are less vivid than those corresponding directly to sensory experiences.[41] This rationalist dislike of imagination was echoed in the contemporary writings of Leibniz, Wolff and Spinoza.[42]

Locke's few references to the imagination, too, are deeply disparaging: it is wanton, wandering, extravagant and associated with the ravings of a madman, the source for no more than 'castles in the air'.[43] 'Of what use', he concludes:

> is all this fine knowledge of men's own imaginations to a man that inquires after the reality of things? It matters not what men's fancies are, it is the knowledge of things that is only to be prized: it is this alone that gives a value to our reasonings and preference to one man's knowledge over another's, that it is of things as they really are and not of dreams and fancies.[44]

[36] René Descartes, *The Philosophical Works of Descartes*, trans. E.S. Haldane and G.R.T. Ross, Vol. 1 (Cambridge, 1969), pp. 90, 186.

[37] *Ibid.*, pp. 44, 106, 152, 161.

[38] *Ibid.*, pp. 56, 58–9, 155.

[39] *Ibid.*, pp. 185–6.

[40] *Ibid.*, p. 27.

[41] *Ibid.*, pp. 39, 106, 188.

[42] G.W. Leibniz, *New Essays on Human Understanding*, trans. P. Remnant and J. Bennett (Cambridge, 1996), pp. 137, 261–2, 375, 392, 404, 451–2, 487; C. Wolff, *Psychologia Rationalis* (Leipzig, 1734); and B. de Spinoza, *Ethics Preceded by On the Improvement of the Understanding*, trans. J.E. Woodbridge (New York, 1949), pp. 28–31, 192. Engell has suggested that Leibniz anticipated many Romantic beliefs about the imagination. See J. Engell, *The Creative Imagination: Enlightenment to Romanticism* (Cambridge, MA, 1981), pp. 29–32.

[43] J. Locke, *An Essay Concerning Human Understanding* (Oxford, 1975), §§2.33.7, 4.11.8, 2.11.13, 4.4.1.

[44] *Ibid.*, §4.4.1.

Ironically, though, his empiricist characterisation of the activity of mind as the passive reception of simple ideas or 'appearances' followed by active combination into 'complex' ideas encouraged other writers to endow the imagination with the creative and manipulative features generally ascribed to reason.[45] Berkeley, for instance, argues that if all knowledge derives from sensation and if objects impress on our minds to produce ideas, then we can only know ideas with certainty, not the objects that stimulated them. As a consequence of his equation of the imaginable with the imageable — and alignment with the rationalists that the imagination deals only with particulars — he rejects the idea that the mind can contemplate the abstract.[46] That is, we cannot posit a platonic form of a man, only particular men.[47]

Joseph Addison, too, used Locke's notion of simple and complex ideas as a point of departure for his series of papers on the 'pleasures of the imagination'. Addison's extended discussion on the power of imagination to appreciate that which is great, novel and beautiful and indeed to create works of art, prose and poetry that evoke the same appreciation in others suggests a positive creative power. Imagination not only sometimes rivals reason; on occasion it is preferable to it because it can better help us understand the greatness, novelty and beauty of God's works. It is for this reason that he argues that a poet 'should take as much pains in forming his imagination, as a philosopher in cultivating his understanding.'[48] Addison's positive appraisal of imagination in turn influenced many thinkers, including the poet Mark Akenside, author of *The Pleasures of Imagination*,[49] and the philosopher David Hume.

'Blind, but Indispensable Function'

For Hume, as for Locke and Berkeley, knowledge is built upon the foundation of impressions — stimuli we receive through the senses — and ideas, the mind's reproduction of impressions. This led him

---

[45] *Ibid.*, §§2.10.5, 7; 2.25.6; 2.30.2, 5; 2.31.6; 2.32.1, 3 25; 4.11.1, 5, 6. On this view of Locke, see E.L. Tuveson, *The Imagination as a Means of Grace* (Berkeley, CA, 1960), ch. 1.

[46] G. Berkeley, *Philosophical Commentaries*, in *The Works of George Berkeley*, ed. A.A. Luce and T.E. Jessop, Vol. 1 (London, 1949), §§341, 417–8, 429, 639, 829.

[47] G. Berkeley, *A Treatise Concerning the Principles of Human Knowledge*, in *The Works of George Berkeley*, ed. A.A. Luce and T.E. Jessop, Vol. 2 (London, 1949), introduction, §10.

[48] J. Addison, *The Spectator*, issues 412–421, in D.F. Bond (ed.), *The Spectator*, Vol. 3 (Oxford, 1965), p. 563. See also pp. 535–82.

[49] M. Akenside, *The Pleasures of Imagination: and other Poems* [1744] (London, 1853).

to wonder, beyond Berkeley, how the notion of objects having a continuous existence external to our minds emerges from discrete and discontinuous sense impressions. We blink, we turn away from a tree, yet we still believe it is there even when we do not see it. It is the imagination, he concludes, that produces this belief because there is an alignment of some of its qualities with those of sense impressions. Some impressions 'present themselves in the same uniform manner, and change not upon account of any interruption in my seeing or perceiving them'.[50] If I look from my window, I see two eucalyptus trees; if I look again later, the same trees, in the same relationship to one another, appear again. Such constancy is a feature, Hume believes, of objects that have an external existence to my mind. And even if they undergo changes — for example, one loses a branch — I still believe that they are the same trees. Our sense impressions may change, but they do so in familiar ways that lead us to consider them as coherent.[51] The implications of this view are quite radical, for it is not only object constancy that is unmasked as a fiction of the imagination, but also the succession of memories, impressions and ideas that form the basis of notions of a unified 'mind' or 'self'.[52] Reason, too, is due to the organising activities of imagination, as is sympathy, where we 'enter into the sentiments' of others and 'partake of their pleasure and uneasiness'.[53] Imagination is therefore implicated in the perceptual, mental and emotional activities and identity beliefs of all people. This is a conclusion that troubled Hume, leading him to wonder whether we ought to accept the comfort of the imagination's illusions.[54] But he, like Addison, also sees imagination in the work of the gifted. The imagination not only evokes strong emotions on the part of geniuses, as all ideas are 'attended with some emotion': but they will also be able to stimulate a similarly strong response in others.[55]

Hume's ambivalent view of imagination as the source of comfortable illusions and a creative power was understood by few of his contemporaries. But it became, nevertheless, part of the impetus for Kant's suggestion that the imagination is a 'blind but indispensable function of the soul, without which we should have no knowledge

---

[50]   D. Hume, *A Treatise on Human Nature*, ed. D. and M. Norton (Oxford, 2000), §1.4.2.18. On the alignment of the qualities of sense impressions and the imagination, see §1.4.2.15.

[51]   *Ibid.*, §§1.4.2.19, 1.4.6.12.

[52]   *Ibid.*, §§1.4.6.15–21.

[53]   *Ibid.*, §2.2.5.14.

[54]   *Ibid.*

[55]   *Ibid.*, §2.2.10.9.

whatsoever, but of which we are scarcely ever conscious'.[56] Kant's descriptions of the imagination are scattered and varied, but the main characterisation that emerges from his more extended comments in the *Critique of Pure Reason* and *Critique of Judgement* is that of mediator. Sensory experiences provide the content of our reasoning and reasoning supplies the categories with which we grasp sensory content. It is the imagination, Kant believes, which presents sensory impressions in a form that the intellect can work with.[57] It does not do so necessarily in a discursive fashion, but more in an intuitive and immediate way. That is, unlike Hume, the imagination does not create coherent impressions out of discontinuous and chaotic sensory impressions on the basis of past experience; rather, it provides the prior spatio-temporal structuring of our sense impressions without us having any control over it. We cannot but apprehend objects that are located in space and time. Such pre-cast impressions are then gathered into images (synthesised) and past images are reproduced in accordance with rules guaranteeing the 'affinity' of appearances, though no consciousness of these rules is required.[58] As a final step, these images may then be conceptualised (e.g. seeing a dog *as a dog*).[59] These activities of the reproductive, empirical imagination are common to all people. But imagination is also involved in works of genius and taste: works by those who either create or appreciate beautiful or sublime objects. Genius, to Kant, is a '*talent* for producing that for which no definite [prior] rule can be given' and is characterised by exemplary originality.[60] Genius 'reveals a new rule that could not have been inferred from any earlier principles or examples', meaning that although the genius is guided by some idea of what they want to produce, the internal pattern, completeness or rule is only expressed through the production of the object. The free play of the imagination both of the artist in forming and the critic in finding the rule internal to an object evokes the pleasure of beauty.[61] The sublime is evoked when the genius or critic create or appreciate that which the imagination cannot apprehend fully: we are in awe of

---

[56] I. Kant, *Critique of Pure Reason*, trans. N. Kemp Smith (London, 1929), A78.

[57] *Ibid.*, A99, 121, A77/B103.

[58] *Ibid.*, A102, A123.

[59] *Ibid.*, A121. On the status of imagination as prior to conceptualisation, see S. Gibbons, *Kant's Theory of Imagination: Bridging Gaps in Judgement and Experience* (Oxford, 1994), ch. 1.

[60] I. Kant, *Critique of Judgement*, trans. J. C. Meredith (Oxford, 1928), §§307–7. Kant's emphasis.

[61] *Ibid.*, §§217, 309, 314–5, 318.

the power of reason that keeps us from being overwhelmed.[62] How exactly the imagination achieves all of these things is unclear to Kant, hence his conclusion that it is 'an art, concealed in the depths of the human soul whose real modes of activity, nature is hardly ever likely to allow us to discover'.[63] He is convinced, though, that at least the perceptual imagination is *a priori* because it is a universal and necessary condition of both sensory perception and cognition and is not, as Hume suggests, derived from experience.[64] It is one of the conditions 'upon which the possibility of experience rests, and which remain as its underlying grounds when everything empirical is abstracted from appearances'.[65]

In the writing of Fichte and Schelling, the locus of mental power is further shifted in the direction of *Einbildungskraft* or imagination. In their view, we do not order sensory impressions by means of the categories of understanding: we create the things themselves. As with Kant, this creative power functions without our being aware of it. When we become conscious of its activities, what results is reconciliation of opposites such as freedom and necessity, the universal and the particular or humanity and nature, and the creation of novel images, concepts and means of investigating people and their place in the universe. Seen thus, the imagination is philosophical, even metaphysical, a mirroring of the creative power of God. But to Schelling, the philosophical imagination is ultimately inadequate because it cannot put the images and concepts it creates into a form external to the mind; for that, we must call upon the creative power of art.[66]

The Romantic Imagination

Not surprisingly, Schelling's aesthetic imagination became one of the key sources for contemporary Romantic novelists and poets like Coleridge and Wordsworth. To them, the work of the artist mirrored the creative work of God. They also drew together and conveyed to a wider audience at least five other philosophical characterisations of imagination already in circulation. First, the imagination is the point of connection between the self and the outside world. Second, differ-

---

[62] *Ibid.*, §§245–6.
[63] I. Kant, *Critique of Pure Reason*, B181.
[64] *Ibid.*
[65] *Ibid.*, A96, A2/B3–4.
[66] F.W.J. Schelling, *System of Transcendental Idealism (1800)*, trans. P. Heath (Charlottesville, VA, 1978), pp. 72, 176, 230–1; J. Engell, *The Creative Imagination*, pp. 225–31, 301–27.

ent levels or degrees of imaginative operations can be identified, from the involuntary, unconscious conversion of sensations into images to the conscious deconstruction and reformation of sensory impressions into images and symbols that have no presence in the natural world. Third, it can foster sympathetic identification with an object, with others or with our own future state. Fourth, it is gendered female because it is thought prone to wayward acts; and fifth, it can stir in us strong emotions and help us to understand the beautiful and the sublime.[67] To all of this they added, though, a strong claim for the place of imagination in childhood and education. To Coleridge, for instance, people who were rationally educated:

> were marked by a microscopic acuteness, but when they looked at great things, all became blank and they saw nothing, and denied (very illogically) that anything can be seen . . . and called the want of imagination judgement and the never being moved to rapture philosophy.[68]

'King without a Country'

At the end of the nineteenth century, it seemed that little was not made possible by the imagination. It was, if not the source, then at least the shaper of sensory perceptions, images, concepts, symbols and thoughts, creative ideas and works, and understanding of others and self. The existentialist writers who succeeded the Romantics also saw the imagination as king of life, but a 'king without a country'.[69] Kierkegaard, for example, characterised the first of the three stages on life's way — aesthetic, ethical and religious — as dominated by an imagination that produces lofty ideals and thus blinds us to the pain and finitude of the real world.[70] Nietzsche also considered the imagination to be the producer of fictions. Unlike Kierkegaard, however, he located it at the entry point of authentic life, for he believed its acknowledgement of fictions *as* fictions to be

[67] S.T. Coleridge, *Collected Works: Volume 7 Biographia Literaria* (I) (London, 1983), 168–70, 293, 296–306; (II) 16–18, 150, 295; W. Wordsworth, *Prelude* [1805] (London, 1932), I, 582–3, II, 266, 277, 409–11, III 124–7, XII 54–5 XIII 82–95, 167–70, 185–8, XIV 188–9; *Prose Works*, ed. W.J.B. Owen and J.W. Smyser (Oxford, 1974), III, 33; 'Tinturn Abbey', *Ode on Immortality and Lines on Tinturn Abbey* (London, 1885), II. 95–9. See also J. Engell, *The Creative Imagination*, chs. 18 and 21; and M. Warnock, *Imagination* (London, 1976), part III.

[68] S.T. Coleridge, *Collected Letters of Samuel Taylor Coleridge*, ed. E. Griggs, Vol. 1 (London, 1956), pp. 209–10.

[69] S. Kierkegaard, *Fear and Trembling and Sickness Unto Death*, trans. W. Lowrie (Princeton, NJ, 1944), p. 203.

[70] S. Kierkegaard, *Training in Christianity*, trans. W. Lowrie (Oxford, 1941), pp. 185–90.

more honest than the cultural conventions or fictions that masquerade as the truths of transcendental philosophy and Romanticism. For Nietzsche, there is no steady foundation of truths for people to stand on, only the many fictions they invent for themselves in order to experience meaning and certainty.[71] Sartre, too, saw life as an imaginative project. To him imagination is a productive act or even a condition of consciousness, producing ideas, hopes and values that are projected onto and which negate the real world. It is narcissistic and pathological, a project where we fruitlessly build ourselves and our world out of unreality or 'nothingness'. We are, unmasked, all dreamers who choose 'from the storehouse of accessories the feelings [we wish] to put on and the objects that fit [us], just as the actor chooses his costume'.[72]

Unlike his predecessors, Sartre's theory was built upon a detailed description of 'imaging'. In this endeavour he was joined by contemporaries Ryle and Wittgenstein, though their descriptions arise in part or whole from analysis of concept usage, not just the phenomenological observation of imaging characteristics.[73] Despite their varying approaches, all three agree that there are several differences between the objects of sense and the objects of imagination. First, there are ways we can be mistaken in sensory perception that do not apply to images: for example, I cannot mistake an image of a spider for an image of a twig as I might mistake seeing a twig as a spider. Second, when I have a mental image or imagine the sound of a particular tune, I cannot crane my head or adjust the way that I look at it to see it or hear it more clearly.[74] Third, images manifest temporal and spatial unreality: moving images may be slowed down or accelerated at will, repeated or considered in reverse sequence and we might 'see' the front and back of an object at the same time and look upon ourselves from the position of an outside spectator.[75] Fourth, in comparison to perceptions, images are impoverished

[71] F. Nietzsche, *The Will to Power*, trans. W. Kaufmann and R. Hollingdale (New York, 1967), §§13, 452, 539, 552.

[72] J.-P. Sartre, *The Psychology of Imagination*, trans. anon (New York, 1972), p. 212. See also pp. 18, 29, 179, 205.

[73] *Ibid.*, pp. 3, 130; L. Wittgenstein, *Philosophical Investigations*, trans. G.E.M. Anscombe, ed. G.E.M. Anscombe, R. Rhees and G.H. von Wright (Oxford, 1953), §§316, 317, 370, 383; G. Ryle, *The Concept of Mind* (Harmondsworth, 1949), p. 232.

[74] J.-P. Sartre, *The Psychology of Imagination*, p. 87; G. Ryle, *The Concept of Mind*, p. 256; L. Wittgenstein, *Remarks on the Psychology of Philosophy*, ed. G.E.M. Anscombe and G.H. von Wright (Oxford, 1992), vol. 2, §§63–104.

[75] J.-P. Sartre, *The Psychology of Imagination*, pp. 103, 105; L. Wittgenstein, *Remarks on the Psychology of Philosophy*, Vol. 2, §§100–4.

because we cannot learn anything new from them. For instance, when I look at the page of a book, I can locate a certain word, but if, on the other hand I was to entertain an image of the same book and I do not know the location of a certain word, then my image will not provide me with this information.[76] Fifth, when we entertain images, we are aware that we are doing such. As Sartre writes: 'we seek in vain to create in ourselves the belief the object really exists . . . We can pretend for a second, but we cannot destroy the immediate awareness of its nothingness'.[77] Sixth, images are always images of something; as with emotions, they are 'intentional'. That is, the features of the image are the features I imagine the object to have, and, as a result, I can be requested to entertain an image but not to see ordinarily. I cannot help seeing a spider before me, but I can help 'seeing' one.[78] Finally, and most importantly, images are a form of consciousness, not objects of consciousness or pictures 'in the mind'.[79] Such reflections on imaging are echoed in philosophies of imagination that followed. Mary Warnock, for instance, combined these insights with those of Hume and the Romantic writers to argue that imagination — in connection with the emotions — is fundamentally involved in creating coherence and meaning at the level of perception.[80]

Psychological Research

A strong interest in imaging may also be found in contemporary psychological research. Psychologists tended, however, to affirm the view of mental images as entities that their philosophical counterparts tried to attack. Early in the twentieth century, Galton noted that capacity for mental imaging declined with age and varied according to gender, class and perception: women and children had a greater capacity for mental imaging (eidetic imaging) than his professional colleagues.[81] The seemingly subjective nature of the reports that Galton worked with, though, led the founder of behaviourism, John Watson, to rule out imagery as a topic in a discipline that sought a solid foundation of confirmable facts. For these

[76] J.-P. Sartre, *The Psychology of Imagination*, pp. 12–13.
[77] *Ibid.*, p. 13.
[78] *Ibid.*, pp. 1–3, 181–243; L. Wittgenstein, *Remarks on the Psychology of Philosophy*, Vol. 1, §§314, 400, 653, 663, 759–60, 1052, 1132; Vol. 2, §§89, 121, 725–7; id., *Philosophical Investigations*, §344; G. Ryle, *The Concept of Mind*, p. 248.
[79] J.-P. Sartre, *The Psychology of Imagination*, pp. 5, 44, 59, 138, 157, 212–9; G. Ryle, *The Concept of Mind*, p. 232.
[80] M. Warnock, *Imagination* (London, 1976), pp. 146, 176.
[81] F. Galton, *Inquiries into Human Faculty and Development* (London, 1907).

reasons, Gardner writes, 'the ghostly image was exorcised for half a century from respectable academic psychology'.[82] What discussion there was on imagination was restricted to Freud's connection of daydreaming, imagination and creativity and clinical use of ambiguous materials like Rorschach inkblots to stimulate fantasy processes and reveal personality traits.[83] Growing interest in cognitive psychology in the 1960s and 1970s put imagery back on the research agenda. In *The Art of Memory*, for instance, Yates argued that subjects could remember long lists of items by imaging each item in a known frame of reference, such as connecting items to rooms in one's house.[84] Also interested in memory was Paivio, who, through the development of a catalogue of 925 words in which measures of imagery are noted, discovered that words that elicited clear images quickly (e.g. 'cat') are more memorable than those which cannot be so readily imaged (e.g. 'beauty').[85] Much work was also done on the manipulation or scanning of images. Studies reported by Block and Kosslyn, for instance, suggested that the rotation of mental images of three-dimensional figures takes approximately the same time as the physical manipulation of figures.[86] More recent studies using functional magnetic resonance imaging have shown that visual mental images use the same brain areas and pathways as sensory perceptions of objects.[87] And Richardson claimed to demonstrate the practical value of imagery, arguing that people who image successful sports skills improve their sporting performances more than people who do not.[88]

The Labyrinth of Mirrors

While mental images are still a popular topic in psychological research, the latter half of the twentieth century saw what Alan White calls 'the death of the image' in philosophical discourse. Taking on board the arguments of Sartre, Ryle and Wittgenstein, philos-

[82]   J.B. Watson, *Behaviour: An Introduction to Comparative Psychology* (New York, 1914), p. 18; H. Gardner, *The Mind's New Science* (New York, 1985), p. 324.

[83]   S. Freud, 'Creative Writers and Daydreaming', *The Standard Edition of the Complete Psychological Works of Sigmund Freud*, ed. J. Strachey, Vol. 9 (London, 1962), pp. 99–140.

[84]   F. Yates, *The Art of Memory* (Chicago, 1966).

[85]   A. Paivio, *Imagery and Mental Processes* (New York, 1971).

[86]   N. Block (ed.), *Imagery* (Cambridge, MA, 1981); and S. Kosslyn, *Image and Mind* (Cambridge, MA, 1980).

[87]   See for example K. O'Craven and N. Kanwisher, 'Mental Imagery of Faces and Places Activates Corresponding Stimulus-Specific Brain Regions', *Journal of Cognitive Neuroscience*, Vol. 12 (6) (2000), pp. 1013–23.

[88]   A. Richardson, *Mental Imagery* (New York, 1969).

ophers turned their attention to meanings of imagination that do not entail imaging. For example, White is not unusual in his assertion that:

> a vivid imagination is not the ability to 'see' or 'hear' things clearly in our mind, nor, as philosophers from Descartes to Hume thought, merely to rearrange 'ideas', that is, material previously received through the senses, but to think of varied, detailed, and perhaps, unusual and unthought of possibilities, whether or not these included perceptual, imageable features.[89]

Later twentieth century philosophy might have questioned the role of imaging in imagination, but postmodern thought goes one step further, unmasking the very notion of imagination as a romantic humanist illusion. Lacan, for instance, sees the conscious, creative, autonomous self as an imaginary ego formation that conforms to 'the normal'. The 'imaginary' is no more than a storehouse of recycled illusions or mirages of 'the normal' and it is thus the business of the analyst to dismantle it.[90] Extending Lacan, Althusser identifies the notion of the human subject or self as nothing more than an ideological, imaginary assemblage which bourgeois society utilises to elicit subjection to the *status quo*.[91] This suggests a new reading not only of the present, but also of the past:

> Since Copernicus, we have known that the earth is not the 'centre' of the universe. Since Marx, we have known that the human subject, the economic, political or philosophical ego is not the 'centre' of history — and even . . . that history has no 'centre' but possesses a structure which has no necessary 'centre' except in ideological misrepresentation.[92]

Humanist history is at an end for Foucault too: it, and the notion of the creative self that it reifies, can be erased 'like a face drawn in sand at the edge of the sea.'[93] Barthes is in agreement with Althusser and Foucault that the creative self is the product of bourgeois ideology. One of the recurring themes of his writing is the death of the author: the idea that works of literature do not originate with nor are the product of the writer's creative imagination. Authors are no more

[89] A. White, *The Language of Imagination* (Oxford, 1990), p. 192.

[90] See for example, J. Lacan, *The Seminar of Jacques Lacan*, Vol. 2, *The Ego in Freud's Theory and in the Technique of Psychoanalysis 1954–1955*, trans. S. Tomaselli (New York, 1955), pp. 36, 37, 178.

[91] L. Althusser, 'Ideology and Ideological State Apparatuses (Notes Towards an Investigation)', *Lenin and Philosophy and Other Essays*, trans. B. Brewer (London, 1971), pp. 152–6.

[92] L. Althusser, 'Freud and Lacan', *Lenin and Philosophy and Other Essays*, p. 201.

[93] M. Foucault, *The Order of Things*, trans. anon (London, 1970), p. 387. See also p. xxiii.

than channels for larger socio-cultural forces and their readers impute meanings to texts regardless of the author's intentions. Barthes writes:

> We know that a text is not a line of words releasing a single 'theological' meaning (the 'message' of the Author-God) but a multi-dimensional space in which a variety of writings, none of them original, blend and clash. The text is a tissue of quotations drawn from innumerable centres of culture.[94]

The imagination is no more than a bourgeois myth that has become so much a part of our cultural furniture that it has been 'naturalised'.[95]

In the writings of Barthes, Foucault and Althusser, as well as those of Deleuze and Guattari, the end of imagination is implied in the end of the humanist self.[96] In the writings of Derrida, however, the imagination comes under direct focus. All theories of imagination, Derrida contends, are characterised by logocentrism: the desire to identify origins, fix points of reference or certify truths. In Plato's theory, the products of imagination point to transcendental forms: in the works of the Romantics, they point to the transcendental origin of meaning in the self. Both enshrine a distinction between what is imitated and what imitates, and assert that the former is anterior and superior; the only difference is that the Romantics interiorised the origins of truth in the self.[97] It is in the name of *logos* or truth, Derrida writes, 'that mimesis is judged, proscribed or prescribed'.[98] What he seeks to question is whether any mode of representation — books or images — refers to some real meaning external to language, whether it be a transcendental truth or human subjectivity. At best, texts bear the traces of and constantly refer to other texts in a parodic circle.[99] We enter here, he tells us, 'a textual labyrinth panelled with mirrors'.[100] Without beginnings and ends, texts are without imagination, without authors, without even readers. Deconstruction it seems marks the end of imagination.

[94] R. Barthes, 'The Death of the Author', *Image Music Text*, trans. S. Heath (London, 1977), p. 146.
[95] R. Barthes, *Mythologies*, trans. A. Lavers (London, 1973), p. 11.
[96] G. Deleuze and F. Guattari, *Capitalism and Schizophrenia*, Vol. 1, *Anti-Oedipus*, trans. R. Hurley, M. Seem and H. Lane (New York, 1977).
[97] J. Derrida, 'The Double Session', *Dissemination*, trans. B. Johnson (London, 1981), p. 191.
[98] *Ibid.*, p. 193.
[99] R. Kearney, *The Wake of Imagination*, p. 252.
[100] J. Derrida, 'The Double Session', p. 195.

The Form of the Content: A Metareflection

Thus far, our account follows the contours sketched out by Abrams, Cocking, Engell, Kearney, Egan and Alan White.[101] These writers narrate a linear account of the rise and fall of the humanist self and imagination, or the near circular movement from imagination as mirror then lamp then hall of mirrors. Whether they are linear or near circular, though, their accounts are all suggestive of an evolutionary continuum: that is, the transformation from Platonic mimesis to Derridean deconstruction involves continuous change within a coherent lineage. Such continuous history ought to attract the criticism of Foucauldians, who favour *epistêmic* ruptures. But it should also attract the wrath of Derrideans, not only because of its tidy linearity — and thus privileging of the singular over the multivalent — but also because it is very easy to slip into seeing a line as a point of origin to which other notions of imagination must connect and even refer back. This has important consequences for usages of 'imagination' preceded by adjectives. For instance, this arrangement of materials suggests that the historical imagination is ancillary or even a 'sub' concept. This might explain why nothing is said about usages with preceding adjectives in the accounts of imagination cited above. But are such usages peripheral, second order or 'branches' to the main 'trunk'? Do all notions of the historical imagination always refer back to imagination? Might the meanings of imagination have been coloured by those of 'historical imagination'? Might some writers see the historical imagination as the imagination?

There are many other possibilities available for the arrangement of this conceptual history. There might be more than one 'trunk' or no solid 'trunk' at all. There may be just branches connected by a single 'essence' or point. More radically, usages may be connected only by a network of overlapping similarities and valued equally. There must be some relation between the activities of the imagination or the historical imagination for them to be given the conceptual label. That relation, though, does not have to be one of a chronological framework. The time has thus come for us to think about both the content *and the form* of the imagination. We could retrace our steps and arrange our account of the imagination according to another organising principle. As no extensive account of the historical imagi-

---

[101] M.H. Abrams, *The Mirror and the Lamp: Romantic Theory and the Critical Tradition* (New York, 1958); J. M. Cocking, *Imagination*; J. Engell, *The Creative Imagination*; R. Kearney, *The Wake of Imagination*; K. Egan, *Imagination in Teaching and Learning* (London, 1992), ch. 1; and A. White, *The Language of Imagination*.

nation has been offered to date, however, we have here the opportunity to cast a new account according to a new form.

If we depart from the linear chronological approach favoured by writers on the imagination, what might we discover? Can such a departure be made and historical differences still be respected? It can, as was demonstrated first by the Chinese historian Sima Qian over two thousand years ago. Qian's history of China and its neighbouring lands from the reign of the legendary Yellow Emperor (c.2697 BCE) to his own times is organised into five sections which look at dynastic houses, chronological tables, topic essays, the histories of prominent families and notable individuals respectively. His thematically chronological *Shi ji* is anything but easy to read, but the overlaps and contradictions between sections foster an enriched and multi-dimensional understanding of the past. Such a thematic chronological approach can also be used with conceptual analysis, as the following shows.

The Historical Imagination

References to the 'historical imagination' abound in historical scholarship. Relatively few writers, however, have gone to the trouble of explicitly elaborating the meaning of the concept for their readers. Most would not even need to do so, as in the main, it seems that it is used to presage no more than a judgement of approval or disapproval. Works bearing the traces of the historical imagination are either the best or the worst that the profession has to offer. Those who use the concept pejoratively do so generally to draw a sharp distinction between works that represent past reality and those that are fictive. To them, the 'historical imagination' denotes uncontrolled flights into fancy, invention, fiction.[102] Underlying this usage is thus the assumption, as Henderson has argued, that historical knowledge precedes and even precludes rhetorical art.[103]

Of those who employ the concept in a more positive fashion, it is possible to identify four major usage groupings. First, the 'historical imagination' is viewed as a means to understanding past events and situations. Second, it is that which enables historians to establish connections between items of evidence. Third, it denotes the use of figurative language and styles to construct historical works; and

---

[102] See for example L. von Ranke, 'Preface to *Histories of the Latin and Germanic Nations from 1494–1514*', in F. Stern (ed.), *The Varieties of History: From Voltaire to the Present* (New York, 1973), p. 241.

[103] H. Henderson, *Versions of the Past: The Historical Imagination in American Fiction* (New York, , 1974), p. xvii.

fourth, it is connected with the production of innovative knowledge, research methods and writing. The fourth of these usages is the most popular though the least explained, while the third has come to the forefront as the result of the recent linguistic turn in historiography. It is important to note, too, that writers frequently mix meanings, or offer multiple meanings.

Historical Imagination and Understanding

The usage of 'historical imagination' to denote the capacity to achieve an understanding of past events and situations was introduced to historiography in the eighteenth century by Giambattista Vico. In the 1744 edition of *The New Science*, he identifies *fantasia* as the medium through which understanding of past civilisations can be achieved. It succeeds, Vico argues, because history is a human artefact:

> Whoever reflects on this cannot but marvel that the philosophers should have bent all their energies to the study of the world of nature, which, since God made it, he alone knows; and that they should have neglected the study of the nations, or civil world, which since men have made it, men could come to know.[104]

Put simply, mind can best know what mind has made. This principle is also at work in the writings of nineteenth century German philosophers like Dilthey, who were interested in *Verstehen* (understanding). Dilthey, for instance, writes:

> we are at home everywhere in this historical and understood world; we understand the sense and meaning of it all; we ourselves are woven into this common sphere.[105]

We recall from chapter two, though, that Dilthey connected understanding not with imagination but with 're-feeling' or 're-experiencing'. And we also recall that it was the translation of Dilthey's works, among others, into English that resulted in the ambiguous relation of understanding, empathy, sympathy and re-enactment with imagination. Herbert Butterfield, for instance, is not unusual in writing of the importance of 'sympathetic imagination' in historical understanding.[106]

---

[104] G. Vico, *The New Science of Giambattista Vico*, trans. T.H. Bergin and M.H. Fisch (London, 1968), §331. See also C. Miller, *Giambattista Vico: Imagination and Historical Knowledge* (New York, 1993).

[105] W. Dilthey, *Selected Writings*, trans. H.P. Rickman (Cambridge, 1976), p. 191.

[106] H. Butterfield, *History and Human Relations* (London, 1951), p. 146.

As with Vico, the bulk of twentieth century writings on the historical imagination and understanding see the former as the means through which the latter can be achieved. Abel, for instance, argues that we use our imagination to ascribe generalised rules of behaviour derived from our own experiences to the behaviour of others. Such understanding serves only as an aid to 'preliminary explorations of a subject', however, because its basis in reflections on our own experiences means that it cannot serve as a means for new knowledge. That is, I cannot use it to comprehend that which I have not experienced. Further, it only generates possible explanations, not probable ones. Probable explanations, he asserts, require the application of 'objective methods of observation' such as experiments and statistical analyses.[107] Abel's characterisation of imagination as subjective and as not connected with novelty echoes both the conservative criticisms of British history education policy outlined in chapter one and Sartre's notion of the poverty of images. For Abel, as for other writers like Hempel, Beard and Hook, the historical imagination functions as no more than a heuristic device, a speculative formulation that serves as a guide or sets limits in the search for more certain understanding.[108]

Detractors from Abel's view are not hard to find. Trevor-Roper, Miller and Smith, for instance, question the connection of imagination with only familiar knowledge, arguing that the 'curious imagination' of the historian is sparked by confrontation with different and even uncongenial minds.[109] Others take issue with the setting up of imagination as a preliminary aid to what Abel calls rigorous 'scientific analyses'. Beer, for example, argues that the recreation, reconstruction or re-enactment in imagination of various states of mind, changes in states of mind and emotions of historical agents can complement the causal explanations favoured by advocates of 'scientific

[107] T. Abel, 'The Operation Called *Verstehen*', *American Journal of Sociology*, Vol. 54 (1948-9), pp. 211–18. See also B. Norton, 'Historical Reality and the Quest for Meaning', *Journal of International and Comparative Studies*, Vol. 4 (1) (1971), pp. 28–37.

[108] C.G. Hempel, *Aspects of Scientific Explanation and Other Essays in the Philosophy of Science* (London, 1965), p. 161, 163, 239–40, 257–8; C.A. Beard and S. Hook, 'Problems of Terminology in Historical Writing', *Theory and Practice in Historical Study: A Report of the (U.S.) Committee on Historiography* (New York, 1946), pp. 127–30.

[109] H.R. Trevor-Roper, 'Historical Imagination', *The Listener*, 27 February 1958, p. 358; J.C. Miller, 'Presidential Address: History and Africa/Africa and History', *American Historical Review*, Vol. 104 (1) (1999), p. 25; and R. Smith, 'Reflections on the Historical Imagination', *History of the Human Sciences*, Vol. 13 (4) (2000), pp. 105–6.

history' like Hempel.[110] Dray goes even further, seeing the covering law explanations of scientific historians as offering a conceptual barrier to understanding. Understanding, he contends, is achieved when the historian imaginatively reconstructs other peoples' experiences from the inside and 'can see the reasonableness of a man's doing what this agent did, given the beliefs and purposes referred to'.[111] That Dray also describes this activity as 'rational explanation' implies that he sees no incompatibility between imagination and intellect, though he does note that the imagination of the historian has to be held in check.[112]

These varied connections of imagination with understanding share a concern with the actual experiences of historical agents. A less popular, but clearly related notion of the imagination — epitomised in the writings of Trevor-Roper — considers both the actual and counterfactuals. Too many historians, he laments, see each historical situation as the inevitable result of prior situations, leaving no room for the contemplation of what might have happened. Trevor-Roper thus sees the historical imagination as working with the actual and the possible. Such a consideration of counterfactuals is sought not for methodological reasons, but to prevent the practical outcome where people see historical events as inevitable and surrender their free will. While this claim is clearly dubious, the connection he draws between the 'determinist' writings of Marx and Spengler and the German people's 'surrender without struggle' to Hitler to support the claim is even more questionable.[113] In the later re-statement of his views, Trevor-Roper substitutes his point about defeatism for the more general claim that the historical imagination helps historians to discern 'the hidden forces of change'.[114] Trevor-Roper's presentist concerns in turn draw attention to another related notion: that connecting the historical imagination with self-understanding. While Abel saw this as a limitation of the historical imagination, Hughes, Richards, Hart and Good see it as a positive feature, helping historians to become aware of their own thoughts and feelings, to orient themselves, identify moral lessons and to marshal the past to

[110] S.H. Beer, 'Causal Explanation and Imaginative Re-enactment', History and Theory, Vol. 3 (1) (1963), pp. 6–29.

[111] W.H. Dray, 'The Historical Explanation of Laws Reconsidered', in S. Hook (ed.), Philosophy and History: A Symposium (New York, 1963), pp. 132–3.

[112] W.H. Dray, Laws and Explanation in History (Oxford, 1964) [revised edition of 1957 monograph], pp. 129–31.

[113] H.R. Trevor-Roper, 'Historical Imagination', pp. 358, 371.

[114] H. R. Trevor-Roper, 'History and Imagination', in H. Lloyd-Jones, V. Pearl and B. Wurden (eds.), History and Imagination: Essays in Honour of H.R. Trevor-Roper (London 1981), p. 368.

address topical concerns and issues.[115] A basic assumption here is that the understanding furnished by the historical imagination is not only scholarly, but also useful.

While clearly there are some important differences among writers on the role and certainty of understanding assisted by the historical imagination, they all share a concern to access what Weinstein — with a nod to Collingwood — calls the 'inside' of history.[116] The term 'inside', as we saw in chapter two, is problematic, as it is suggestive of 'private minds'. Further, they all neglect to explain why the concept of the 'historical imagination' is to be preferred over those of empathy or sympathy. Indeed, most of the writers in this category treat the terms as synonymous and assume others accord with that view. For example, in his analysis of the historical research of Tilly and Walzer, Beer talks of Walzer's account of the 'powers of the imagination', even though Walzer only employs the term 'empathy'.[117] This same conflation of terms is also present in commentaries on Collingwood. Nor are we given any clue as to how the historical imagination develops: Curtis, Trevor-Roper and Hughes, for example, are content to describe it as a 'sixth sense', form of 'intuition' or 'gift' that historians either have or they do not.[118]

Historical Imagination and Connection

For this usage we also start with Vico, because given that his notion of *fantasia* implies — among other things — images, it is likely that it represents an extension to the longstanding view of imagination as the power to connect and combine images. In *On the Most Ancient Wisdom of the Italians*, he identifies *ingenium* – the power of connecting disparate and diverse elements — as a component of imagination.[119] Later, and independently, Wilhelm von Humboldt also

[115] H.S. Hughes, *History as Art and as Science: Twin Vistas on the Past* (London, 1964), p. 13; G. Richards, 'Varieties of Historical Imagination: Imagining Life without Freud', *History of the Human Sciences* Vol. 13 (4) (2000), p. 110; A.B. Hart, 'Imagination in History', *American Historical Review*, Vol. 15 (1910), p. 240; and J. Good, 'Introduction: The Historical Imagination and the Human Sciences', *History of the Human Sciences*, Vol. 13 (4) (2000), p. 99.

[116] M.A. Weinstein, 'The Creative Imagination in Fiction and History', *Genre*, Vol. 9 (1976), p. 271.

[117] S.H. Beer, 'Causal Explanation and Imaginative Re-enactment', p. 25.

[118] L.P. Curtis, 'Of Images and Imagination in History', *The Historian's Workshop* (New York, 1970), pp. 274; H.R. Trevor-Roper, 'Historical Imagination', p. 357; and H.S. Hughes, 'The Historian and the Social Scientist', *American Historical Review*, Vol. 66 (1960), p. 46.

[119] G. Vico, *On the Most Ancient Wisdom of the Italians, Unearthed from the Origins of the Latin Language*, trans. L.M. Palmer (Ithaca, NJ, 1988), 7.IV.

characterised the historical imagination as a constructive mental activity, but was careful to distinguish it from the activities of poets. The historian, he writes, is:

> Active, even creative — not by bringing forth what does not have existence, but in giving shape by his own powers to that which by mere intuition he could not have perceived as it really was. Differently from the poet, but in a way similar to him, he must work the collected fragments into a whole. It may seem questionable to have the field of the historian touch that of the poet at even one point. However, their activities are undeniably related. For if the historian, as has been said, can only reveal the truth of an event by presentation, by filling in and connecting the disjointed fragments of direct observation, he can do so, like the poet, only through his imagination. The crucial difference, which removes all potential dangers, lies in the fact that the historian subordinates his imagination to experience and the investigation of reality.[120]

The historical imagination is thus characterised as active, creative, more than intuition and firmly rooted in reality. Attempting to strike a more poetic note, Hart used his presidential address to the American Historical Association in 1909 to argue that it is the power of the imagination to 'assemble the dry bones [of the past] and make them live' that brings about the transformation of 'the lifeless lead of the annals into the shining gold of the historian'.[121] Subsequent writers repeat Hart's formula of connection producing a life out of dry bones, but nothing more expansive is said until Collingwood's work on the topic in the mid-1930s. Saving our account of his 'a priori historical imagination' for the next chapter, I note simply the influence that he exerted on the many writers interested in the idea of history as construction ('constructivism') in the latter part of the twentieth century. Some, like Weinstein, speak of the reality of the historian as an 'imaginative construct', but many more opted to speak of construction without the concept of the 'historical imagination'.[122] Outside of discussions specifically directed towards constructivism, scattered references to the connective historical imagination are still to be found, as for instance in Richards' suggestion that it works to generate connections that historical agents were perhaps unaware of.[123]

[120] W. von Humboldt, 'On the Historian's Task' [1821], *History and Theory*, Vol. 6 (1967), p. 58.
[121] A.B. Hart, 'Imagination in History', p. 246.
[122] M.A. Weinstein, 'The Creative Imagination in Fiction and History', p. 270.
[123] G. Richards, 'Varieties of Historical Imagination: Imagining Life Without Freud', p. 110.

Historical Imagination and Literary Style

A common assumption in accounts of the connective historical imagination is that histories owe their character and meaning to the links historians themselves construct between items of evidence. To describe the origin and nature of those links, historians have drawn parallels with the activities of both scientists and novelists, but in the nineteenth and twentieth centuries the historical imagination came to be firmly associated with the 'literary side' of history. George Eliot, for instance, describes the 'historic' imagination as an 'application of art' in which the historian is free from the 'vulgar coercion of conventional plot'.[124] Similarly, Macaulay suggests that historians must possess an imagination powerful enough to make their narratives 'effecting and picturesque' but that they must 'control it so absolutely' as to prevent themselves from filling in gaps with fictive additions.[125] Conversely, criticisms of an historian's historical imagination connote a lack or loss of control.[126] The role of the historical imagination in historical style was by no means seen as necessary, though, for the bulk of the writings on this topic make either no or only passing reference to it. At best, it was seen as something that was brought into operation once the facts had been established. This continued to the end of the 1960s, despite the rather lively historiographical debate that raged on whether history corresponded to the construction of narratives.[127]

Given that context, Hayden White's *Metahistory: The Historical Imagination in Nineteenth-Century Europe* (1973) marks a watershed. Not only did White bring the historical imagination back into focus in discussions on historical form, he also connected it with contemporary literary criticism, a connection that remains unbroken today.

---

[124] G. Eliot, 'Historic Imagination', in T. Pinney (ed.), *Essays of George Eliot* (London, 1963), p. 446; see also T. Deegan, 'George Eliot's Novels of The Historical Imagination', *Clio*, Vol. 1 (1) (1972), pp. 21–33.

[125] T.B. Macaulay, 'History', in F. Stern (ed.), *The Varieties of History*, pp. 72–3. See also H. Butterfield, *History and Human Relations*, p. 232.

[126] See for example Kitson Clark's criticism of Macaulay, in C.K. Clark, *The Critical Historian* (London, 1967), pp. 101, 107.

[127] See for example A. Danto, *Analytical Philosophy of History* (Cambridge, 1965); W.B. Gallie, *Philosophy and the Historical Understanding* (New York, 1964); W.H. Dray, 'On the Nature and Role of Narrative in History', *History and Theory*, Vol. 10 (1971), pp. 153–71; L.J. Goldstein, *Historical Knowing* (Austin, TX, 1976); M. Mandelbaum, 'A Note on History as Narrative', *History and Theory*, Vol. 6 (1967), pp. 413–9; C.B. McCullagh, 'Narrative and Explanation in History', *Mind*, 1969, vol. 78 (n.s.), pp. 256–61; and M. White, 'A Plea for an Analytic Philosophy of History', *Religion, Politics and the Higher Learning* (Cambridge, MA, 1959), pp. 61–74.

In *Metahistory*, White's aim is to chart the 'deep structure of the historical imagination' in the works not only of nineteenth century historians such as Michelet, Ranke, Burkhardt, Hegel and Nietzsche, but also — by extrapolation — the works of all historians. For White, the historical imagination is not something that historians consciously apply once the factual framework of their research is set. It denotes, rather, the more or less unconscious application of rhetorical conventions — conventions of explanation by argument, emplotment and ideological implication — to *pre*figure (explain or represent) historical data. In the 'poetic', 'imaginative' act which, he writes, 'precedes the formal analysis of the field, the historian both creates his object of analysis and predetermines the modality of the conceptual strategies he will use to explain it'.[128] This is no act of originality, though, for how the historian *pre*figures the past is simply a reflection of culturally dominant figurative language. Thus the historical imagination is a symptom of the 'linguistic determinism to which the conventional narrative historian remains enslaved'.[129]

Most of the current literature on the historical imagination owes its focus and shape to the work of Hayden White. Henderson, Ritter, Ostrowoski, Kelley, Sachs and Klein are some of the many historians who have applied White's taxonomy of the historical imagination to the works of a wide range of historians from different periods.[130] Others have highlighted the applicability of White's ideas to other fields, as with Smith's analysis of the historical imagination of social and natural scientists.[131] And Mink and Munslow use Hayden White's ideas to chart the historiographical anatomy of the historical imagination. Mink has highlighted what he sees as a basic tension between the claims to truth attached to historical content and the individual and therefore incomparable products of the historical

---

[128] H. White, *Metahistory: The Historical Imagination in Nineteenth-Century Europe* (Baltimore, MD, 1973), p. 31; see also pp. ix–xii.

[129] H. White, 'Historicism, History, and the Figurative Imagination', *Tropics of Discourse: Essays in Cultural Criticism* (Baltimore, MD, 1978), p. 17.

[130] H.B. Henderson, *Versions of the Past*; H. Ritter, 'Progressive Historians and the Historical Imagination in Austria: Heinrich Friedjung and Richard Charmatz', *Austrian History Yearbook*, Vol. 19–20 (1) (1983–4,) pp. 45–90; D. Ostrowski, 'A Metahistorical Analysis: Hayden White and Four Narratives of "Russian" History', *Clio*, Vol. 19 (1990,), pp. 215–36; D.R. Kelley and D.H. Sachs (eds.), *The Historical Imagination in Early Modern Britain* (Cambridge, 1997); and K.L. Klein, *Frontiers of Historical Imagination: Narrating the European Conquest of Native America 1890–1990* (Berkeley, CA, 1997).

[131] R. Smith, 'Reflections on the Historical Imagination', p. 108.

imagination.[132] Munslow has offered a more extensive statement, arguing that 'historical knowledge is primarily, or in substantial part, the metaphoric creation of the historical imagination' and that historians should reorient themselves to think of form as anterior to content, not the other way around. To Munslow, the metaphoric process — the application of a term or phrase to something not apparently applicable in order to suggest a resemblance — 'permits the historian to 'see' and compose/configure a set of relationships that did not previously exist between events'.[133] It needs to be stressed, however, that these examples represent only a small fraction of the scholarship on White: as with the literature on constructivism, the historical imagination seems to have disappeared after serving as an preliminary focal point. Perhaps in these two cases, the historical imagination has, as Hempel and Abel believed, served as a heuristic device, but in historiography, not history.

Historical Imagination and Innovation

By far the most popular usage of the concept of 'historical imagination' denotes the production of innovative, creative or novel knowledge, research methods and writing. It is also the least historiographically explored, probably because most historians consider it to be no more than a superlative to be used in reviews. It might also be thought that innovative or creative thought equates with individual thought, thus making a general account of the creative historical imagination impossible or at least undesirable. From the writings that offer some kind of historiographical analysis of this usage, two features stand out. The first is the emphasis placed on the notion of freedom, and more particularly the freedom *from x* rather than the freedom *to do x*. Eliot, we recall, saw the imagination as bringing freedom from the 'vulgar coercion of conventional plot'; Trevor-Roper saw it as playing a key social role in freedom from determinism. Thus we can say that writings on the historical imagination define it more by what it departs from than by what it goes towards. The second interesting feature of this usage is its appeal to psycho-historians and psychotherapists. Stannard, for example, sees the activity of the historical imagination as corresponding to the

[132] L.O. Mink, 'Narrative Form as a Cognitive Instrument', in R. Canary and H. Kozicki (eds.), *The Writing of History: Literary Form and Understanding* (Wisconsin, WI, 1978), pp. 129–49.
[133] A. Munslow, *The Routledge Companion to Historical Studies* (London, 2000), pp. 124–130.

willingness to ask different questions; Goldwert as the rapid movement from one idea to another; and Still as a breaking free from repetitive and compelling patterns of thought and feeling. All three agree, though, that psychoanalysis or psychotherapy can awaken imaginative activities, and that they can be a form of therapy.[134] This is a long way from the views of Lacan, who saw it as the business of the analyst to dismantle the 'normalising' influence of imagination.

Most historiographical writings on this usage, however, serve to refute it. We recall Abel's claim that the historical imagination cannot produce new knowledge of the experiences of others because it is limited by our prior experiences. To this we can add Soffer's analysis of the writings of interwar British historians like Collingwood and Butterfield to demonstrate that the historical imagination can encourage 'comfortable confirmation' of historiographical beliefs rather than divergent ideas.[135] On a more epistemological tack, there is also Vico's connection between imagination and memory on the grounds of the analogous argument that 'no painter has ever painted any kind of plant or animal that nature has not produced'. Even fantastic creatures like centaurs 'are true to nature but falsely mixed.'[136] Here, of course, Vico echoes the primary characterisation of mental imaging that both pre- and post-dates him: our images cannot teach us anything that we have not already experienced and known. It is also not hard to envisage the combination of Hayden White's views with Derrida's refutation of 'origins'.

The Historical Imagination of Historical Imagination Scholars

As I hope will be clear from these accounts of 'imagination' and 'historical imagination', both content *and* form shape meaning and character. If we take away the overarching chronological framework of traditional accounts of the imagination, we see not linear evolution, but a great tangle of meanings, not all of them complementary. Indeed, it often seems that 'imagination' is characterised by dichotomies. Recall that the historical imagination has been viewed as,

[134] D.E. Stannard, *Shrinking History: On Freud and the Failure of Psychohistory* (Oxford, 1980), p. 155; M. Goldwert, 'Creative Imagination in the Historian: A Leap of Faith Toward Interpreting Evolution', *Journal of Unconventional History*, Vol. 6 (2) (1995), p. 68; and A. Still, 'Psychotherapy and the Historical Imagination', *History of the Human Sciences*, Vol. 13 (4) (2000), pp. 115–20.

[135] R.N. Soffer, 'The Conservative Historical Imagination in the Twentieth Century', *Albion*, Vol. 28 (1) (1996), pp. 1–17.

[136] G. Vico, *On the Most Ancient Wisdom of the Italians*, 7.III.

among other things, a source of innovation and novelty *and not*, a conscious controllable activity *and not*, firmly rooted in reality *and not* and a means for understanding others *and not*. For the conceptual analyst, it is tempting to try and sort the mess out, to adjudicate on the basis of logic or perhaps even popularity on what side of the contradictions a more rigorous account of the concept might fall. Such adjudication, though, is an exercise of Hayden White's notion of the 'historical imagination' because very little connection or even adjudication among usages is to be found inside the relevant literature itself. While a few of the writings on the historical imagination post more than one meaning, no one as yet has offered an account of the nature of the relation between those meanings. Moreover, and ironically, writers on the historical imagination have paid little cognisance to earlier — and perhaps contradictory — usages. Nor has there been account of the relation of the historical imagination to the imagination, indeed, many writers treat them as synonymous. This last point may be a trivial matter: the decision on the part of a writer, for example, that the terms 'historical imagination' are just too wordy to employ all the time. But it might also suggest that the 'historical imagination' is, at base, just the 'imagination' at work in a particular context. More radically, though, we might read that claim in reverse, suggesting that the 'imagination', is at base the 'historical imagination'. The traditional scholarship on the imagination suggests that the former is more likely, but that, as I have argued, is a product of the historical imagination. Another historian's imagination — like that of Collingwood — might see the matter differently. In the next chapter, we will find revealed an account of the historical imagination that is innovative in both content and form.

Chapter V

Collingwood's Historical Imagination

German philosophies, when they die, it has been said, go to Oxford . . .[1]

In 'The Principles of History' (1939), Collingwood tells us that the 'reconstruction' of the thoughts of historical agents from traces left by them entails imagination.[2] He then passes on, never to return to such a potentially important point, which deserves some pause. The time has come for us to draw together Collingwood's many scattered comments on history, re-enactment and imagination, to see how they relate and what roles they play in the activities of the mind. In our hunt for information, we will look across the length and breadth of Collingwood's writings, from his unpublished manuscripts to his Waynflete lecture, 'The Historical Imagination'. This, we shall see, will be well worth the effort, for we will be rewarded with an account of the imagination that is innovative in both content and form.

Imagination and Historical Imagination

Collingwood's interest in the imagination can be traced back at least as far as his translation of and commentary on book three of Aristotle's *De Anima* from 1913–14.[3] Scattered references to the imagination are located throughout his published and unpublished works to

[1]   R.G. Collingwood, 'The Metaphysics of F.H. Bradley, An Essay on *Appearance and Reality*' [1933], Ms Collingwood Dep. 29.

[2]   R.G. Collingwood, 'The Principles of History' [1939], *The Principles of History and Other Writings*, ed. W.H. Dray and W.J. van der Dussen (Oxford, 1999), p. 49.

[3]   R.G. Collingwood, '*Aristotelis De Anima Libri Tres* — Translation and Commentary' [1913–14], Ms Collingwood, Dep. 11.

1939,[4] but his most extensive comments are to be found in the rough and published forms of 'The Historical Imagination' − a lecture given to mark his appointment as Waynflete Professor of Metaphysical Philosophy at Oxford University in 1935 − and in *The Principles of Art* (1938).[5] Key among Collingwood's writings on imagination are the rough and published versions of 'The Historical Imagination' for, as will be argued in this chapter, they offer us the most expansive account of the content and form of his views. Furthermore, it will be demonstrated that for Collingwood, 'imagination' is 'historical imagination'. For that reason, Collingwood's Waynflete lecture will serve as the departure point of our analysis, and a reference to which his other writings on imagination will be referred.

In the published form of his Waynflete lecture, 'The Historical Imagination', Collingwood begins by telling us that historians had, in the last century and a half, worked out a distinct technique that had 'profoundly influenced philosophy'.[6] He then offers an account of that 'technique' through a developmental analysis of historical knowledge and the imagination. Most people, when they first reflect on the nature of history, adopt a 'common-sense' or 'scissors and paste' view. On this view, the historian is a cipher and compiler of statements by historical agents. For example, if Cicero reports that he met Caesar on a certain date and in a certain place, then the historian must accept that report as true and add it to their compilation.[7] There are, Collingwood argues, two major problems with this view of historical knowledge. First, common-sense historians can do

---

[4]   See for example, R.G. Collingwood, 'Words and Tune' [1918], Ms Collingwood Dep. 25(1), p. 9; 'Outline of Lectures on the Philosophy of Art Delivered T[rinity] T[erm] 1924', Ms Collingwood Dep. 25 (2), pp. 4–15, 37–42; 'The Nature and Aims of a Philosophy of History' [1924–5], *Essays in the Philosophy of History*, ed. W. Debbin (New York, 1965), pp. 45–8; 'Some Perplexities About Time: First Draft of a Paper to the Aristotelian Society, 1925', Ms Collingwood 18(1), p. 9n. 4; 'Aesthetic' [annotated galley proofs of a lecture published in *The Mind: A Series of Lectures Delivered in King's College, London*, ed. R.J.S. McDowall, 1927], Ms Collingwood Dep. 25 (3), pp. 4a–9a; 'Notes Towards a Metaphysic: B' [1933–4], Ms Collingwood Dep. 18 (4), p. 42a; and 'Central Problems in Metaphysics: Lectures Written April 1935, for Delivery in T[rinity] T[erm] 1935', Ms Collingwood Dep. 20 (1), pp. 76–7, 96.

[5]   R.G. Collingwood, 'Inaugural: Rough Notes' [1935], *The Principles of History and Other Writings*, pp. 143–69; *The Historical Imagination: An Inaugural Lecture Delivered. Before the University of Oxford on 28 October 1935* (Oxford, 1935); and *The Principles of Art* (Oxford, 1938). While there are some minor differences between the published form of the inaugural lecture and 'The Historical Imagination' in *The Idea of History*, page references in this chapter refer to the latter.

[6]   R.G. Collingwood, *The Idea of History*, p. 232.

[7]   R.G. Collingwood, 'Inaugural: Rough Notes', *The Principles of History and Other Writings*, pp. 143–4.

nothing to protect their compilations from the omissions, concealments, distortions or even lies on the part of historical agents. Second, common-sense historians find themselves in a bind when it comes to the selection of evidence: if they do not make selections, their works will be nothing more than 'a mere chaos of disconnected details', but if they do make selections, they challenge the authority of historical agents.[8] Once we recognise those problems, Collingwood tells us, the common-sense view of historical knowledge gives way to a 'critical' one. Critical historians abandon the passive attitude of common-sense historians and demonstrate 'autonomy' in at least three ways. First, and most importantly, they treat historical agents not as authorities but as witnesses that can be questioned critically. Second, they select information according to their interests or in order to address questions; and third, they interpolate, filling in gaps in evidence with ideas reached inferentially.[9]

Here Collingwood, echoing Kant, uses 'autonomy' to signal that historians are bound only by principles that are self-authorised.[10] Unlike Kant, however, these principles are not universal and invariant. Nor do they correspond, as Bradley claims in his account of critical history, to the universal laws of the natural sciences.[11] Does this therefore mean that historical thought is a matter of 'anything goes'? By what right is the historian entitled, for example, to question the accounts of historical agents? In response, Collingwood shows how critical history becomes 'constructive' history through the recognition of a temporal 'a priori imagination' as the criterion of historical thought. Before describing Collingwood's account of the a priori imagination, it is worth drawing out what he means by 'a priori'.

[8]   *Ibid.*, pp. 144–6; *The Idea of History*, pp. 234–5.
[9]   R.G. Collingwood, 'Inaugural: Rough Notes', *The Principles of History and Other Writings*, pp. 146–50; *The Idea of History*, pp. 237–8.
[10] R.G. Collingwood, *The Idea of History*, p. 236; I. Kant, *Grounding for the Metaphysics of Morals* [1785], trans. J. W. Ellington (Indianapolis, 1993), p. 432. Page number corresponds to the 1903 Berlin Akademie version of the work, which is included in the Ellington translation.
[11] R.G. Collingwood, *The Idea of History*, pp. 238–41. See also F.H. Bradley, *The Presuppositions of Critical History and Aphorisms* [1874], ed. G. Stock (Bristol, 1993).

A Priori

Traditionally, the modifier 'a priori' connotes knowledge, concepts, or justifications that do not depend on evidence from sensory experiences. It thus contrasts with a posteriori knowledge, which is based on evidence from sensory experience. This distinction derives in the main from Kant's *Critique of Pure Reason*.[12] Kant, along with many subsequent writers, holds that a priori knowledge is to be found only in analytic truths: that is, the statement 'All triangles have three sides' is true in virtue of the meanings of its constituent terms. Synthetic truths, in distinction, are true not just because of the meanings of their constituent terms: for example, the truth of the statement 'There is a eucalyptus tree outside my window' requires observational justification. They are 'ampliative': they 'add to the concept of the subject a predicate which has not been in any wise thought in it, and which no analysis could possibly extract from it'.[13] While some philosophers, like Kripke, contest Kant's denial that any synthetic truth is knowable a priori, others have been more interested to describe the role of a priori knowledge in human activities.[14] Kant's a priori 'modes of knowledge' point to universal, invariant categories of mind. Lipps, on the other hand, asserts that a priori truths are those that our psychological constitution precludes us from considering as false.[15] Along similar lines, Ayer, with other linguisticists, holds to the view that a priori truths are those that rules of coherent language-use preclude us from considering as false.[16] Lewis contends that a priori truths are those that describe a person's pragmatically guided intention to use a particular conceptual scheme for the organization of experiences. And Chisholm claims that true propositions are a priori if our understanding those propositions is all the evidence we need to see that they are true.[17] Rich as this variety of views is, none of them cover Collingwood's and, as we shall see, Wittgenstein's accounts.

As was suggested in chapter three, in Collingwood's view there are fundamental presuppositions in every field of knowledge. These

[12] I. Kant, *Critique of Pure Reason*, trans. N. Kemp Smith (London, 1929), Introduction, §§1–4.

[13] *Ibid.*, A7/B11.

[14] S. Kripke, *Naming and Necessity* (Cambridge, MA, 1980), pp. 53–8.

[15] R.M. Chisholm, 'The Truths of Reason', *A Priori Knowledge*, ed. P.K. Moser (Oxford, 1987), pp. 130–4.

[16] A.J. Ayer, *Language, Truth and Logic*, (2nd edn., London, 1946), pp. 71–87; reprinted in *A Priori Knowledge*, pp. 26–41.

[17] C.I. Lewis, 'A Pragmatic Conception of the A Priori' and R. M. Chisholm, 'The Truths of Reason', *A Priori Knowledge*, pp. 15–25, 112–44.

principles cannot be established empirically, but are a priori. Since the Greeks, he writes in his lectures of 1936:

> people have been accustomed to recognise two kinds of knowledge, the empirical knowledge of what is given in perception [a posteriori knowledge] and the a priori knowledge of eternal and necessary truths . . . truths of fact and truths of reason, intuition and conception, matters of fact and relations between ideas, and so on.[18]

The principles of history, however, fall within neither category. History does not 'proceed by way of perception' and is therefore not built upon a posteriori truths. It is 'not present, and cannot be empirically perceived. Historical knowledge is not immediate; its object is not given, it must be arrived at by reasoning'.[19] Nor does history fall under the traditional idea of the a priori, for although its truths are necessary, they are not 'something eternal and indifferent to space and time'. Collingwood thus concludes that '[n]either perception nor thought, as traditionally conceived, can give us historical knowledge'.[20]

In other words, the a priori principles of history are themselves historically grounded. Their meaning and truth do not depend simply on their correspondence with permanent, abstract, universal truths that are exterior or interior to humans. For this reason, the principles of history are never final. Ideas of history may come under strain, collapse and be replaced. In defending the rigour of the historian's enterprise, though, Collingwood is clear that this temporal view of principles does not result in an 'anything goes' situation. If historians stray from the a priori principles or presuppositions that are at work in the scholarly activity of history, then they produce historical fictions, not historical explanations.[21] Here Collingwood prefigures Wittgenstein in his suggestion that general agreement in the results that one gets at different times is *necessary* for there to be historical inquiry at all.[22] In line with the analysis of presuppositions offered in chapter three, Collingwood's remark suggests that the source of the requirement that the historian's work be rigorous is that an activity in which just any results were allowed

[18] R.G. Collingwood, 'Lectures on the Philosophy of History', Ms Collingwood Dep. 15 (3); as quoted in W.J. van der Dussen, *History as a Science: The Philosophy of R.G. Collingwood* (The Hague, 1981), p. 285.

[19] *Ibid.*; see also R.G. Collingwood, *The Idea of History*, pp. 233, 307, 482.

[20] *Ibid.* On this point, see also L.O. Mink, *Mind, History and Dialectic: The Philosophy of R.G. Collingwood* (Bloomington, IN, 1969), p. 185.

[21] R.G. Collingwood, *The Idea of History*, p. 241; see also L. Wittgenstein, *Remarks on the Foundations of Mathematics*, ed. G.H. von Wright, R. Rhees and G.E.M. Anscombe (Oxford, 1965), I, §116.

[22] R.G. Collingwood, *The Idea of History*, pp. 244–6; 'Observations on Language' [n.d.], Ms Collingwood Dep. 16 (3), p. 1.

would not be called 'history'. We follow the principles of history as we work; we do not posit and decide to accept or reject them before application. Consequently, Collingwood's a priori imagination thus is historical in two senses: first, because it describes the activities of historians, and second, because what it entails is subject to change.

In chapter three, a temporal foundationalism was revealed in the writings of Collingwood and Wittgenstein. We recall that our pre-suppositions are not static but dynamic, changing with time as with the flow of a river and shift in its bed. On the basis of this view, it is possible to distinguish at least two senses of the modifier a priori. First, one can speak of an existential a priori. Here, the matrix of human activities structures and conditions experience, giving it a particular form. Human life displays recurrent patterns, identifiable structures, regularities, and particular ways of being and doing. For example, one might ask if we could think of a humanity in which the experience of time plays no part. We might with difficulty be able to imagine similar beings without a temporal sense, but such things would be far from what is 'human'. The experience of time is tied up with the very definition, the very form of human life. Certain activities give the human way of being its characteristic form, and are rooted so deeply in our lives that imagining them altered would entail imagining radically different kinds of lives. This is not to say, though, that they are exempt from change. Echoing Vico and setting himself against Kant, Collingwood presents human nature as an historical artefact.[23] Thus to Collingwood and Wittgenstein, the modifier 'a priori' refers to particular presuppositions that could not be changed without radically transforming the human way of being.[24]

Secondly, people are born into, and are capable of being socialised into, a context of meanings. The a priori in this sense constitutes a form of being that is like that of a species within a certain environment. All meaning, thinking and knowing are grounded in such a form of life. The structure or order that is known is not already independently given, but comes into being as people engage in activities. Further, it is not an a priori which circumscribes the space of all possibilities. This can be seen as follows. Because of specific historical

---

[23] R.G. Collingwood, *The Idea of History*, pp. 203–7. See also G. Vico, *The New Science* [1744], trans. T.G. Bergin and M.H. Fisch (Ithaca, NJ, 1968), §§120–2.

[24] R.G. Collingwood, 'Reality as History', Ms Collingwood Dep. 12 (9), pp. 21–9; *The Idea of History*, pp. 208–9. See also L. Wittgenstein, *Philosophical Investigations*, ed. G.H. von Wright, R. Rhees and G.E.M. Anscombe (Oxford, 1992), II, §§122, 174, 200; *Remarks on the Foundations of Mathematics*, §123; *On Certainty*, trans. D. Paul and G.E.M. Anscombe, ed. G.E.M. Anscombe and G.H. von Wright (Oxford, 1969), §§80, 94, 95, 102, 126, 141–3, 211, 225, 358–9.

and cultural situations and the problems and interests they invoke, particular forms of life take on a structure. For example, people are socialised into patterns of grief, pain and sorrow. Different cultures or social groupings may find different arrangements expedient given the particular conditions they face, but such variation is a variability within the limits of more long term presuppositions. For example, we are able to recognise that our world is not like the medieval European world. This might be taken to mean, for instance, that whereas people looked to Christianity as a source of orientation in medieval life, science is a source of orientation today. Given the variability of forms of life, certain activities may not make sense without careful study — the kind of study promoted in history. This second class of a priori presupposition is subject to far more rapid change than those of the first class. It is important to recall, though, that there is no sharp distinction between them. Thus Collingwood and Wittgenstein posit an a priori that has come to be established and can be replaced, and has its origins in time.

A Priori Historical Imagination

Once we recognise that the principles of history are a priori but also historical then we move from holding a 'critical' to a 'constructive' view of history. The constructive historian, like the critical one, is selective, critical in their attitude towards sources and able to interpolate between gaps in evidence. Importantly, though, the resulting history is neither a compilation of statements by authorities nor the 'mosaic' of sources fashioned by a critical historian.[25] It is, Collingwood tells us, something fashioned according to a self-authorised criterion: that of the a priori historical imagination. In the rough draft of his Waynflete lecture — 'Inaugural: Rough Notes' — Collingwood instructs us that:

> It will be useful to distinguish three forms of imagination. First, there is the wholly free or pure imagination whose specialised development is seen in the activity of the artist. Secondly, there is the perceptual imagination, as I shall call it, which presents to us the objects of possible perception which are not actually perceived; the under-side of this table, the back of the moon, the inside of an unopened egg. How important this 'blind but indispensable' faculty is, Kant has shown in a famous passage. Thirdly, there is what I shall call the historical imagination, which presents to us the past: not an object of possible perception, since it does

[25]   R.G. Collingwood, 'Inaugural: Rough Notes', *The Principles of History and Other Writings*, p. 150.

not exist to be perceived, but none the less able, through the activity of imagination, to become an object of our thought.[26]

Collingwood's account of the 'pure or free' imagination of the artist is not restricted to his writings on history. In *Speculum Mentis* (1924), for instance, he writes that art is 'purely' imagination.[27] By this he means an attitude towards the world in which the artist is not constrained by concepts of reality or unreality or even utility.[28] It is also an attitude that does not require awareness, and as such may appear out of the artist's control. As he writes in his lectures on the philosophy of art from 1924:

> If [the artist] simply imagines without realising that he is imagining, his imaginations rise up before him in a mysterious and unexplained way, and their beauty, that is, their aesthetic power or value, seems to be something independent of himself, something which comes from outside and takes possession of his soul without his cooperation or permission.[29]

It also differs from thought in that when we think *x* we consider it in relation to other things; when we imagine *x* in a pure or free fashion, we consider it in isolation. What matters therefore is that the artist's imaginative products are internally, not externally coherent.[30] For example, Tolkien's imaginative skill is seen in his creation of 'Middle-Earth', a complex and internally consistent secondary world. In 'The Historical Imagination' too we are told that the novelist and artist, like the historian, aim to construct a picture that is coherent and consistent. Both novels and histories are thus the product not of arbitrary activities, but of self-authorised presuppositions belonging to the constellation of the pure imagination.[31] Where they differ, though, is in the presuppositions of truth that bind them.[32] If the artist or novelist create something that is internally coherent and consistent, then it is true. As Collingwood advances in *The Principles of Art*: '[s]o far as the utterance is a good work of art, it is a true utterance; its artistic merit and its truth are the same thing'.[33] For a history to be true, however, it needs to be both internally *and* externally

---

[26]   *Ibid.*, p. 166.
[27]   R.G. Collingwood, *Speculum Mentis* (Oxford, 1924), p. 61.
[28]   R.G. Collingwood, 'Aesthetic' [1927], pp. 6, 4a.
[29]   R.G. Collingwood, 'Outline of Lectures on the Philosophy of Art Delivered T[rinity] T[erm] 1924', p. 9.
[30]   *Ibid.*, p. 6a; see also *Outlines of a Philosophy of Art* [1925] (Bristol, 1993), pp. 99–100.
[31]   R.G. Collingwood, *The Idea of History*, pp. 242, 245–6.
[32]   *Ibid.*, p. 246; see also 'The Nature and Aims of a Philosophy of History' [1925], *Essays on the Philosophy of History*, ed. W. Debbins (New York, 1965), p. 48.
[33]   R.G. Collingwood, *The Principles of Art*, p. 287.

coherent and consistent. External consistency follows from at least three principles. First, a history must have a definite spatio-temporal location on Earth. Second, as there is only 'one historical world' everything in it must stand in consistent relation to everything else: for example, the same person named Captain Cook cannot have lived 240 years ago and a million years ago, as with some Australian Aboriginal histories.[34] The secondary or imaginary worlds of artists and novelists, on the other hand, need not be drawn together. Third, a history must agree with the traces of the past left in evidence. What Collingwood means by 'evidence' will be unpacked in our accounts of the perceptual imagination and historical imagination that follow.

Collingwood's account of the pure or free imagination can clearly be located in the tradition of writings on the imagination of artists and geniuses by, among others, Addison, Akenside, Hume, Kant, Fichte, Schelling, Coleridge and Wordsworth. His alignment with Kant and Coleridge on two points, however, is worth noting in particular. First, we recall that, for Kant, artistic genius entails breaking free from prior rules and forming new rules or patterns that are internal to a work. This view is clearly echoed in Collingwood's connection of the pure or free imagination with the production of internally consistent works of art. Second, while most accounts of the artistic imagination see it as evidenced by only a few gifted individuals, Collingwood holds with Coleridge that it can be found in the activities of children. This is, why, for instance, Collingwood claims in his lectures on the philosophy of art from 1924 that 'the child's life of imagination is a training for the adult life of thought' and thus that 'we must learn to imagine before we can know'.[35] We will discuss Collingwood's views on imagination and education more fully in the following chapter; for now it will suffice to note that he finds imagination in more that just the works of exceptional adults.

It is also important to recognise that Collingwood was not the first writer to draw a parallel between the imagination of the artist and that of the historian: for example, Hume and George Eliot refer to histories as well as novels in their writings on imagination. Nor is Collingwood the first writer to note that the match between the imagination of the artist and that of the historian is not exact: for example, we recall Macaulay's instruction that historians should

[34] R.G. Collingwood, *The Idea of History*, p. 246; and D.B. Rose, 'Ned Kelly Died for Our Sins', *Oceania*, Vol. 65 (2) (1994), pp. 175–86.
[35] R.G. Collingwood, 'Outline of Lectures on the Philosophy of Art' [1924], p. 42.

control their imagination in order to prevent flights of fancy.[36] What is innovative in his thought, though, is first, the specification of a requirement that historians produce works that are internally and externally coherent and consistent; and second, the identification of additional forms of imagination at work in the activities of the historian.

The second form of imagination that Collingwood identifies in 'Inaugural: Rough Notes' is the 'perceptual imagination'. This 'presents to us the objects of possible perception which are not actually perceived', like the back of this page. As with the pure and free imagination, Collingwood's comments on the perceptual imagination are not restricted to his writings on history. In his lectures on Metaphysics from 1935, for example, he tells us that 'the very act of seeing a white ball on a green table' is 'an act of imagination'.[37] For him, as for Hume and Kant, the notion of persistent and solid objects is actuated by the imagination.[38] Further, it presents to us objects of possible perception like the back of the moon and the inside of a closed matchbox,[39] and an impression of persistence even if our perceptions have been interrupted, as with the eucalyptus trees outside my window that I look at only intermittently. In 'The Historical Imagination', Collingwood offers a more complex example of the latter when he suggests that if we look out at sea and see a ship and then look again later and see it occupying a different location 'we find ourselves obliged to imagine it as having occupied intermediate positions when we were not looking'.[40] Persistence is thus assumed even with a shift in spatial location. Moreover, as this example also shows, imagination actuates the interpolation of possible perceptions. Hume, for example, suggested that imagination makes possible the positing of a shade of blue between two others derived from sensory experience.[41] This example, like others involving possible perceptions, shows us that the perceptual imagination is in some sense indifferent to the distinction between the real and unreal.[42] In distinction from Hume, Collingwood does not hold that coherent

---

[36] Collingwood indicates his awareness of Macaulay's essay 'History' on p. 241 of *The Idea of History.*

[37] R.G. Collingwood, 'Central Problems in Metaphysics' [1935], p. 77.

[38] R.G. Collingwood, *The Principles of Art*, pp. 192, 210.

[39] *Ibid.*, p. 192.

[40] R.G. Collingwood, *The Idea of History*, p. 241.

[41] D. Hume, *A Treatise on Human Nature*, ed. D. and M. Norton (Oxford, 2000), §1.1.1.1; as noted in R.G. Collingwood, 'Inaugural: Rough Notes', *The Principles of History and Other Writings*, p. 150.

[42] R.G. Collingwood, *The Principles of Art*, pp. 136-7; 'Outline of Lectures on the Philosophy of Art' [1924], p. 4; and 'Aesthetic' [1927], p. 6.

perceptions emerge only from past experiences. For like Kant, Collingwood holds that imagination provides the prior structuring of our sense impressions: we cannot but apprehend objects that are structured by a priori categories of mind or presuppositions. For example, we cannot help but see the white ball on a green table as located in space and time.

Imagination provides the structuring of our perceptions without us having control over it and without us even necessarily being aware of it. Our perceptions are active rather than passive, though, because even if they are beyond our control, they are still something we do; they are not something done to us.[43] A further extension of the same structuring, Collingwood contends, is to be found in the activities of historians.[44] It is the imagination that allows historians to interpolate with 'perfectly good conscience' between two pieces of evidence; such as finding 'themselves obliged' to imagine that Caesar travelled from Rome to Gaul when they are told that he was in those two places at successive times.[45] In saying 'obliged', Collingwood here signals the status of the imagination as a priori: we do not decide to accept or reject the process of interpolation in advance of our using it. Indeed in 'The Historical Imagination' he acknowledges that historians may even be unaware of its operation.[46] As a final point, we should also note that as with the comparison of the historian and artist in our account of the pure or free imagination, there is the requirement upon historians that they produce interpolations that are both internally and externally coherent and consistent. It would not do, for instance, for Caesar to be in both Rome and Gaul at the same time, or for the historian to pad out a narrative with details not suggested by the evidence such as what Caesar ate during his journey. Nor presumably would it be acceptable to suggest that Caesar drove a motor car to Gaul or caught a lift with passing aliens. The positing of historical interpolations entails some indifference to judgements of reality and unreality, but not to the same degree as the postulations of novelists.

As we have seen, Collingwood's notion of the perceptual imagination clearly derives from the writings of Hume and Kant. Vico and

[43] R.G. Collingwood, *The Principles of Art*, pp. 196–7.
[44] R.G. Collingwood, 'Inaugural: Rough Notes', *The Principles of History and Other Essays*, p. 151; and *The Idea of History*, p. 241.
[45] R.G. Collingwood, *The Idea of History*, p. 241. In 'Inaugural: Rough Notes', he offers the example of Tacitus positing that Suetonius Paulinus rode from Anglesey to London in response to Boudicca's rebellion. See *The Principles of History and Other Writings*, p. 152.
[46] R.G. Collingwood, *The Idea of History*, p. 241; see also *The Principles of Art*, p. 224.

Humboldt, too, precede him in the suggestion that the historical imagination is implicated in the connection of fragments of evidence. Additionally, Humboldt must be credited for pointing out that while poets and historians may connect fragments, historians must subordinate their imagination to the investigation of reality. What is novel about Collingwood's work is his combination of ideas on perception and imagination with those on connection and the historical imagination. To be sure, as noted in the previous chapter, there is an oblique connection between imagination and perception in Vico's writings. This is by virtue of the fact that in contemporary thought 'imagination' was almost exclusively thought of in terms of imaging, and imaging was not clearly distinguished from perception. In Collingwood's writing, though, the connection is explicit. Importantly, too, we cannot assume that imaging and perception are the same thing for him.

Collingwood's views on the relation between imaging and perception are laid out in chapters nine and ten of *The Principles of Art* (1938). At first sight, what he has to say there seems not to sit with his views expressed elsewhere. This, I believe, is mainly a terminological problem. Although these chapters are undoubtedly about the particular activities of imaging and perception, Collingwood opts to apply the more general label of 'imagination' to both.[47] Why? Wading against the tide of twentieth century philosophy and psychology, Collingwood complains that in ordinary usage, 'image' implies an analogous relation between an object and the image made of it. When we 'imagine' an object, he points out, we cannot also hold up for mental inspection the object that it is an image of. Technically, Collingwood is right, but no other writers on imaging assume a strict concurrent bond between image and object. Saying that something is an image suggests some connection with sensory experience: no theorist holds that an image can be entirely uncoupled from it. That does not mean, however, that the connection is tested every time we entertain an image. Regardless of its merits, though, Collingwood's opting for 'imagination' over 'imaging' may lead readers to mistakenly conclude that he is addressing all activities of imagination, like the ones described above, not just a limited range.[48]

---

[47] R.G. Collingwood, *The Principles of Art*, pp. 191–2.
[48] Von Leyden's account of Collingwood's views is based almost exclusively on *The Principles of Art*. See W. von Leyden, 'Philosophy of Mind: An Appraisal of Collingwood's Theories of Consciousness, Language and Imagination', *Critical Essays on the Philosophy of R.G. Collingwood*, ed. M. Krausz (Oxford, 1972), pp. 20–41.

After outlining theories of imaging by Descartes, Hobbes, Spinoza, Leibniz, Berkeley, Locke and Hume, Collingwood dismisses the claims that, first, perceptions and mental images are indistinguishable, and second, that they can be distinguished on the grounds of being lively or dull, subject to the laws of nature or wild or involuntary or voluntary.[49] In agreement with Kant, he sees them as differing in 'degree', where:

> each 'degree' is at once a fuller realisation of the essence of knowledge than the one below (more certain, less liable to error) and also a fresh kind of knowledge.[50]

We will have more to say later on the form of Collingwood's concept of imagination suggested here. How perceptions and images differ, though, is in the involvement of understanding. Whereas sensations undergo interpretation by the understanding, allowing judgements of reality and unreality, images have not undergone that process of interpretation, and are therefore prior to judgements of reality and unreality.[51] This is the case with Hume's example of the interpolated shade of blue described above. So what does the process of interpretation involve? First, 'appreciation': distinguishing an object as a thing in itself such as a white ball distinct from the green table that it sits on. Here, we divide our field of vision into objects. Second, 'thinking': abstracting from or classifying an object such as applying the concepts of 'whiteness' or 'ball'. What is important in the second process is that we consider the object in relation to other objects — eg. 'white' objects — and to 'an established system of colours with established names'.[52] While thinking presupposes appreciation, it can follow it or even take place concurrently. Both imply consciousness in the sense that we can come to be aware of our activities, but this is not the same as freedom of consciousness where we exercise choice.[53] That freedom, as we shall ascertain in chapter six, comes with higher degrees of intellectual activity.

Collingwood's suggestion that images differ from perceptions in degree of intellection is astute: Sartre, Ryle and Wittgenstein all note, for instance, that perceptions are subject to error and correction in a way that images are not. Collingwood's reservation of appreciation and thinking for perception, though, is clearly wrong. When we entertain an image, as Sartre, Ryle and Wittgenstein point out, we

---

[49]   R.G. Collingwood, *The Principles of Art*, pp. 174–85.

[50]   *Ibid.*, p. 187n.1.

[51]   *Ibid.* See also *Outlines of a Philosophy of Art*, p. 95.

[52]   *Ibid.*, p. 212.

[53]   *Ibid.*, pp. 203, 207–8.

'see' objects — not undifferentiated fields of colour, say — and we can abstract from them or classify them. We use concepts like colour concepts to describe our images: we can image a white ball on a green table as well as see one. What matters is that we cannot be mistaken in our images and we cannot learn anything new from them as we can from perceptions. For example, I cannot mistake an image of this page, but if I do not know all the words on it, then my image will not tell me. For these reasons, and for others that will become apparent when we consider the form of Collingwood's concept of imagination, I believe that we ought to modify his claim that the activity of imaging is prior to interpretation by the understanding. In the activity of imaging, interpretation by the understanding is not absent, but *minimally present*.

While Collingwood's use of highly visual examples in the rough draft and published versions of 'The Historical Imagination' suggests the involvement of what we would call mental imaging in historical activities, the above discussion on interpretation by the understanding means that they are of little use to historians. Mental imaging, though an activity of imagination, is of a lower degree than activities entailing perceptual imagination because it is insufficiently critical. For Collingwood as for Alan White, then, there is much more to imagination than imaging. He thus cannot be aligned with the move towards the 'death of the image' in twentieth-century philosophical thought, but he certainly downplays its contribution to the activities of the mind.

For Collingwood, the very act of perceiving objects — including text on a page — is an act of imagination. In *Speculum Mentis* he even goes so far as to argue that imagination is a 'factor in every single cognitive act'.[54] A similar view is echoed in the works of Warnock and Little.[55] A further extension of the same process of 'image-making', as Warnock calls it, enables the interpretation of what we perceive as 'signifying something beyond itself, perhaps something other than the kind of which it is a member'.[56] That is, the imagination not only makes it possible for us to see marks on paper or an arrangement of stones as a document or as a building, but also as evidence of the past. Such an activity is implied, I believe, by Collingwood's distinction between 'data' and 'evidence', which is explained below. However, like Wittgenstein, he would object to the

[54] R.G. Collingwood, *Speculum Mentis* (Oxford, 1924), p. 83.
[55] M. Warnock, *Imagination* (London, 1976); and V. Little, 'What is Historical Imagination?', *Teaching History*, no. 36 (1983), pp. 27–32.
[56] M. Warnock, *Imagination*; as quoted in V. Little, 'What is Historical Imagination?', p. 27.

labelling of all these activities as 'imaging' because that would suggest that they are prior to judgements of reality. Further, while Collingwood and Wittgenstein hold to a kinship between seeing and 'seeing as' or seeing and 'visualisation' they do not — like Warnock, Munslow and Wisner — see them as synonymous.[57] When I look at a spoon, for instance, I do not say 'I see this *as a* spoon'. Wittgenstein writes:

> One doesn't 'take' what one knows as the cutlery at a meal *for* cutlery; any more than one ordinarily tries to move one's mouth as one eats, or aims at moving it.[58]

Of course I only know that a spoon is a spoon because I have been socialised into seeing it as such. But Collingwood clearly holds that the activities of the historical imagination go beyond the obvious and conventional; they demand a higher degree of autonomous thought. And autonomous thought emerges from historical socialisation, a process that we will look to in the chapter that follows.

Imagination actuates connection and interpolation. Arising from this is a view of the historian as generating a 'web of imaginative construction stretched between certain fixed points provided by the statements of his authorities'.[59] Another image Collingwood suggests is that of a mosaic, where, we infer, the tiles correspond to pieces of evidence and the arrangement of them and the mortar fixing them are the work of the historian.[60] Collingwood sees this as problematic, though, because the mosaic tiles or fixed points of the web relieve historians of responsibility or diminish their autonomy. This leads Collingwood to offer an apparently radical conclusion,

> that there are for historical thought no fixed points thus given: in other words, that in history, just as there are properly speaking no authorities, so there are properly speaking no data.[61]

His point is that nothing ought to be included in a history that has not been actively interpreted by the historian. It is imagination that helps the historian to actively interpret, because for Collingwood as for Aristotle and many subsequent theorists, it bridges the gap

[57] A. Munslow, *The Routledge Companion to Historical Studies* (London, 2000), pp. 124–130; D.A. Wisner, 'Modes of Visualisation in Neo-Idealist Theories of the Historical Imagination (Cassirer, Collingwood, Huizinga)', *Collingwood Studies*, Vol. 6 (1999), pp. 53–84.

[58] L. Wittgenstein, *Philosophical Investigations*, II, xi, p. 195.

[59] R.G. Collingwood, *The Idea of History*, p. 242.

[60] R.G. Collingwood, 'Inaugural: Rough Notes', *The Principles of History and Other Writings*, p. 146.

[61] R.G. Collingwood, *The Idea of History*, p. 243; see also 'Inaugural: Rough Notes', *The Principles of History and Other Writings*, p. 154.

between sensation and thought.[62] How does this view of imagination apply to the case of historical evidence? All evidence, Collingwood is adamant, must be perceptible to the historian. And it is the imagination that provides the prior structuring of the historian's perceptions. It is thus the imagination that helps the historian to see that the marks on a page are letters; that they make words that have meaning in a language; that they convey an historical agent's view of events; and that the historical agent's view coalesces with other evidence. As with other activities of imagination, this structuring is a priori. Thus:

> Freed from its dependence on fixed points supplied from without, the historian's picture of the past is thus in every detail an imaginary picture, and its necessity is at every point the necessity of the a priori imagination. Whatever goes into it, goes into it not because his imagination passively accepts it, but because it actively demands it.[63]

Imagination makes possible active connection, interpolation, 'reading' and 'reading as'.

A similar account of the activities of the imagination underpins Collingwood's accounts of 'reading' and 'historical reading' in *The Principles of Art* and 'The Principles of History'. We recall from chapter two Collingwood's characterisation of historians studying traces of thought as 'reading'. Reading entails both establishing whether evidence is genuine and decoding text. 'Historical reading', though, also requires bringing to light both the thoughts and emotions and even the relative and absolute presuppositions of historical agents. This would explain Collingwood's comment at the beginning of 'The Historical Imagination' that the development of the a priori historical imagination had 'profoundly influenced philosophy'. This point is reinforced in *The Principles of Art*, where Collingwood suggests that the interpretation of thought as expressed in language is a function of imagination.[64] Moreover, we can now return to the point from 'The Principles of History' with which this chapter began. I now quote that point in full:

> If the actions studied by the historian are actions in which thought is recognisably at work, it follows that the evidence for them must be something which reveals to him the presence of thought. In other words, it must be expressions of thought, or language: either language itself, the bodily gestures by which a thinker expresses his thought to himself and to others, or a 'notation' of language, the traces left by these gestures in

---

[62] R.G. Collingwood, *'Aristotelis de Anima Libri Tres* — Translation and Commentary'* [1913–14], p. 117; and *The Principles of Art*, p. 171.

[63] R.G. Collingwood, *The Idea of History*, p. 245.

[64] R.G. Collingwood, *The Principles of Art*, pp. 225, 251.

the perceptible world, or a trustworthy copy of these traces, from which a person able to read them can reconstruct the gestures in his imagination, and so reconstruct as an experience of his own the thought they express.[65]

Put simply, imagination actuates the detection and illumination of thoughts and presuppositions and can involve 'reconstruction'. As 'reconstruction' is one of Collingwood's cognates for 're-enactment', here we have an oblique connection posited between re-enactment and imagination. Collingwood does not need to make a direct connection, though, because we now know that the interpretation of thought traces in re-enactment *requires* imagination. Conversely, imagination does not require re-enactment. Thus for Collingwood, re-enactment can be a part of the activities of imagination, but the terms are not synonymous. To see what more there is to imagination, we will have to describe Collingwood's understanding of the concept in both content and form.

The Content and the Form

In the rough draft of the Waynflete lecture and *The Principles of Art*, Collingwood talks of 'forms' and 'branches' of imagination.[66] These terms may suggest little to readers today, perhaps only the idea that they are different but equal expressions of imagination. Closer acquaintance with Collingwood's more general philosophical writings — especially *Speculum Mentis* (1924), *An Essay On Philosophical Method* (1933) and *An Essay on Metaphysics* (1940) — however suggests that they are signals for his view of concepts. And that, as we shall see, lends his theory of historical imagination a form quite unlike that of any other writer.

Concepts are commonly viewed as the constituents of thought, as tools for categorising the world both singly and in combination. Further, few philosophers would object to the view that all concepts are and must be governed by sets of properties or criteria.[67] There is in philosophical discourse, though, considerable diversity in views of the nature and form of concepts. As Weitz tells us, ontological theories range from:

> concepts as supersensible entities, such as universals, meanings, abstract objects, definitions, and predicates and relations to concepts as

[65] R.G. Collingwood, 'The Principles of History', *The Principles of History and Other Writings*, p. 49.

[66] R.G. Collingwood, 'Inaugural: Rough Notes', *The Principles of History and Other Writings*, pp. 146, 150, 151, 165, 166.

[67] M. Weitz, *Theories of Concepts: A History of the Major Philosophical Tradition* (London, 1988), p. xvi.

mental entities or states, such as composite images, ideas, thoughts, conceptions, or innate ideas; or concepts as neutral entities between words, thoughts and things; or concepts as abstractible items from families of sentences or as extracted features of similar things; or concepts as human or animal skills or abilities, only one of which is the ability to wield linguistic expressions; or concepts as the roles of certain expressions *tout court*.[68]

Of these, the view that concepts are entities, whether sensible or supersensible, dominated philosophy from Plato through Frege, Russell, Moore and Wittgenstein of the *Tractatus*. This is, however, neither the view of Collingwood, nor of the later Wittgenstein. For them, we recall from chapter two, concepts are not things but activities governed by rules.[69] Dominant, too, has been the view that concepts are governed by definitive sets of necessary and sufficient properties, conditions or criteria. Here, calling a phenomenon an instance of a concept equates with the identification of a necessary and sufficient condition in all and only the phenomena so labelled. This condition is called the generic essence. Frege epitomises this view in his suggestion that:

A definition of a concept (of a possible predicate) must be complete; it must unambiguously determine, as regards any object, whether or not it falls under the concept (whether or not the predicate is truly assertible of it). Thus there must not be any object as regards which the definition leaves in doubt whether it falls under the concept; though for us men, with our defective knowledge, the question may not always be decidable. We may express this metaphorically as follows: the concept must have a sharp boundary.[70]

This discrete view of concepts is at work, for instance, in Alan White's conclusion that 'imagination' can be encapsulated in the formulation that 'to imagine something is to think of it as possibly being so'.[71] Against this view, other philosophers have adopted a more open view of concepts: the identification of a large number of similarities among instances of a phenomenon that are incapable of encapsulation in a definite description. This is epitomised by Wittgenstein's later writings on 'family resemblances' and 'games'.

Wittgenstein counters the essentialism of writers like Frege and White with the suggestion that a network of overlapping similarities unites instances of a concept. For example, the activities we call

---

[68]   *Ibid.*, p. 260.
[69]   R.G. Collingwood, *The New Leviathan* [1942], ed D. Boucher (rev. edn., Oxford, 1992), §7.22; and L. Wittgenstein, *Philosophical Investigations*, §43.
[70]   G. Frege, *The Foundations of Arithmetic*, trans. J. L. Austin, Vol. 2 (Oxford, 1950), §56.
[71]   A. White, *The Language of Imagination* (Oxford, 1990), pp. 184, 186.

games need not all share something in common by which they may thus be described, but the unity of the concept is founded in a series of criss-crossing similarities, like the fibres overlapping in a rope.[72] Just as there may be no one feature or set of features common to all the members of a family, there may be a distinction in varying ways of facial characteristics which allows a person to be recognised as a member of it.[73] Some of the openness of Wittgenstein's view of concepts is also to be found in the writings of Collingwood. Wittgenstein's formulation, however, does not entirely cover the contribution of Collingwood, for as we shall see, he introduces a temporal, developmental aspect.

To Collingwood, concepts cannot be rigidly defined. Nor are they 'families' of equal and overlapping properties. Moreover, they are not invariant. Rather, he holds that they describe both activities of becoming and past activities and take the shape of a 'scale of forms'. The idea of a scale of forms has a long history in philosophical thought. Plato, for example, formulated scales of the forms of knowledge, being, pleasure and political constitutions.[74] It is in Hegel's writings that the dialectical development of concepts takes on the shape of a linked hierarchy of forms. The dialectic is a process of logic by which we deduce from our experience the ideas that lead to the absolute idea, or truth itself. In the logic of the dialectic, we start with a thesis, or a position put forward for an argument. Opposed to this is a contrary idea, or antithesis. Out of their opposition comes a synthesis that incorporates both. But the first synthesis may not offer us an account of truth, and consequently, forms a new thesis. This process continues until we reach the absolute idea.

Collingwood is partial to such a view of concepts, but does not consider it to be free of problems. In *An Essay on Philosophical Method*, he focuses on two. First, the idea of a scale of forms is fairly easy to accept when the generic essence of the concept is one thing, and the variable another. In such a case, every instance of a concept is an equal embodiment of the essence. For example, whilst water, steam and ice are apparently different, they all share the same generic essence of the concept of H_2O and they share it fully.[75] But in pursuing his account of those concepts in which the generic essence is itself

[72] L. Wittgenstein, *Philosophical Investigations*, §§65–7. See also *The Blue and Brown Books* (Oxford, 1958), p. 87.

[73] L. Wittgenstein, *The Blue and Brown Books*, p. 17, 87, 124; see also *Philosophical Investigations*, §67; and *Philosophical Grammar,* ed. R. Rhees, trans. A. Kenny (Oxford, 1974), p. 75.

[74] Plato, *Republic*, trans. D. Lee (Harmondsworth, 1955), §§477–8, 532b–c, 510–21.

[75] R.G. Collingwood, *An Essay on Philosophical Method* (Oxford, 1933), pp. 59–60.

subject to variation, Collingwood raises a criticism: if the generic essence of a concept varies, will the activities at the 'bottom' of a concept's scale of forms exemplify the concept *at all*?[76] Second, there is the question of why forms succeed one another in a scale of forms.[77] Collingwood's solution to these two problems comes from his adoption of Croce's modification of the Hegelian idea of the dialectic.

For instance, if we consider a scale of forms of the concept 'selflessness', then activities we label 'selfless' would be at the top of the scale, those we label 'selfish' would be at the bottom of the scale, and any intermediate activities will come between the top and the bottom. But if the variable is identical with the essence of the concept, then 'selfish action' cannot be on the scale of forms of 'selfless action' because it does not share any of the essence of 'selfless action'.[78] This leads Collingwood to draw on Croce's suggestion that the relation between the forms of concepts is one of *distinction* rather than *opposition*.[79] Each scale begins not with a concept in which the essence of the concept is not embodied, but with a form in which the essence of the concept is *minimally embodied*.[80] The lowest member of the scale is in some way a realisation of the essence of the concept, and is distinct from other realisations; but it is an extreme, and thus opposite relatively to the rest of the scale.[81] For example, beauty, Croce advances, is what it is because of its denial of the ugly, and good is such because it denies evil. The positive and the negative are inherent in the same concept. That is, we cannot understand 'evil' without having 'good' to oppose it.[82] Collingwood follows Croce in his suggestion that within a scale of forms, 'selfless' and 'selfish' action are exhibited in varying degrees according to the place on the scale from which the essence of the concept is viewed. In other words, the lower of two levels in a scale takes on the character of 'selfishness' in comparison to the one above.[83]

---

[76] *Ibid.*, p. 62.

[77] *Ibid.*, p. 63; D. Boucher, *The Social and Political Thought of R.G. Collingwood* (Cambridge, 1989), p. 29.

[78] R.G. Collingwood, *An Essay on Philosophical Method*, p. 81.

[79] B. Croce, *What is Living and What is Dead in the Philosophy of Hegel*, trans. D. Ainslie (London, 1915), pp. 9–10; *Logic of the Science as a Pure Concept*, trans. D. Ainslie (London, 1917), p. 93; and *Aesthetic as a Science of Expression and General Linguistic*, trans. and ed. D. Ainslie (New York, 1953), p. 61.

[80] R.G. Collingwood, *An Essay on Philosophical Method*, p. 81.

[81] *Ibid.*, p. 82.

[82] M.E. Moss, 'The Crocean Concept of the Pure Concept', *Idealistic Studies*, Vol. 17 (1) (1987), pp. 45–50.

[83] R.G. Collingwood, *An Essay on Philosophical Method*, p. 82.

In light of these modifications, we now look to Collingwood's solution to the second problem raised by the idea of a scale of forms: namely, its failure to explain how the forms relate to one another. Collingwood's view of the scale of forms suggests differences of *degree* and *kind* and the relations of *distinction* and *opposition*. The higher form on a scale belongs to the same concept as the lower, but it differs in degree as a more adequate embodiment of the generic essence as well as in kind as a specifically different embodiment. It follows from this that forms are not only distinct from one another, as one specification from another, but also opposed to one another, as a higher specification to a lower, a more to a less adequate embodiment.[84] Higher forms, however, do include aspects of lower forms. Thus each form is a culmination of the concept to date.[85] Collingwood's point is that each form of a concept represents the best embodiment of the concept until it is revealed as inadequate. When that inadequacy is exposed, we adopt a new or modified view of the concept. Thus the overlap consists in the lower being contained in the higher, the higher transcending the lower and adding to it something new.

The concept of imagination also bears the shape of a scale of forms. Imaging, pure or free imagination, perceptual imagination and the historical imagination are not coordinate species of a genus, each autonomous and valid as a limited range of mental activities. Each form of imagination is inadequate on its own, Collingwood argues, and so gives way to another that stands above it in a hierarchical and cumulative scale.[86] While Collingwood did not specify a particular order of forms, I believe that it is possible to build one up on the basis of his comments about the degree of intellection in the particular activities of imagination. We recall, for instance, Collingwood's presentation of imaging and perceptual imagination as differing in 'degree' on the grounds that the latter was a fuller realisation of interpretation by understanding. Perceptual imagination entails a greater degree of thinking and consciousness. Similarly, in the rough and published versions of the Waynflete lecture, Collingwood locates the imagination in a discussion on the development of autonomous thought. I therefore believe that conscious — but also autonomous — thinking forms the generic essence of the concept of imagination. That is, higher forms on the scale of imagination

[84] *Ibid.*, p. 88.
[85] *Ibid.*, p. 89.
[86] R.G. Collingwood, 'Inaugural: Rough Notes', *The Principles of History and Other Writings*, pp. 150, 158.

embody the activities of conscious, autonomous thought more adequately than lower ones. At the bottom of the scale is imaging, in which conscious, autonomous thought is minimally present. Further, it is apparent from the rough and published versions of 'The Historical Imagination' that the historical imagination both emerges out of and incorporates the activities of the pure and free and perceptual imagination. It thus stands above them in the scale, because it embodies autonomous thought more adequately. Locating the intermediate forms — pure and free and perceptual — is more difficult, because there is no clear statement by Collingwood setting one above the other. That ordinary activities of perception — as distinct from the activities of the artist — are subject to judgements of reality or unreality probably puts them closer to the activities of the historical imagination. This order is also confirmed by Collingwood's low designation of art in the forms of experience, as shown in the chapter that follows. Overall, then, I believe that Collingwood's concept of imagination takes the form suggested in figure 1.

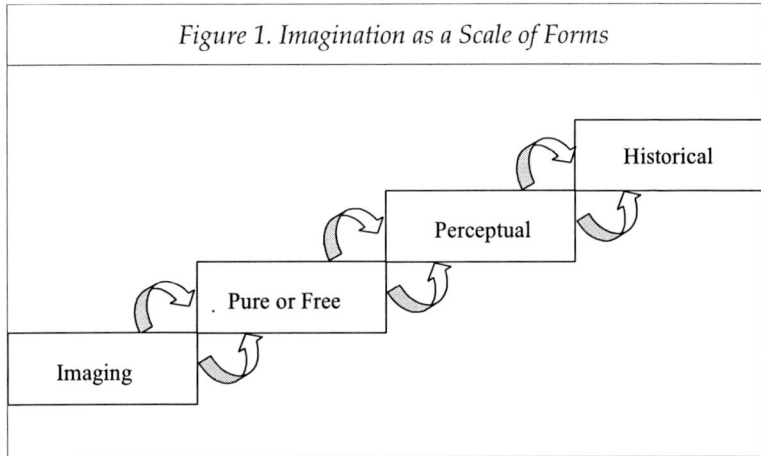

Figure 1. Imagination as a Scale of Forms

Rubinoff was the first writer to suggest that Collingwood's concept of historical imagination should be regarded as a scale of forms.[87] We are, however, at a far remove from Rubinoff's conception of the scale. First, Collingwood's scale describes not a movement from methodology to the fundamental aims of history — as Rubinoff asserts — but from lower to higher degrees of autonomous thought.

---

[87] See also L. Mink, 'Collingwood's Historicism: A Dialectic of Process', in M. Krausz (ed.), *Critical Essays on the Philosophy of R. G. Collingwood* (Oxford, 1972).

Second, the scale outlined above offers a fuller account of the activities of imagination than can be gleaned from looking at the Waynflete lecture alone. Put simply, Rubinoff offers a scale of the forms of the historical imagination, whereas I am outlining Collingwood's scale of the forms of imagination *per se*. Third, Rubinoff did not have the opportunity to see Collingwood's direct account of the structure of the concept of imagination in the rough version of the Waynflete lecture. We no longer have to rely on indirect evidence for such an arrangement from Collingwood's more general writings on concepts. And finally, whereas Rubinoff described the succession of forms according to the Hegelian idea of the dialectic, I have suggested succession according to Croce's modification of this idea.[88]

Further, the forms of imagination may be located in a broader conceptual scale of forms: that of the various views of history described in the rough and published forms of the Waynflete lecture. Imaging is clearly a pre-historical activity and thus at the bottom of the scale and the historical imagination is found in the work of constructive historians at the top of the scale. In the middle are the pure and free and perceptual activities of imagination, which are found in the work of critical historians. That leaves common-sense history, which does not immediately match with any one form of imagination. This, I believe, is a proto-historical activity. Common-sense history requires historical perception — as with seeing Cicero's writings as describing a past world — so it demands a higher degree of interpretation by understanding than imaging. As it does not involve judgements of reality and autonomous thought, though, it clearly comes before the pure and perceptual activities of the critical historian. I therefore suggest that it may be described as a form of 'historical imaging'. This scale of forms nested within another scale of forms is outlined in figure 2.

The form of Collingwood's ideas in the rough and published versions of 'The Historical Imagination' is clearly reminiscent of the introduction to Hegel's lectures on the philosophy of history. In that work, Hegel details the three stages in the search for more adequate 'categories' of historical research and arranges them as a hierarchy of forms. Original historians primarily describe events as contemporary witnesses, critical historians restrict their attention to the ideas that have given shape to past history writing and philosophical historians reason about the history of reason in order to illuminate and

---

[88] L. Rubinoff, *Collingwood and the Reform of Metaphysics* (Toronto, 1970), p. 281.

contribute to the development of the one reality that is 'Mind'.[89] Collingwood's scale also describes movement towards reason, but it is not a simple echo of Hegel's idea. I mention here again Collingwood's use of Croce's modification of the Hegelian idea of the dialectic. More importantly, though, Collingwood diverges from Hegel in seeing imagination as intimately connected with the development of reason.

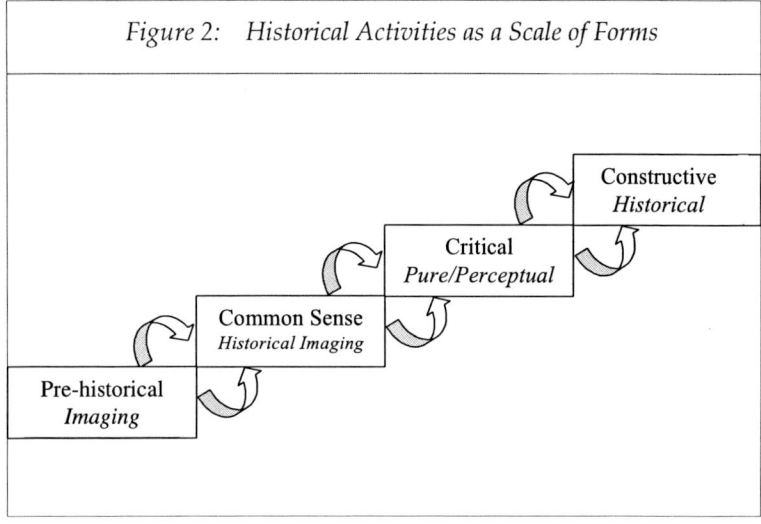

Figure 2: Historical Activities as a Scale of Forms

Further, Collingwood's suggestion that imagination is embodied in different levels of activity is not in itself original. We recall from the previous chapter, for instance, the Romantic identification of different levels or degrees of imaginative activity, from the involuntary, unconscious conversion of sensations into images to the conscious deconstruction and reformation of sensory impressions into images that have no likeness in the world. Collingwood's scale, like the Romantic view, suggests a shift from passivity to activity: the higher the form of imagination, the more we consciously do. Where they differ is in value judgements of function, Collingwood preferring an imagination that informs us about the world — past and present — to one that departs from it. Hence his designation of imaging as a lower form of mental activity than perception. This judgement is also evident in his complaint in 'Aesthetic' about contemporary psychological views of the imagination as the source of

[89] G.W.F. Hegel, *The Philosophy of History*, trans. J. Sibree (New York, 1956), pp. 1–3, 8, 9, 11, 19.

uncontrollable 'pathological' or 'diseased' fancies. If imagination is a pathological activity, he argues, then 'the whole intellectual activity of the modern world is faced with bankruptcy'. This is because to him, imagination is a 'normal activity':

> an activity which instead of impeding the formation of knowledge actually advances it and, in fact, constitutes its initial stage. When we find this faculty operating, we shall not instantly despair of sanity; on the contrary, we should despair of sanity, if for a moment it ceases operating.[90]

In this work, Collingwood clearly has his eye fixed on more than the activities of historians. It is, he tells us, a 'normal' activity that advances knowledge, a declaration that clearly sets him apart from postmodern critics of the imagination like Althusser and Deleuze. What we have so far pieced together of Collingwood's view of imagination is therefore not enough: we also need to articulate its place in the activities of all people, not just historians. Additionally, we are still to explain why Collingwood values it so highly. Having attended to these issues, we will be in a position to assess what Hayden White would see as Collingwood's historical imagination. That will be the function of the next chapter.

Historical Imagination as Imagination

Before concluding this chapter it is important that we return to a question posed in both chapters one and two: what is the relationship between the historical imagination and imagination *per se*? If we were to read Collingwood's work in the tradition suggested by Abrams, Cocking, Engell, Kearney, Egan and Alan White, then we would consider the 'historical imagination' to be a particular expression of or ancillary to imagination *per se*. We might even present it as one of a number of different species or kinds, along with, say, the scientific imagination or the artistic imagination. Collingwood's view, however, does not fit with that tradition. Here we see the force of the conclusion of chapter four: theories of imagination are about form as well as content. They may suggest a form only implicitly, as with the majority of theorists. Or they may do so explicitly, as with Collingwood. To him, the historical imagination is not just one of a number of equal manifestations of imagination. It is located at the top of a hierarchical, cumulative scale of forms and is thus the best embodiment of that concept. In employing the modifier 'a priori' as well as 'historical', too, he reminds us that it is the best embodiment

---

[90] R.G. Collingwood, 'Aesthetic', Ms Collingwood Dep. 25 (3), p. 8. See also pp. 7–8a.

to date and that it is subject to change. For Collingwood, therefore, the historical imagination is *the* imagination.

What is the Historical Imagination?

With every step we take in the analysis of Collingwood's ideas, the wider our lens of view becomes. Re-enactment does not stand alone as a methodological tool, but can be connected with the activities of the historical imagination. Indeed, we have discovered that re-enactment requires historical imagination. Historical imagination itself is not a methodology, but a scale of forms of intellectual activity. Moreover, these intellectual activities are fundamental activities of mind, and as we shall see, play a basic part in both education and the shaping of civilisation. However, little hint of this broader context is offered in scholarship on Collingwood's views of imagination. To von Leyden, for instance, Collingwood's theory of imagination is to be thought of almost exclusively in terms of imaging and perception[91], Walsh considers 'historical imagination' as 'only another name for the historical judgement' and Wisner sees it as a form of visualisation.[92] Though apparently different, these views have in common the collapsing of historical imagination to a single or limited function. As I hope is now clear, Collingwood's view cannot be so reduced. The imagination is none of these things, or more specifically none of them in isolation. Imagination certainly entails imaging, perception and judgement but it also includes connection, inference, 'reading as' and 'historical reading'. Donagan's alignment of imagination with thinking[93] is closer to the mark, but it too is inadequate because, as we have seen, different degrees of thinking are possible.

Nor can Collingwood's contribution to theories of imagination be reduced — no matter what his contemporaries thought or he himself joked — to a colourless redescription of a moribund German philosophy. While some ideas such as those of Kant, Hume, Hegel and Croce loom large in his writings, his drawing together of these with many others results in a theory of imagination quite unlike any other in form and content.

[91] W. von Leyden, 'Philosophy of Mind: An Appraisal of Collingwood's Theories of Consciousness, Language and Imagination', pp. 20–41.

[92] W.H. Walsh, 'R.G. Collingwood's Philosophy of History', *Philosophy*, Vol. 22 (1947), p. 158; and D.A. Wisner, 'Modes of Visualisation in Neo-Idealist Theories of the Historical Imagination', pp. 53–84.

[93] A. Donagan, 'Editor's Introduction', *Essays on the Philosophy of Art by R.G. Collingwood* (Bloomington, IN, 1964), p. xii.

Chapter VI

'How Good an Historian Shall I Be?'

Imagination and Education

When we think of history as merely a trade or profession, a craft or calling, we find it hard to justify our existence as historians. What can the historian do for people except turn them into historians like himself? And what is the good of doing that? It is not simply a vicious circle, whose tendency is to overcrowd the ranks of the profession and to produce an underpaid 'intellectual proletariat' of sweated teachers. This may be a valid argument against the multiplication of historians, if history is merely a profession, but it cannot be if history is a universal human interest; for in that case there are already as many historians as there are human beings, and the question is not 'Shall I be an historian or not?' but 'How good an historian shall I be?'[1]

In January 1945, Wittgenstein concluded his preface to *Philosophical Investigations* by commenting 'It is not impossible that it should fall to the lot of this work, in its poverty and in the darkness of this time, to bring light into one brain or another — but, of course, it is not likely'.[2] By all accounts, Wittgenstein and Collingwood's times were times of 'darkness'. For example, of the approximately 15,000 Oxford men — past and present students — who enlisted for military action in the war of 1914–18, at least 2,857 were killed and many

[1]   R.G. Collingwood, *The Philosophy of History*, 1930, p. 3.
[2]   L. Wittgenstein, *Philosophical Investigations*, trans. G.E.M. Anscombe, ed. G.E.M. Anscombe, R. Rhees and G.H. von Wright (Oxford, 1953), p. viii.

more were seriously wounded. Seventy percent of those killed were under the age of thirty.[3] Harold Macmillan later wrote 'I did not go back to Oxford after the war . . . To me it was a city of ghosts'.[4] At least another 1,719 were killed in the war of 1939–45, which Collingwood did not live to see the end of.[5] Such losses, however, were a symptom of, not the cause of the darkness. To Wittgenstein and Collingwood, the cause was to be found in the failing health of Western civilisation.[6] In distinction from Wittgenstein, though, Collingwood was not so pessimistic about the possibility of encouraging people to take remedial action. In this chapter we shall see evidence that Collingwood marshalled his views across a wide range of subjects — including history and imagination — to an educative purpose: the development of a healthy civilisation via the promotion of self-knowledge and freedom of the will. Although some features of Collingwood's thought may seem outmoded to educators today, I believe that his views on history education are worth taking seriously.

Collingwood on Education

'No serious explanation of R.G. Collingwood's philosophy of education has yet been undertaken'.[7] So began Stanage in 'Collingwood's Phenomenology of Education' in 1972. Despite the attention given to Collingwood's accounts of the many activities of the mind, Stanage's observation is still surprisingly true. Boucher has tried to explain this neglect by suggesting that Collingwood's strong views on the English public school system, along with his argument that parents should educate their own children in order to save them from educators, have been viewed with incredulity and have acted as a barrier to any serious exploration of his ideas on education.[8]

---

[4] J.M. Winter, 'Oxford and the First World War', *The History of the University of Oxford*, ed. B. Harrison, Vol. 8 (Oxford, 1994), pp. 18–19, 21. Estimates for those killed in the first and second world wars are acknowledged to be low because they do not, for instance, include Oxford scholars who served in the German forces.

[5] As quoted in B. Harrison, 'College Life, 1918–1939', *The History of the University of Oxford*, ed. B. Harrison, Vol. 8 (Oxford, 1994), p. 81.

[6] P. Addison, 'Oxford and the Second World War', *The History of the University of Oxford*, ed. B. Harrison, Vol. 8 (Oxford, 1994), p. 181.

[6] P. Lewis, 'Collingwood and Wittgenstein: Struggling with Darkness', *Collingwood Studies*, Vol. 5 (1998), p. 28.

[7] S. Stanage, 'Collingwood's Phenomenology of Education: Person and the Self-Recognition of the Mind', *Critical Essays on the Philosophy of R.G. Collingwood*, ed. M. Krausz (Oxford, 1972), pp. 268–95.

[8] See for example R.G. Collingwood, *The New Leviathan* [1942], rev. edn., ed. D. Boucher (Oxford, 1992), §37.35; and D. Boucher, 'The Place of Education in Civilisation' (unpublished ms, 1994).

Although a number of reviews of *The New Leviathan* do express scorn about Collingwood's educational suggestions, I do not agree with Boucher that this is the primary reason why they remain relatively unknown.[9] Rather, I think that the enormous amount of attention that educators have given to his ideas on art and history has led them to neglect his wider views on personal and social development. Furthermore, Collingwood's views on education are not to be found in any one work or even under clearly identifiable educational headings. On the contrary, as we shall see, a wide range of his writings are tied together by an implicit educational purpose.

Following Boucher's lead, I believe that it is useful to divide Collingwood's views on education into three main areas: first, the aims of education; second, the nature and content of the curriculum; and third, the means by which education is to be brought about. These areas are by no means sealed off from one another. Moreover, we shall discover that Collingwood's understanding of 'education' and 'curriculum' is wider than that of professional educators today. In sketching his views, we shall find education described as a process of historical socialisation that reaches beyond educational institutions and into families. And this view of education, I will argue, explains why Collingwood wants each of us to ask 'How good an historian shall I be?'

The Aims of Education

For Collingwood, education refers both to institutions and to the wider process by which individuals become citizens of a society.[10] In this respect, Collingwood follows Plato, Aristotle, Hegel and Green in holding that the best education a person can have is to be brought up in a civilised nation state. For example, in *Elements of the Philosophy of Right*, Hegel advances that the fundamental purpose of education is to liberate people from ignorance and help them to see that a civilised state is an expression of freedom of the will.[11] The role of the educational process in Collingwood's thought should not be underestimated. Indeed, in the *New Leviathan* he tells us that it is the means 'by which a civilisation keeps itself alive from one generation to the

[9] See for example Anon., 'Review of *The New Leviathan*', *The Scotsman*, 20 August 1942, pp. 40; G. Catlin, 'Review of *The New Leviathan*', *Political Science Quarterly*, Vol. 57 (3) (1943), p. 436; W. Dewar, 'Review of *The New Leviathan*', *Time and Tide*, 15 August 1942, p. 660; and J. Laird, 'Review of *The New Leviathan*', *Philosophy*, Vol. 18 (1) (1943), p. 79.

[10] D. Boucher, 'The Place of Education in Civilisation', p. 357.

[11] G.W.F. Hegel, *Elements of the Philosophy of Right*, trans. H.B. Nisbet, ed. A. Wood (Cambridge, 1991), §24.

next'.[12] It facilitates the transmission of the presuppositions that shape a civilisation to succeeding generations, and aims to help each student to 'grow into an active and vigorous contributor to the life of the world'.[13] Education, therefore, does more than help the student to master reading, writing and arithmetic. The prime task of the educator is to help the student achieve freedom of the will, and to be a good citizen. How is this to be done? Primarily, Collingwood tells us, through the development of self-knowledge. In 'Human Nature and Human History', for instance, he writes:

> Man, who desires to know everything, desires to know himself. Nor is he only one (even if, to himself, perhaps the most interesting) among the things he desires to know. Without some knowledge of himself, his knowledge of other things is imperfect: for to know something without knowing that one knows it is only a half-knowing, and to know that one knows is to know oneself. Self-knowledge is desirable and important to man, not only for its own sake, but as a condition without which no other knowledge can be critically justified and securely based.[14]

At first glance, this appears to be a highly individual ethic, suggesting that students should take an interest only in themselves. A closer look at Collingwood's writings, however, shows that this is not the case, for he is adamant that individuals cannot but be members of a community.

The Self

When we talk of the 'self', Galen Strawson tells us, we commonly have in mind

> The sense that people have of themselves as being, specifically, a mental presence; a mental someone; a single mental thing that is a conscious subject of experience, that has a certain character or personality, and that is in some sense distinct from all its particular experiences, thoughts, and so on, and indeed from all other things.[15]

The self is thus conceived of as a discrete entity, separate from other things, including other selves. Such a view rests upon an epistemological error and a psychological error. The epistemological error is epitomised in the writings of Descartes. In *Meditations*, Descartes convinces himself that he can doubt whether the physical world exists, and whether he has a body. Out of this doubt

---

[12]   R.G. Collingwood, *The New Leviathan*, §39.18.
[13]   R.G. Collingwood, *Speculum Mentis* (Oxford, 1924), p. 316.
[14]   R.G. Collingwood, *The Idea of History* [1946], rev. edn., ed. W.J. van der Dussen (Oxford, 1993), p. 205.
[15]   G. Strawson, 'The Self', *Journal of Consciousness Studies*, Vol. 4 (5–6) (1997), p. 406.

arises the conviction that 'I am'. Here, 'I' refers only incidentally to the body. Moreover, 'I' is not identical with the mind. Attempts to flesh out the Cartesian 'I', however, run into three problems. The first concerns the relation of the 'I' to the body from which it is distinguished. How can the 'I' act upon or be acted upon by the body? This is the problem captured in Ryle's characterisation of this view as the 'dogma of the ghost in the machine'.[16] Second, on what grounds does Descartes justify his assumption that 'I' brings continuity to successive mental states?[17] Third, how can Descartes justify his claim that the 'I am' cannot be doubted? We cannot be the sole arbiters about statements that we make about what we think. For example, suppose that yesterday I said 'I am overjoyed' and today I say with sincerity that 'I believe now that I was mistaken in asserting that I was overjoyed yesterday'? To resolve the conflict between these two statements, I might need the help of others.

The second, psychological error in the common view of the self arises from empiricist philosophy after Locke. The self, as an inner subject, can clearly not be discovered by the outer senses, which perceive only the visible, audible and tangible exterior of things. But it cannot be discovered by inner sense either. This led Hume to conclude, after failing to locate the self, that it corresponded to 'bundles' or 'collections' of perceptions and experiences structured by the imagination. A similar view, we shall see, might be imputed to Collingwood.

In its most basic sense, Collingwood sees self-knowledge as 'knowledge of oneself living in . . . activities'.[18] We recall from chapters three and five that there are presuppositions that are fundamental to human beings. These presuppositions are so deeply rooted in the human way of being that they are not consciously chosen or affirmed, debated or questioned. For Collingwood, one such presupposition is a certain continuity of individual character through time.[19] Wittgenstein arrives at a similar point in *The Blue and Brown Books*:

> Imagine that it were usual for human beings to have two characters, in this way: People's shape, size and characteristics of behaviour periodically undergo a complete change. It is the usual thing for a man to have two such states, and he lapses suddenly from one into the other. It is very

[16] G. Ryle, *The Concept of Mind* (Harmondsworth, 1949), p. 23.

[17] On this issue, see G.E. Myers, *Self: An Introduction to Philosophical Psychology* (New York, 1969), ch. 1.

[18] R.G. Collingwood, *The Idea of History*, p. 297.

[19] *Ibid.*, pp. 292–4.

likely that in such a society we would be likely to christen every man with two names, and perhaps talk of the part of persons in his body.[20]

Wittgenstein's point is that variance from continued self-identity would be judged as a disturbance, a deviation from what normally characterises the human. If similar alterations occurred throughout the human community, our understanding of 'self' would be radically altered.[21]

Though both Collingwood and Wittgenstein recognise the idea of the self, it is not the discrete entity that philosophers have traditionally assumed. Rather, the self is to be found in the presuppositions that people hold as a consequence of the activities they participate in. These presuppositions will be a combination of the recurrent patterns, regularities and ways of being and doing that the human form of life displays, and the particular activities that people have been born and socialised into. These presuppositions, it was suggested in chapter three, are immanent in language and thus open to 'reading' by anybody who comprehends the rules of the language in which they are embedded. And 'reading', it was further argued in chapter five, is an extension of the activities of the perceptual imagination. Thus imagination has an important part to play in the achievement of self-knowledge and knowledge of others. Moreover, if we follow Collingwood's line of thinking on perceptual imagination and combine it with his view of an historicized human nature, it is possible to argue that our notion of the self also results from the activities of imagination. That is, imagination provides the prior structuring of memories, perceptions, and experiences as a unified 'self'. This activity of imagination, like those of the historian, is a priori: we do not decide to adopt or reject it prior to application. Further, it has its origins in time and is subject to change. Accordingly, the self, like human nature, is an historical artefact presented to the intellect by imagination.

This characterisation of the self as the historical product of human activities is not too far removed from the views of Foucault, Derrida, Lacan, Althusser, Deleuze, Guattari and Barthes. These thinkers, we learned in chapter four, are associated with the postmodern dismantling of the self. In distinction from them, though, Collingwood sees our notion of self not as pathological or self-deceptive but as a positive feature of our lives.

---

[20] L. Wittgenstein, *The Blue and Brown Books* (Oxford, 1958), p. 62.
[21] L. Wittgenstein, *Philosophical Investigations*, §207.

Education and the Development of Self-Knowledge

In Collingwood's view, education should be geared to help the student to achieve freedom of the will and to be a good citizen. In order to realise this aim, students must be guided to rational consciousness. Rational consciousness is seen in the recognition that one's life is given shape by presuppositions, and that these presuppositions are historical artefacts. Rational consciousness, though, is not easy to achieve, for it stands at the top of a cumulative scale of forms of 'freedom of will' analogous to the conceptual scales of forms described in the previous chapter. The first form that Collingwood specifies is simple capricious choice. Caprice is 'uncomplicated by any reason why it should be made this way and not that'.[22] We begin to leave caprice behind once we seek reasons for both our choices and our actions. There are three kinds of reason, Collingwood tells us, that can be given to justify an activity. First, I can say that I did it because it was useful (utilitarian action); second, because it was right (regularian action); and finally, because it was my duty (dutiful action). Of these, only dutiful action equates with rational consciousness. We will return to this scale of forms in our discussion on Collingwood's view of the curriculum.

Collingwood's use of the word 'duty' points us to courses of action that he believes will most contribute to the good of civilisation. Why he is interested in civilisation will become clearer in the later part of this chapter. What is not clear, though, as Helgeby points out, is why Collingwood thinks that we will act in such a way. Helgeby clarifies this matter by pointing to Collingwood's contention that if we understand ourselves then we know what we must do. Arising from this are two sources of compulsion. First, we are compelled to act because our choice comes at the end of a process of reasoning, and if we reject it, we no longer act rationally. Second, we are compelled because our choice is tied up with self-knowledge, and if we reject it, we turn our back on what we have become. We are compelled to act, therefore, because we do not want to be either capricious or insincere.[23] Rational choice is a duty because irrational choices jeopardise one's and others' freedom of the will. Here, Collingwood follows Hegel's suggestion that 'no man can think himself free except as an integrated in a context of other free men

[22]   R.G. Collingwood, *The New Leviathan*, §13.12.
[23]   S. Helgeby, 'Action, Duty and Self-Knowledge in R. G. Collingwood's Philosophy of History', *Collingwood Studies*, Vol. 1 (1994), pp. 104–5.

constituting with himself a society'.[24] This is crucial for Colling-wood's view of society. Each person must recognise that it is the activities that humans share that give rise to the rules that are bind-ing upon everyone, and this is not mutual slavery because individu-als follow the rules of their own free will.[25] As we saw in our analysis of Collingwood's views of public language in chapter two, the self and society are inextricably bound together. Thus as Green puts it, the self:

> is not an abstract or empty self. It is a self already affected in the most primitive forms of human life by manifold interests, among which are interests in other persons. These are not merely interests dependent on other persons for means to their gratification, but interests in the good of those other persons . . . Thus man cannot contemplate himself as in a better state, or on the way to be best, without contemplating others, not merely as a means to that better state, but as sharing it with him.[26]

Collingwood holds that society is a mixed community comprised of both individuals displaying freedom of will in their activities and those who do not. Those people lacking freedom of will are incapa-ble of leading because leading presupposes freedom of choice. Non-social communities thus cannot rule themselves, but must be ruled by others. Collingwood calls this transeunt rule. A society, on the other hand, exercises self or immanent rule. To Collingwood's view, immanent rule is superior to transeunt rule.[27] 'Civilisation' is the term that Collingwood uses to describe the process of socialising a non-social community into a society.[28] This process entails at least three things. First, it involves helping members of a community to behave civilly to one another: that is, refraining from acting in ways that might diminish the self-respect or freedom of will of others. Sec-ond, it involves civility towards nature. Here, people are to be helped to understand the natural world and to make use of it in an intelligent fashion. This requires scientific knowledge, but also prac-tical knowledge such as:

> things which it is useful for a hunter or a shepherd or a fisherman or a farmer or a sailor or a miner or the like to know: things about the seasons, the weather, the soil, the subsoil, the habits of game and fish and domes-

[24] R.G. Collingwood, *The New Leviathan*, §21.76; see also G.W.F. Hegel, *Elements of the Philosophy of Right*, p. 182.

[25] R.G. Collingwood, 'Rule Making and Rule Breaking' [1935], Ms Collingwood Dep. 1 (9), p. 11.

[26] T.H. Green, *Prolegomena to Ethics* (Oxford, 1883), §99.

[27] R.G. Collingwood, *The New Leviathan*, §§20.36–20.39, 20.42.

[28] *Ibid.*, §37.22; see also 'Science, Religion and Civilisation: A Sermon Preached in Coventry Cathedral' [1930], Ms Collingwood Dep. 1 (7).

tic animals and vermin; how to get materials for the implements needed in these various crafts, and how to work them up into finished articles and how to use and keep and mend these articles when made . . . [29]

Third, it involves helping people to display a 'civil demeanour' towards members of another community. Fundamentally, this means that people outside of our community may display freedom of will in their activities or be capable of doing so. And practically, this means refraining from exploitation, the use of force and talking about others in patronising ways.[30]

In sum, then, the purpose of education is to socialise students through the development of civil behaviour, and this, in turn, rests on the development of self-knowledge. Self-knowledge brings freedom of the will, and the recognition that others are also capable of such freedom. This leads students to see that it is their duty to help others to achieve freedom of will, and that 'others' ultimately refers to humanity as a whole. Having clarified this fundamental aim, what kind of curriculum will help to realise it?

The Curriculum

Collingwood's writings contain little explicit discussion on the content and nature of a socialising curriculum.[31] It is possible, though, to construct an account on the basis of his writings on the forms of experience, particularly *Speculum Mentis* (1924). In *Speculum Mentis* Collingwood argues that the concept of experience is constituted by a cumulative scale of forms, and identifies the forms as art, religion, science, history and philosophy. Debate abounds about whether Collingwood held to the separate identity of history and philosophy in all his writings. What are neglected in this debate are Collingwood's own strong views against the fragmentation of knowledge into boundary-defending disciplines. This view is explicitly present in *Speculum Mentis*, but is also implicitly conveyed in the staggering range of topics that he obviously felt comfortable writing on. The forms of experience are not distinct subjects in an institutional curriculum: they are constellations of activities whose names are historical artefacts and are thus open to change. In offering a link between re-enactment, imagination and presuppositions, we have identified common ground between what we traditionally regard as 'history' and 'philosophy'. As will be shown, it is this area

[29]   R.G. Collingwood, *The New Leviathan*, §36.32.
[30]   *Ibid.*, §§35.38–35.93.
[31]   D. Boucher, 'The Place of Education in Civilisation', p. 375.

of overlap that is crucial in Collingwood's view of education. I have therefore opted to talk of history/philosophy to signal not a merger between distinct subjects, but shared activities. And overlap is the right thing to stress here, for as with all forms of a concept, there is common ground to be found between all the various forms of experience.

Collingwood considers art to be the initial form of experience out of which other experiences emerge.[32] Fundamentally, he does not think of the aesthetic experience:

> as an attempt to investigate and expound certain verities concerning the nature of an eternal object called Art, but as an attempt to reach, by thinking, the solution of certain problems arising out of the situation in which artists find themselves here and now.[33]

Furthermore, he thinks that aesthetic experience has consequences bearing not only on the way that we ought to approach the creation of works of art, but also on the very shape of our lives.[34] This is because art is fundamentally geared towards self-knowledge. Good art, Collingwood maintains, derives from rational consciousness and freedom of the will; bad art arises when people lose sight of their duty to help others socialise. Here, artists pursue only their own interests.[35] As Rubinoff points out, not only is it impossible to have bad art in a well-balanced or healthy society, it is likewise impossible to have good art in a bad or corrupt society.[36] In order to combat this corruption, art must establish contact with its audience. To achieve this, the artist must abandon imaginative activities that are prior to judgements of reality or unreality and begin to help others to understand themselves by describing their world:

> The artist must prophesy not in the sense that he foretells things to come, but in the sense that he tells his audience, at the risk of their displeasure, the secrets of their hearts. His business as an artist is to speak out, to make a clean breast. But what he has to utter is not, as the individualistic theory of art would have us think, his own secrets. The reason why they need him is that no community altogether knows its own heart; and by failing this knowledge a community deceives itself on the one subject

---

[32] R.G. Collingwood, 'Aesthetic' [annotated galley proofs of a lecture published in *The Mind: A Series of Lectures Delivered in King's College, London*, ed. R.J.S. McDowall, 1927], Ms Collingwood Dep. 25(3), p. 9a; see also *Outlines of a Philosophy of Art* [1925] (Bristol, 1993), pp. 95–6.

[33] R.G. Collingwood, *The Principles of Art* (Oxford, 1938), p. vi.

[34] *Ibid.*, pp. vii, 325.

[35] *Ibid.*, p. 285.

[36] L. Rubinoff, *Collingwood and the Reform of Metaphysics* (Toronto, 1970), p. 132; see also R.G. Collingwood, *Ruskin's Philosophy: An Address Delivered at the Ruskin Centenary Conference, Coniston 8 August 1919* (Kendal, 1922), pp. 34–6.

concerning which ignorance means death. For the evils which come from that ignorance the poet as prophet suggests no remedy, because he has already given one. The remedy is the poem itself. Art is the community's medicine for the worst disease of the mind, the corruption of consciousness.[37]

By corruption of consciousness, Collingwood means the denial of emotions and intellectual activities that prompt dutiful action. It is important to note here that Collingwood is not suggesting that *everything* that artists do should be directed towards the process of civilisation. Socialising others is the prime duty of artists, not the only one. Socialising others will also be the prime duty of art educators, though their job is not just to help students to create works of art, but also to read the 'secrets' of others' works. Those secrets, I think it is right to argue, are none other than the presuppositions that shape a society's forms of life. And to 'read' them, students will need more than just the experience of art: they will also need the experience of history/philosophy. The problem is that art fosters *utilitarian* action. Here, the useful is the good, and action entails the choice of both a means and an end. Utilitarian action fails because there is nothing that ties the means with the end: nothing can tell us what means to use to achieve an end, or indeed, what end to choose. How does the artist justify their choice of a particular medium to make a point? How does the artist justify the ends chosen?[38] These are questions that the utilitarian view leaves unanswered. As with the common-sense historian, the artist must recognise that autonomy — regulation by self-authorised principles — is required. That comes, as we have seen, with a critical historical approach towards activities.

Collingwood's views on the social utility of art as a medium for the expression of presuppositions mark a strong departure from the views of his contemporaries. For example, Green holds that unless one is gifted, one should not engage in the activity of the arts:

It is not time to enjoy the pleasures of eye and ear, the search for knowledge, of friendly intercourse, of applauded speech or writing, while the mass of men whom we call our brethren, and whom we declare to be with us for eternal destinies, are left without the chance, which only the help of others can gain for them, of making themselves in fact what in possibility we believe them to be.[39]

In distinction from Green, Collingwood holds that all students should be given the opportunity to both learn to appreciate the

[37] R.G. Collingwood, *The Philosophy of Art*, p. 336.
[38] R.G. Collingwood, *The New Leviathan*, §§15.6–15.8.
[39] T.H. Green, *Prolegomena to Ethics*, p. 270.

works of artists — past and present — and engage in the activities of artists. What makes possibility fact here is the imagination, the activities of which are to be found in all children as well as creative geniuses. Art is not an ancillary activity open only to the fortunate few, but part of a continuum of intellectual activities out of which more complex activities grow. Hence Collingwood's conclusion in his lectures on the philosophy of art from 1924 — which was introduced in the previous chapter — that 'art is the kingdom of the child' and that 'the child's life of imagination is a training for the adult life of thought, and the specialised imagination of the artist is a training for the specialised thought of the scientist'.[40]

The passage from experience of art to experience of science, though, can only take place through the mediatory experience of religion. Hence Collingwood's suggestion in the lectures on art from 1924 that 'the place of religion in the life of the spirit may be defined either as a transition from art to science, or as the antithesis to art which in science is reconciled with its opposite'.[41] In 'Reason is Faith Cultivating Itself', Collingwood advances that reason is no more than the development of faith into an articulated system:

> Reason itself is henceforth seen to depend for its cogency on the immediate and indemonstrable certainty which is faith; faith is henceforth no longer severed from reason or given an idea of its own to operate by itself, but becomes as it were the soul of which reason is the body.[42]

Faith and reason are interdependent in that, first, it is only through reason that faith can reveal its nature to mind, and second, all scientific and philosophical ideas are initially presented to peoples' minds in the form of religious beliefs.[43] In *Speculum Mentis*, Collingwood characterises religious beliefs as conventional beliefs. Importantly, these conventions emanate from without, not from within, individuals. Religious action is thus 'the type of action in which the agent does a given thing not because he chooses it, but because his society chooses it'.[44] This is clearly different to the activities of artists, who seek only internal consistency. Neither artistic nor religious experience, though, can be described as autonomous, for they do not entail critical self-rule in accord with principles. Rather,

[40] R.G. Collingwood, 'Outline of Lectures on the Philosophy of Art Delivered T[rinity] T[erm] 1924', Ms Collingwood Dep. 25 (2), pp. 37, 42.

[41] *Ibid.*, p. 43.

[42] R.G. Collingwood, 'Reason is Faith Cultivating Itself', *Hibbert Journal*, Vol 26 (1927), p. 9.

[43] *Ibid.*, pp. 13–14; see also *An Essay on Metaphysics* [1940], rev. edn., ed. R. Martin (Oxford, 1998), p. 198 and *The Idea of History*, pp. 255–6.

[44] R.G. Collingwood, *Speculum Mentis*, p. 135; see also *The New Leviathan*, §18.43.

art and religion are like the extremes of freedom identified by Hegel in ancient Rome and Greece, one ruled by individual preferences and one ruled by convention.[45] Moderation between these two extremes requires a higher level of experience: that offered by science.

Religion, like art, has a part to play in education. In the minimal sense, this means helping students to make clear the conventions that bind their activities. More specifically, Collingwood points to the conventions of Christianity. Christianity, Collingwood contends, lies at the heart of Western civilisation because of its association with freedom of the will, speech and inquiry and respect for others. In order to maintain these values, 'the inward flame of religion . . . must always be kept burning in the heart of civilisation'.[46] Collingwood's views on Christianity would not attract much favour among educators today. His connection of religion in general with 'regularian' activities, though, allows for its location in a socialising curriculum. And what is expected of religious education is that students begin to see the problems of *right* action. In right action, we identify a rule and choose whether or not to follow it. There are at least two problems with this. First, given that a variety of actions might be instantiations of the same rule, on what grounds do I choose one over another?[47] Second, given that rules might clash, on what grounds do I choose one over another? Citing Kant's well-known example, Collingwood asks whether I should tell a person the whereabouts of another person if they mean to do them harm.[48] Again, as with common-sense historians and artists, those engaged in religious activities must recognise that autonomy is required for reasonable action, and that the development of autonomy requires a higher level of experience.

The third form of experience is science. We have already seen the importance that Collingwood places on a person's relationship with the natural world; natural science fosters the intelligent use of resources. Communities accumulate an enormous amount of knowledge relating to the seasons, the soil, livestock, and so on. Passing on this information contributes to the survival of civilisation. Here, Collingwood echoes Fichte's suggestion that, in education:

[45] G.W.F. Hegel, *Lectures on the Philosophy of History*, trans. J. Sibree (New York, 1956), pp. 256–332; *Elements of the Philosophy of Right*, §15.
[46] R.G. Collingwood, 'Science, Religion and Civilisation' [1930], p. 16.
[47] R.G. Collingwood, 'Goodness, Rightness, Utility: Lectures Delivered in H[ilary] T[erm] 1940', Ms Collingwood Dep. 9, p. 59; *The New Leviathan*, §16.63.
[48] R.G. Collingwood, *The New Leviathan*, §§16.64, 16.75.

pupils must understand the principles of what they do, and that they have already received the information necessary for their occupations concerning the growth of plants, the characteristics and needs of the animal body, and the laws of mechanics . . . [49]

Urbanisation, Collingwood argues, alienates people from the land, and this leads to a breakdown in civility. Here Collingwood is not unusual: many of his contemporaries, including Tolkien, lamented the loss of countryside to urban development. Additionally, though, he feared that inability to comprehend mechanical advances would lead to blind acceptance — the kind of acceptance that makes possible the ascendance of nazism, fascism or any other kind of 'barbarism' which is the antithesis of civilisation.[50]

Science does not only refer to practical matters, for Collingwood also uses the term — most famously in *The Idea of History* — to describe 'any organised body of knowledge'.[51] Science education thus has to be 'predominantly a method for inducing habits of orderly and systematic thinking'.[52] This refers not only to the natural sciences, but also to the human sciences such as geography, sociology and psychology. Indeed, this form of experience would cover most of the subjects given discrete identity in curricula today, including 'history'. All of these subjects, however, are dependent on history/philosophy. Collingwood writes:

Natural science as a form of thought exists and has existed in a context of history, and depends on historical thought for its existence. From this I venture to infer that no one can understand natural science unless he understands history: and no one can answer the question of what nature is unless he knows what history is.[53]

How does science depend on historical thought? The connection is seen when we consider *dutiful* action. Dutiful actions, we recall, come at the end of and are consistent with a process of reasoning. They are self-authorised and autonomous actions, for we consciously choose them and are responsible for them.[54] These are actions in which, Collingwood tells us, the 'element of why' is more prominent than lower forms of experience.[55] Further, these are

[49] J.G. Fichte, *Addresses to the German Nation* [1807–8] (New York, 1968), pp. 424–5.
[50] R.G. Collingwood, 'Art and the Machine' [n.d.], Ms Collingwood Dep 25 (8); see also *The New Leviathan*, §34.51.
[51] R.G. Collingwood, *The Idea of History*, p. 249.
[52] R.G. Collingwood, *An Essay on Metaphysics*, p. 134.
[53] R.G. Collingwood, *The Idea of Nature* (Oxford, 1945), p. 177.
[54] R.G. Collingwood, *The New Leviathan*, §§17.1–17.81.
[55] R. G. Collingwood, 'Central Problems in Metaphysics — Lectures Written April 1935, for Delivery T[rinity] T[erm] 1935', Ms Collingwood Dep. 20 (1), p. 114.

actions that entail the imagination. As Collingwood writes in 'Aesthetic':

> a scientist without imagination is a scientist sterilised, a scientist with no power of initiating new scientific ideas or of discovering hitherto unknown laws; and . . . a man of action without imagination is a man who acts in the dark, a mere blind force, not active in the proper sense of the word at all, but the dupe of his opponents and the plaything of circumstance.[56]

Here again, we see the imagination at play in the activities of more than just a select group of gifted individuals. As with critical historians, scientists are selective, critical in their attitude towards information and able to interpolate between gaps in evidence, as with plotting a line between two data points. And like critical historians, they lack an awareness of, first, the fact that the principles which guide their actions are a priori but also historical, and second, the role of the imagination in their activities. That awareness comes only with the experience of history/philosophy, and the historicized dutiful action that it entails.

From the above discussion, it should be abundantly clear that aesthetic, religious and scientific education presuppose historical/philosophical education. History/philosophy takes us to self-knowledge and dutiful action via the activities of the a priori historical imagination. This, in turn, helps us to see our duty to socialise others. This is the reasoning behind his suggestion that:

> Historical knowledge is no luxury, or mere amusement of a mind at leisure from more pressing obligations, but a prime duty, whose discharge is essential to the maintenance not only of any particular form or type of reason, but of reason itself.[57]

Given that civilisation presupposes rational consciousness, there can be no civilisation without the experience of history/philosophy. Civilisation, for Collingwood, is thus 'historical civilisation'.[58]

History/philosophy has aims that are superordinate to those of the basic curriculum. This means that the prime aims of individual subjects are instantiations of the wider aims of history/philosophy. This is not to suggest that subjects are devoid of their own particular aims, but that history provides the link between subjects and the curriculum as a whole. On this point, Collingwood speaks to the pres-

---

[56]   R.G. Collingwood, 'Aesthetic' [1927], p. 6a.
[57]   R.G. Collingwood, *The Idea of History*, pp. 227–8.
[58]   R.G. Collingwood, 'Notes On Historiography' [1938–9], *The Principles of History and Other Writings*, ed. W.H. Dray and W.J. van der Dussen (Oxford, 1999), p. 246.

ent-day issue of the fragmentation of the curriculum. Many educators today consider subjects to be independent principalities, each on guard against subsumption or being squeezed out of the curriculum altogether. Collingwood does not ask us to abandon our attempts to understand the activities entailed in different subjects; he simply reminds us to give more thought to the connections between subjects and education as a whole.

Though Collingwood has much to say on why history/philosophy is important, he offers very little practical advice on how it is to be taught to students. His own lectures on history and philosophy clearly convey the view that the study of both recent and ancient events, and events shaped by presuppositions that are very different or very similar to the student's, can contribute to the development of self-knowledge. The arrangement of his lectures on philosophy, art and history also tell us that he favoured a chronological approach to study. What is most striking about his lectures, though, is that he lived up to his own suggestion to study presuppositions as inherent in human activities, not as separate entities. What general comments he makes arise from concrete examinations of past and present activities. This is why, for instance, Knox did Collingwood a disservice when he extracted 'History as Re-enactment of Past Experience', 'The Subject-matter of History' and 'Progress as Created by Historical Thinking' from Collingwood's lectures from 1936 and included them in the epilegomena of *The Idea of History*. There is no clear demarcation between theory and practice in Collingwood's works. Further, we also know that Collingwood thought that presuppositions could be studied through a wide range of materials. For example, 'The Principles of History' includes discussion of material evidence, and other unpublished manuscripts look to popular cultural evidence such as fairy and folk tales.[59] Clearly for Collingwood there are many avenues to reflection on our own and other peoples' forms of life.

In summary, education aims to develop self-knowledge by helping students to engage with the various forms of experience. Self-knowledge presupposes autonomous thinking and dutiful action, which are present in varying degrees in the forms of experience. Collingwood's socialising curriculum thus has as its foundation the progressive movement through the experiences of art, religion, science and history/philosophy. History/philosophy

[59]   R.G. Collingwood, 'The Principles of History' [1939], *The Principles of History and Other Writings*, pp. 48–9, 66–7; see also 'Fairy Tales' [n.d.], Ms Collingwood Dep. 21 (4–7).

stands at the top of the scale because only this form entails autonomous activities and recognition of historical a priori presuppositions. Importantly, too, this is a curriculum for all, not just a select group of gifted individuals. This explains Collingwood's insistence in the quote that heads this chapter that history is not just a professional activity, but also a universal human interest. To his view, every person has a duty to ask not 'Shall I be an historian or not?', but 'How good an historian shall I be?' To turn our backs on this duty, Collingwood warns us, is no less than to turn our backs on civilisation.

The Organisation of Education

Whilst Collingwood has little to say on the arrangement of his socialising curriculum, he offers what Boucher calls a 'remarkable' account of the practical organisation of education.[60] Central to Collingwood's views on pedagogy is his claim that one of the fundamental faults of civilisation is that the education of children is entrusted to professional educators. As he writes:

> I will begin with the Platonic case . . . where the family suffers . . . destructive interference at the hands of the body politic. The family is here divided into three parts instead of two; we have the parents, who, instead of the richly diversified functions attached to parenthood in a tradition that was already old when Plato wrote, have in this family only the function of producing offspring; we have the children; and we have the nurses or educators provided by the body politic. Why Plato propounded so odd a scheme I will not pause to explain.[61]

In agreement with Boucher, I think it is fair to explain Collingwood's views in part by recalling the extraordinary nature of his home education, as described in the introduction. I do not follow Boucher, though, in judging Collingwood's views to be remarkable. As we will see, they are not so unusual when considered in context.

Until 1870, 'popular' education in Britain was all but equated with denominational education. In 1858, a commission was set up under the chairmanship of Lord Newcastle to 'consider and report what measures, if any, are required for the extension of sound and cheap elementary instruction to all classes of people'.[62] Alongside the claim for basic standards of literacy for all, the provision of elemen-

---

[60] D. Boucher, 'The Place of Education in Civilisation', p. 356.
[61] R.G. Collingwood, *The New Leviathan*, §22.61.
[62] As quoted in P. Gordon and J. White, *Philosophers as Educational Reformers: The Influence of Idealism in British Educational Thought and Practice* (London, 1979), p. 67.

tary education was thought to offer a means to prevent crime, diffuse social unrest and to help newly franchised men to exercise their right to vote wisely. With these aims in mind, Forster shepherded the 1870 Elementary Reform Act through the Commons. Under the provisions of this Act, local school boards were to be encouraged to open schools where denominational provisions were inadequate. Forster's reforms coalesced with the views of British 'new idealists' such as Green, Acland, Haldane, Jones, Sadler and Morant. Initially, these writers favoured the kind of educational reconstruction espoused by Matthew Arnold. Arnold held that nothing less than the reconstruction of British life was necessary, and that this was to be brought about through the provision of education for at least the middle classes.[63] In formulating these views, Arnold looked to the German and French education systems, which he had studied for the Newcastle Commission in 1859 and the Taunton Commission in 1865.[64] Pointing to German educational practices, he argued for a twofold system, divided into academic and technical schemes. This division had its origins in Fichte's suggestion that education should seek to develop moral agents who work for the good of the community, and, at a higher level, scholars to lead the state and foster moral growth in others.[65]

Looking to Green's writings, it is evident that he held in common with Arnold the belief that the first step in the reconstruction of national life was the adequate provision of education.[66] In distinction from Arnold, though, he believed in the extension of the same kind of education to all people. This is because he hoped that educational reform would:

> heal the division between those who angrily look up to others as having the social reputation which they themselves have not, uniting both classes by the free-masonry of education.[67]

Green's views, as well as those of other new idealists, were echoed in the 1918 Education Act. Among other things, the 1918 Act extended the school leaving age and established a national system of secondary education and examinations (the School Certificate).[68]

---

[63]   M. Arnold, *Schools and Universities on the Continent* (London, 1868). See also R.G. Collingwood, 'What "Civilisation" Means', *The New Leviathan*, p. 509.

[64]   P. Gordon and J. White, *Philosophers as Educational Reformers*, p. 48.

[65]   *Ibid.*

[66]   *Ibid.*, pp. 68–70.

[67]   T.H. Green, *Works*, Vol. 3 (London, 1888), p. 460.

[68]   D. Boucher, 'The Place of Education in Civilisation', p. 385; see also H.A.L. Fisher, *Education Reform Speeches* (Oxford, 1918), p. 48.

It was against this background that Collingwood's writings on education appeared. Looking at the new idealist push for a national system of education, it does seem remarkable that Collingwood wanted to place responsibility for education firmly in the hands of parents. What advantages do they offer over an institutional approach to education? Collingwood sees at least two. First, parents have much more power over their children than professional educators do.[69] Handing children over to professional educators results in a division of power that diminishes the strength of both. By power, Collingwood means not total control, for that would go against the socialising aim of education. Rather, I think that Collingwood is suggesting that a strong bond is needed for the educator (professional or parent) to draw a child towards new intellectual challenges. When children are handed over to professional educators, they must take a backward step and build a new bond, and it will not be as strong because it is not undivided. Second, the 'parent as educator has the resourcefulness, the versatility, of a non-specialist'. The parent is free from the sheer mass of demands that plague professional educators, and is thus more open to Collingwood's advice that 'It doesn't matter what you do; you are free to do anything you like; all I ask is that you shall do *something*, and try to do it better than you did last time'.[70] Free from trivial demands, like checking to see if their children's hands are clean, parents are able to concentrate on the more important task of facilitating the identification of presuppositions and the development of dutiful action. Socialisation is not about efficiency, it is about single minded dedication. Put simply, then, to Collingwood's view, 'modern children are grossly and criminally over-taught'.[71]

It is important to note, though, that Collingwood is not advocating a 'general massacre of school-masters and school-inspectors and university teachers'.[72] Educators should be available to teach parents and children who go to them for assistance with specialist subjects. This would leave professional educators with more time to conduct research. Educational institutions would thus exist 'partly as teaching institutions where specialised teaching is on tap for all comers who want it, and partly as institutions of research where science and learning shall be kept alive instead of being, as they too

[69]   R.G. Collingwood, *The New Leviathan*, §37.34.
[70]   *Ibid.*, §37.36.
[71]   *Ibid.*, §§37.92, 37.94.
[72]   *Ibid.*, §37.95.

often are in our educational institutions today, dead'.[73] The above shows that Collingwood thinks that parents are better equipped to bring about the development of self-knowledge, but we have not been offered much of an explanation as to why this is the case. To address this issue, it is necessary to look at Collingwood's ideas on education and society in the context of Hegel's and Green's writings.

Collingwood's and Green's views on society draw much of their direction from the philosophy of Hegel. In turn, Hegel's writings owe much to the ideas of Plato, Aristotle, Herder, Kant, Schelling and Fichte. From Herder, for instance, he adapted the idea that there is a universal history of humanity that exhibits a progression from primitive times to civilisation at the present. The mainspring of this progress is freedom. Also fundamental to Hegel's thought is the notion that everything is interconnected. By contrast, Kant's philosophy stresses the idea of individual autonomy; that moral agents are persons who, through reason, decide what their obligations are. Kantian society is thus an aggregate of autonomous agents.[74] Hegel judges that from the writings of Kant, 'The situation was ideal for the imposition of a new tyranny: absolute freedom'.[75] Kant's social philosophy, Hegel argues, puts too much weight on the autonomy of the individual, and thus underemphasizes the part that each individual plays in society. Thus there is a tension between *Sittlichkeit*, or individual morality, and *Moralität*, or the morality of society. To counterbalance Kant's *Sittlichkeit*, Hegel draws on the Classical Greek idea of *polis*, or society as a systematic whole. In a *polis*, the highest value is attached to the well being of the state as a whole. In order to balance this view with that of Kant, Hegel posits the idea of society as an expression of the Absolute Mind or Spirit. In realising themselves, therefore, people move towards the realisation of Absolute Mind or Spirit. This process of self-realisation is made possible through the logic of the dialectic.

Individuals form part of the Absolute Mind, but this link is mediated by the state. The link to the state is also mediated. Between an individual and the state come an individual's family and social class. Each of these, as well as the state as a whole, brings with it its own customs and rules to guide conduct.[76] By this series of attachments, the individual becomes a member of the state-community. The family provides the individual's first experience of community life. In

[73] *Ibid.*, §37.98.
[74] G.W.F. Hegel, *Elements of the Philosophy of Right*, §§302–3.
[75] G.W.F. Hegel, *Phenomenology of Mind*, trans. J.B. Baillie (Cambridge, 1931), pp. 599–600.
[76] *Ibid.*, ch. 6; see also id., *Elements of the Philosophy of Right*, §§2–3.

the family community, there is no distinction between one's own and others' private interests: every member contributes to and shares in the well being of the family as a whole. This is akin to the idea of *polis*. Beyond the family is what Hegel calls 'civil society'. Civil society is driven by the self-interest of its members. Each member seeks their own ends, with little thought of the wellbeing of the community. People only follow the customs and laws of society in order that they may promote their own interests. Civil society is thus the product of *Sittlichkeit*.

Out of this opposition of the family and civil society comes the state. In the state, individuals work together for a common wellbeing. What controls exist do so for the common good, not for individual gain. Yet this is not at the sacrifice of individual autonomy, for the individual does not blindly accept the rules of the community. Individuals should understand why they should accept a particular rule or custom, and understanding entails seeing its connection with Absolute Mind. As Gordon and White write of Hegel's view of rules:

> although the social maxims which [the individual] follows are not his own in the sense that he has originated them, he is still acting autonomously because he can freely accept them as rationally demanded.[77]

Individuals live in the state because they find reason in its laws and customs. Mobility from the family to the state, Hegel advances, is made possible by education.[78]

Along with Hegel, Green is aware of the importance of mediating communities between the individual and the largest social communities. For instance, he refers to the family, local government and the nation state.[79] The nation state is for him:

> an organization of a people to whom the individual feels himself bound by ties analogous to those which bind him to his family, ties derived from a common dwelling-place with its associations, from common memories, traditions and customs, and from the common ways of thinking and feeling which a common language and still more a common literature embodies. Such an organization of an homogenous people the modern state in most cases is.[80]

Echoing Hegel, Green's account of the state is peopled by individuals who follow rules for the good of the community because they see

---

[77]   P. Gordon and J. White, *Philosophers as Educational Reformers*, p. 15.
[78]   G.W.F. Hegel, *Elements of the Philosophy of Right*, §206.
[79]   T.H. Green, *Prolegomena to Ethics*, §§229, 237; see also *Lectures on the Principles of Political Obligation* [1879] (London, 1937), §119.
[80]   T.H. Green, *Lectures on the Principles of Political Obligation*, §123.

them as rationally required. Green understands the following of such rules as a duty, for the refusal to follow them undermines one's rational development. He writes:

> It is the very essence of moral duty to be imposed by a man on himself. The moral duty to obey a positive law, whether a law of the State or of the Church, is imposed not by the author or enforcer of the positive law, but by that spirit of man — not less divine because of the spirit of man — which sets before him the ideal of a perfect life, and pronounces obedience to the positive law to be necessary to its realisation.[81]

Our principal duty is our own self-realisation. In understanding ourselves, we come to understand the Absolute Mind. At the same time, trying to achieve self-realisation is a step towards the self-realisation of others.[82] The ultimate objective is to develop the intellectual abilities of humanity as a whole. Thus part of our duty of self-realisation involves helping others to realise themselves. Education is the process whereby self-realisation is developed.

Green diverges from Hegel in his account of the emergence of the state. While Hegel saw the state emerging out of the clashes of the dialectic, Green saw it as growing out of a primitive community, differing from it only in the degree of freedom that it entails. By extension, the family is a proto-community out of which the state grows, and thus plays a vital part in the process of socialisation. Green, however, did not think that a parent-based education system was pragmatic. He writes:

> In an ideal society, perhaps the education of all families might safely be left under the control in each case of the parents. In the actual state of English society, however, no one pretends that it can be left, and it is doubtful whether under the modern system of labour in great masses, which draws all those who have to work for their living more and more away from their homes, the fate of the children can ever with safety be left solely in the hands of the parents.[83]

It goes without saying that education is central to Collingwood's theory of society. In line with Hegel and Green, Collingwood tells us that it is education that facilitates the conversion of non-social communities into societies. In placing the family at the centre of that process of conversion, though, Collingwood diverges from Green in a radical way. To Collingwood's view, a family including children is a non-social community over which parents exercise transeunt rule.[84] It is the prime duty of parents, though, to help their children to join

[81] T.H. Green, *Prolegomena to Ethics*, §324.
[82] T.H. Green, *Lectures on the Principles of Political Obligation*, §171.
[83] T.H. Green, *Works*, vol. 3, pp. 431–2.
[84] R.G. Collingwood, *The New Leviathan*, §§22.1, 23.6.

the social community of the state. Parents, like the rulers of states, are pathfinders and setters of examples.[85] Civil and dutiful action is thus acquired through successful modelling.[86] In going through this process of socialisation, joining a social community helps a person to take a step towards the realisation of a worldwide community. Here Collingwood clearly heeds Green's call for a 'world-wide brother-hood'.[87] For Green and Collingwood, education helps people to move beyond adversarial methods of solving disputes, and to adopt a conciliatory approach to problems. Thus civilisation is achieved, or as Green puts it, 'the dream of an international court with authority resting on the consent of independent states may come to be real-ised'.[88] Such a dream may seem far from realisation, but it is not, to the mind of Green and Collingwood, impossible.

In summary, Collingwood advances that there are three reasons why the development of autonomous and dutiful action, and thus civilisation, should be the responsibility of parents. First, parents have a strong relationship with their children, particularly when they are young, and this forms a strong foundation for intellectual and emotional development. Second, parents are more able to focus on the process of socialisation than professional educators, because they are free from demands to simply inculcate information. Third, and most importantly, the family is a form of community out of which a society grows. That is, society rests on a stronger foundation of freedom of the will than the family. In adding a state-run system, Collingwood argues, the bond between the family and the social community is weakened. This is not to say that professional educa-tors play no part in the child's development; it is just that Collingwood thinks that the conversion from non-social to social people is more likely to be achieved through the activities of fami-lies. On these points, Collingwood is not offering anything remark-able or unheard of. He is simply following the lines of argument set down by Hegel and then Green. Where he diverges from these two thinkers is on the extent of the role that the family plays in socialisa-tion. Collingwood, remembering the education that his parents gave him, and mindful of the responsibilities that parenthood bring, clearly thinks that a parent based education system is possible.

Green is right: making parents the primary providers of education is impractical. It is even more so now, when the norm is increasingly

[85] *Ibid.*, §27.12; and 'The Three Laws of Politics', Ms Collingwood Dep. 24 (11), p. 10.
[86] R.G. Collingwood, *The New Leviathan*, §§25.32, 32.31.
[87] P. Gordon and J. White, *Philosophers as Educational Reformers*, p. 31.
[88] T.H. Green, *Lectures on the Principles of Political Obligation*, §175.

that both parents undertake paid employment. This does not mean, though, that Collingwood's arguments are without merit. Today when we think of education, we look almost exclusively to formal institutions such as schools, colleges and universities. Parents and siblings are thought to contribute to education in a limited sense, but we do not think of them as being on a par with professional educators. Some parents even consider education to be the duty of schools alone. For Collingwood, however, *any* social institution is a potential educator, and the educative power of families should not be underestimated. If education is purely a matter of inculcating information to help students to pass examinations, he argues, then we should look no further than British public and state schools. Such a view of education, though, is unlikely to result in the socialisation of students and the halt of the decline of Western civilisation into a state of barbarism.[89] If, on the other hand, education is seen as the process of socialisation, then any individual, group, or institution that contributes the development of autonomous dutiful action should be recognised as educative. Indeed, if individuals achieve any level of autonomous, dutiful action themselves, then they will know that it is their *duty* to foster it in others. Education thus reaches out beyond schools and also beyond the ages that we normally associate with learning. Socialisation is a lifelong process that involves all of us. We are all potential educators, and so Collingwood's question 'How good an historian shall I be?' also means 'How good an educator shall I be?'

Simply Another Idealist?

Collingwood's views on education can clearly be located in the context of idealist and British new idealist writings. I believe, though, that he departs from his predecessors in two important ways. First, he is opposed to the new idealist call for increasing state involvement in education. To Collingwood, such a shift would see an emphasis on the memorising of information at the expense of socialisation. The process of education, he thus believes, should begin with parents and remains their prime responsibility. Second, in distinction particularly from the new idealists, Collingwood suggests that history/philosophy is the backbone of a socialising curriculum. Collingwood recognised the interest of new idealists like Bradley,

---

[89]   R.G. Collingwood, *The New Leviathan*, §34.51.

Green and Bosanquet in history,[90] but believed that it did not permeate their thinking to the extent that it did his own. In a letter to the Italian philosopher de Ruggiero from 1931, for instance, he complained:

> Even the nineteenth century idealists in England were not, in general, historically minded: there are traces of an historical point of view in Bradley and Green, and Caird — but they were not very strong, and in Bosanquet they vanish entirely, and the relics of the [idealist] school in Oxford today are quite out of touch with history. Therefore an historically-minded philosopher here is a *vox clamantis in deserto*.[91]

Telling people about past events does not make you an historian/philosopher. Being an historian/philosopher also requires fostering in yourself and others an historical orientation towards the world. In coming to know ourselves, we obtain a clearer view of the presuppositions that shape our lives. These presuppositions are immanent in any document, piece of material evidence or action that can be 'read'. Both the presuppositions that characterise the human form of life and the particular assumptions that a person is socialised into are historical; they shift and change like a river and its bed. It is through the various forms of experience — art, religion, science and history/philosophy — that we achieve self-knowledge and freedom of the will. This freedom, as we have seen, is linked to the health of Western civilisation. Thus although Collingwood's educational views show something of the influence of idealism and British new idealism, he alone locates history at the heart of civilisation.

Questions

Collingwood's views on education are extensive and innovative. What we now need to do is to ask how viable they are. Whilst his account raises many issues, I would like to briefly examine six.

First, how can education produce a global society? What possibility is there for global dialogue, let alone agreement, disagreement and enrichment? If there is at present no common ground, how and why should people strive towards Oakeshott's 'conversation of mankind' or Green's 'world-wide brotherhood'? In responding to such scepticism, Collingwood asks us not to overlook the historical a priori presuppositions that shape our activities. Some presuppositions, he tells us, vary greatly from culture to culture. Others,

[90] R.G. Collingwod, 'Lectures on the Philosophy of History' [1936–1940], Ms Collingwood Dep. 15 (3), p. 44a.

[91] R.G. Collingwood, 'Letter to Guido de Ruggiero, 3 January 1931', Ms Collingwood Dep. 27.

though, are common to humanity. It is these that give us the common ground required for conversation to begin.

Even if we grant the previous point, are Collingwood's ultimate aims for autonomous, dutiful action and the development of a global historical civilisation beyond the capability of most people? Collingwood believes that education reaches all of us, but will we all be able to grapple with its demands? This question demands a two-fold response. First, we ought not focus on the end point of Collingwood's views of education at the expense of the intermediary points he sketches. He does not expect us to grasp the nature and need for autonomous, dutiful action and a global historical civilisation easily. He believes that we will make progress towards these goals through engagement with the various forms of experience, each of which instantiates autonomous, dutiful activities in some capacity. Further, we begin not with the global community, but learn social action through engagement with progressively larger communities, from the family to the state. Second, Collingwood explicitly recognises a variation in capabilities among people. In *The New Leviathan*, for instance, he notes that intellectually disabled children may not be as capable of achieving rational consciousness as those that are not. Importantly here, Collingwood does not use the word 'incapable', but 'not so capable'.[92] Not everyone may be able to achieve rational consciousness, but that does not mean that we are released from the duty of socialisation. Here perhaps his advice to parents to try to do something with their children as best they can is most pertinent: better to try to socialise others than to do nothing at all. Nor is Collingwood only interested in those people who perform best in institutional education. To his view, being able to memorise and regurgitate information for exams does not make you a good citizen. Street cleaners, farmers, and academics can all become citizens and recognise their duty to socialise others.

Third, does Collingwood overly constrict the scope of education? That is, does Collingwood's view of education exclude all those experiences that may not be closely tied or even tied at all to the end of socialisation? As has been stated a number of times here, Collingwood saw presuppositions at work in every form of experience. In theory, then, engaging in any activity offers us the opportunity to become more aware of our presuppositions. What is implied in this suggestion is that the path to civilisation is a broad one, and that people can express their civility in an endless number of ways. It is worth noting too that Collingwood presents socialisation as the

[92] R.G. Collingwood, *The New Leviathan*, §23.61.

prime aim of education, not the only one. I am not sure, for instance, that Collingwood viewed his interest in recreational sailing as closely tied to the health of Western civilisation, yet he still engaged in it. There is freedom in our activities: all that Collingwood asks is that we do not lose sight of our prime duty to help others and ourselves.

Fourth, is Collingwood's socialising curriculum one that serves only the interests of the state? That is, will education only be directed to the cultivation of patriots and nationalists? Here, objectors might cite the apparently close association between nationalism and acts of violence in the twentieth century. One can dismiss this objection by recalling that Collingwood, along with Green, views the state as only one of a number of communities to which people belong. Families and local communities make up the state, and in turn, the state makes up part of the global community. For Collingwood as for Green then, patriotism and nationalism should thus be viewed as steps towards the embrace of wider perspectives. Gordon and White put this point well:

> The nation state, with its common language, literature, and customs provides one obvious focus for a communal life. If we think so of it that it not only embraces pluralism of values . . . but is also essentially internationalist and humanitarian in its external relations, there is nothing abhorrent which we can see in patriotism of this kind.[93]

Fifth, what roles do women play in Collingwood's views of education? Is Collingwood's global community, like that of Green, simply a 'brotherhood'? While Collingwood has little to say on women in any of his writings, it is clear that he viewed them as both educable and educators firstly by virtue of their roles as children and parents, and secondly because they are capable of the same 'mental maturity' as men.[94] Furthermore, not only are they capable of citizenship, they can also display genius, as was the case with Austen.[95] He does admit, though, that cultural circumstances may work against women achieving freedom of will, as for instance when they are denied education or viewed as chattels acquired in marriage.[96]

Sixth, who controls education? Collingwood is clear that any person or social institution is a potential educator. Further, he locates parents at the heart of the delivery of education. What, however, happens if parents are unable — for whatever reason — to fulfil their

[93]   P. Gordon and J. White, *Philosophers as Educational Reformers*, pp. 245–6.
[94]   R.G. Collingwood, *The New Leviathan*, §23.32.
[95]   R.G. Collingwood, 'Jane Austen' [n.d.], Ms Collingwood Dep. 17 (3), p. 15.
[96]   R.G. Collingwood, *The New Leviathan*, §§23.37, 23.38, 23.4.

duty? To whom does the duty fall? Additionally, who is there to check that parents do the best by their children? Collingwood has no answer to these questions, for as far as he can see, there is no reason why parents cannot educate their children and regulate their own activities. In response to Collingwood, I do not agree that parental control of education is self-evidently a good thing. Parents may not want to see their children socialised as Collingwood does for a host of religious, social and political reasons. Collingwood assumes that parents are rational agents, but they may not be. Nor may they be aware of the range of presuppositions that Collingwood evidently was. Probably the strongest defence of Collingwood's position we can offer is to say that everyone in society has a duty to ensure the socialisation of others. Duty compels us to look out for others, but will there be enough dutiful people out there to look out for everyone?

Collingwood's account of the delivery of education is far from pragmatic. The most positive thing we can say is that he is right to set us thinking about education beyond the gates of educational institutions. This does not mean, though, that his views on the aims, content and processes of education are fatally flawed. In the next chapter, we return to where we began, with a comparison of Collingwood's views against the three thinkers who most shaped history education in Britain in the latter half of the twentieth century: Bloom, Hirst and Bruner. That comparison will lead us to our final conclusion, that Collingwood deserves to be known more than in name.

The Historical Imagination of R.G. Collingwood

Before moving on, however, it is important that we return to Collingwood's concept of imagination. Imagination is not to be found in the activities of geniuses and professional historians alone. In this chapter, it has been argued that it is the mainspring of historical socialisation. Educational decisions are thus to be directed towards the development of imagination as well as the endpoint of historical civilisation. For Collingwood as for Hobbes, then, civility is a product of imagination. But it is only one of many possible products of imagination, so why value it? In asking this question, we become aware that there is at least one more way in which imagination features in Collingwood's work. If we recall Hayden White's observations on the historical imagination, we arrive at the realisation that Collingwood's theory of imagination is itself a product of imagination. Put simply, Collingwood's selection, arrangement and emphasising of particular ideas is actuated by imagination. White would probably see Collingwood's 'historical imagination' as characterised by a 'Romantic' mode of emplotment. That is, across his writings, Collingwood narrates the story of liberation from barbarism and the victory of people over darkness.[97] White's designation does not fit, though, for the 'story' that Collingwood narrates is not finished. At the time that Collingwood wrote, no victory over 'barbarism' was guaranteed. And indeed, there will never be a final victory of civilisation over barbarism, because each person must undertake a personal journey to historical civilisation. Collingwood's theory of imagination is not one of triumph, therefore, but one of becoming and of hope.

---

[97]   H. White, *Metahistory: The Historical Imagination in Nineteenth-Century Europe* (Baltimore, MD, 1973), pp. 8–9.

Chapter VII

Towards an Historical Education

When we find [imagination] operating, we shall not instantly despair of sanity; on the contrary, we should despair of sanity, if for a moment it ceases operating.[1]

In the 1960s, new history education models were built with reference to the ideas of Hirst, Bruner and Bloom. These models were then fleshed out with historiographical suggestions drawn above all from the writings of Collingwood. In the hands of educators, Collingwood's concepts of re-enactment and imagination were conflated and treated as a discrete entity that could be slotted into whatever model prevailed. Why? Many a teacher can recognise and even recite quotes like 'the historian of a certain thought must think for himself that very same thought, not another like it'. Such quotes, though, have been mesmerizing; few have shaken loose from their superficial appeal to wonder about the presuppositions that give them shape. This surface fascination has been sustained by an ahistorical analytical philosophy of education, which has had little capacity to deal with Collingwood's historicized conceptual scales and a priori presuppositions. Moving beyond the surface, we have been rewarded with an account of imagination — and to a lesser extent re-enactment — that is firmly located within an extensive constellation of educational and social thought. We return now to where we began, with the curriculum innovations of Hirst, Bloom and

---

[1]   R.G. Collingwood, 'Aesthetic' [annotated galley proofs of a lecture published in *The Mind: A Series of Lectures Delivered in King's College, London*, ed. R.J.S. McDowall [1927], Ms Collingwood Dep.–25 (3).

Bruner. This time, though, we look to Collingwood as the provider not of a small curriculum component but of a vision of education characterised by a deep commitment to history, the imagination and the creation of a global community.

Hirst and the Forms of Knowledge[2]

'[T]he domain of human knowledge can be seen to be differentiated into a number of logically distinct 'forms', none of which is ultimately reducible in character to any of the others, either simply or in combination'.[3] This brief formulation captures much of Paul Hirst's attempt to grasp the nature of an epistemologically oriented education. Since the appearance of his paper 'Liberal Education and the Nature of Knowledge' (1965), Hirst's 'forms of knowledge' thesis has been widely discussed by educators and used to support innovations such as the British National Curriculum. As Peters comments, 'there is a sense in which anyone working in the field has to take up some stand with regard to the 'forms of knowledge''.[4]

In 'Liberal Education and the Nature of Knowledge', Hirst spells out his vision of education for the 'good life'. The good life, he argues, is achieved through the pursuit of reasonable knowledge.[5] In order to achieve reasonable knowledge, students should be immersed in and made aware of the various forms of knowledge: mathematics, the physical sciences, the human sciences, history, religion, literature and the fine arts and philosophy. These are not curriculum subjects or collections of information 'but the complex ways of understanding experience which man has achieved, which are publicly specifiable and which are gained through learning'.[6] They may be distinguished from one another on the grounds of characteristic concepts and relations of concepts (logical structure), truth tests and particular skills and techniques. For example, gravity has a

---

[2]   In this section, we concentrate on Hirst's early writings, culminating in the 1974 paper 'The Forms of Knowledge Revisited'. In his later writings, Hirst moves away from an emphasis on epistemology in education and stresses instead desire satisfaction, practical reasoning and social practices. See for example P.H. Hirst, 'Education, Knowledge and Practices', *Beyond Liberal Education: Essays in Honour of Paul H. Hirst*, ed. R. Barrow and P. White (London, 1993), pp. 184–99.

[3]   P.H. Hirst, 'The Forms of Knowledge Re-visited', *Knowledge and the Curriculum* (London, 1974), p. 84.

[4]   R. Peters, 'Preface', in *ibid.*, p. viii.

[5]   P.H. Hirst, 'Liberal Education and the Nature of Knowledge', *Knowledge and the Curriculum*, p. 43.

[6]   *Ibid.*, p. 34.

specific meaning in physics, and ideas in physics are testable in experiments and observations.[7]

Writing on the influence of Hirst's thesis, Peters has suggested that:

> There is, of course, little that is philosophically original in Hirst's general thesis that such distinct forms of knowledge exist. Indeed it is almost a stock-in-trade of the idealist tradition. Modern examples are Michael Oakeshott's *Experience and its Modes*, John MacMurray's *Interpreting the Universe* and R. G. Collingwood's *Speculum Mentis* ... What is distinctive about Paul Hirst's handling of the forms of knowledge is first his application of this general thesis in epistemology to problems of the school curriculum. Whitehead once said that philosophy never recovered from the shock of Plato. My guess is that curriculum theory will never recover from the shock of Hirst. Second, there is Paul Hirst's great lucidity and intellectual power.[8]

While Peters' second claim is difficult to debate, I think that a revision of the first is needed. The necessity for revision will become apparent when we explore the philosophical relation between Collingwood's and Hirst's views. Though there are many points that can be drawn out of this comparison, I have chosen four: first, why Collingwood talks of experience and Hirst of knowledge; second, what status the forms of experience or knowledge have; third, what can be said about the inter-relationships between the forms; and fourth, how strong the relationship between education and the forms of experience or knowledge is in their respective writings. In attempting to unravel the relationship between these two theses, it will become apparent that there is a strong difference in purpose between Collingwood's and Hirst's writings.

For Hirst, the realm of knowledge is the realm of true propositions or statements.[9] As an account of true propositions, Hirst argues, his writings on knowledge also provide an account of the concepts applied in those propositions.[10] From this it follows:

> That if one holds, as I hold, that all forms of experience are intelligible only by virtue of the concepts under which we have them, a classification of forms of knowledge provides also a classification of forms of experience.[11]

---

[7] *Ibid.*, pp. 44–5.
[8] *Ibid.*, p. viii.
[9] P.H. Hirst, 'The Forms of Knowledge Re-visited', *Knowledge and the Curriculum*, p. 85.
[10] *Ibid.*, p. 91.
[11] *Ibid.*

Collingwood's account of the forms of experience also includes propositions and statements, but both true and false ones. When we begin to reflect on the knowledge we possess, he tells us, we soon realise that it is fallible. This thought of fallibility teases us, and so we seek grounds or reasons for our propositions.[12] Once we start to examine and seek reasons for our propositions, we take the further step of trying to illuminate both relative and absolute presuppositions. Herein lies a clear difference between Collingwood's and Hirst's projects. Whereas Collingwood's forms of experience entail — among other things — absolute presuppositions which are prior to judgements of truth or falsity, Hirst regards the forms of knowledge to be constituted solely by *true* propositions. Collingwood would consider Hirst's forms of knowledge to be complexes of true relative presuppositions, and thus only the starting point in the search for self-knowledge. In order to realise self-knowledge, Collingwood asks us to take a further step back and look to our absolute presuppositions. Put simply, then, Hirst's forms of knowledge are constituted by propositions that we are aware of as true, and Collingwood's forms of experience are constellations of activities shaped in part by presuppositions that we may not be aware of.

This leads us to the second point of comparison. For Collingwood, the absolute presuppositions that constitute the forms of experience are historically grounded. Hirst also tries to avoid presenting his forms as invariant. He and Collingwood are thus in agreement that the forms of knowledge or experience are not immune to change.[13] Because of particular historical and cultural situations and the issues and interests they raise, different forms will take shape. Yet both writers recognise that the variation in the number, nature and grouping of forms is a variation within limits. This is because human activities display recurrent patterns, identifiable structures and regularities. It follows, as Hirst points out, that:

> These common features would seem to cast doubt on the view that major forms of thought of different communities are mutually incomprehensible. There may be considerable difficulty in understanding the conceptual schemes of another society without comprehensive immersion in its culture. Yet in so far as its purposes and context are shared with one's own, the fundamental basis for understanding would seem to be there.

---

[12] R.G. Collingwood, *The New Leviathan* [1942], rev. edn., ed. D. Boucher (Oxford, 1992), §§14.2–14.29.

[13] P.H. Hirst, 'The Forms of Knowledge Re-visited', *Knowledge and the Curriculum*, p. 92.

The idea of total lack of communication in many areas of life would seem unlikely.[14]

Thus both Collingwood and Hirst recognise that, although the forms are subject to change, they are not entirely socially relative.

Third, it should be clear from chapters five and six that Collingwood gave a great deal of thought to the task of clarifying the interrelations between the various forms of experience. In contrast, Hirst is more interested in spelling out the points of distinction between the various forms of knowledge.[15] This difference, I believe, can be explained in two ways. First, the views of concepts that underpin Collingwood's and Hirst's theses are very different. We recall that for Collingwood the forms of experience are not coordinate species embodying equally the essence of the concept: they are arranged in a cumulative scale. Each of the forms of experience is related to the others as a greater or lesser instantiation of the concept. For example, the activities of an historian/philosopher embody autonomous, dutiful action more adequately than those of the scientist. Collingwood thus places history/philosophy above science in the scale because he sees experience as being essentially about dutiful action. Ostensibly, Hirst's view of the forms of knowledge is non-hierarchical: each is considered distinct and equal.[16] There is, though, an implicit hierarchy at play in his thesis, for each of the forms is identified and distinguished through philosophy.[17] Here it is implied that philosophy has a superior status to all the other forms. Unfortunately Hirst does not offer us any reason why they ought to be distinguished by philosophy, rather than say, by longevity or even popular consensus. Are we to take it that Hirst sees philosophy as providing the epitome of knowledge?

On the fourth point of comparison, and most importantly for our purposes, I contend that the agenda of Collingwood's work differs dramatically from that of Hirst's. While I think Peters is correct to suggest that Hirst gave more thought to the application of his thesis to the school curriculum, Collingwood's work bears a stronger educational agenda. For Hirst, the endpoint of education is reasonable knowledge, for this equates with the good life. Collingwood is also interested in the cultivation of reasonable knowledge and action, but as an intermediary step towards the realisation of freedom of the

[14] *Ibid.*, pp. 94–5.
[15] *Ibid.*, pp. 90–1.
[16] P.H. Hirst, 'Liberal Education and the Nature of Knowledge', *Knowledge and the Curriculum*, p. 41.
[17] P.H. Hirst, 'The Forms of Knowledge Re-visited', *Knowledge and the Curriculum*, p. 85.

will and a global community. To him, the most valuable knowledge is that which contributes to the health of Western civilisation. Thus the forms of experience are not to be held up as ideals but as symptoms of a fragmented mind and civilisation. Collingwood puts this point explicitly in *Speculum Mentis* when he writes that during the renaissance, each of the forms:

> Tended to become a specialised activity pursued by specialists for the applause of specialists, useless to the rest of mankind and unsatisfactory even to the specialist when he turned upon himself and asked why he was pursuing it. This is the point to which we have come today.[18]

Unity of experience is achieved when we recognise the historical/philosophical presuppositions that shape all of our activities. Hirst has his eyes set on the curriculum, not the society beyond it, but does at least recognise that immersion in the forms of knowledge does not represent a total education. He admits, for instance, that his view of education displays a lack of concern for moral commitment.[19]

Superficially, the resemblances between Hirst's and Collingwood's ideas are many. Looking deeper, though, we have discovered two quite different accounts of what the aims of education should be. As we shall see, the distance between Collingwood's and Bloom's ideas is even greater.

Bloom and the Taxonomy of Educational Objectives

Bloom's *Taxonomy of Educational Objectives*, the first part of which was published in 1956, is familiar to educators around the world.[20] We recall from chapter one that participants in the project sought to plot out and classify the observable and describable cognitive and affective behaviours of students. They did so, Bloom tells us, for two major reasons: first, to develop a precise, standardised list of observable behaviours that could be used to develop examinations, and second, to broaden the range of skills tested by examiners beyond that of information recall.[21] This list was to be purely descriptive and

---

[18] R.G. Collingwood, *Speculum Mentis*, p. 34.

[19] P.H. Hirst, 'The Forms of Knowledge Re-visited', *Knowledge and the Curriculum*, p. 96.

[20] While over thirty people contributed to the construction of the taxonomy, it is generally connected with the name of its editor, Benjamin S. Bloom.

[21] B. Bloom (ed.), *Taxonomy of Educational Objectives: The Classification of Educational Goals, Handbook 1: Cognitive Domain* (London, 1956), pp. 2, 4. See also B. Bloom, 'Reflections on the Development and Use of the Taxonomy', *Bloom's Taxonomy: A Forty-year Retrospective*, ed. L.W. Anderson and L.A. Sosniak, Ninety-third

thus 'neutral' as to the value or quality of the behaviours included or as to their ranking in the taxonomy.[22] No list, though, can be free of judgements of value and quality.[23] Bloom's taxonomy places the development of examinations above other possible aims, and also ranks analysis as a greater cognitive skill than description. Collingwood, on the other hand, wrote on education not to make the lot of examiners easier; indeed, he abhorred the idea of education being equated with examination outcomes. To his view, education by examination would leave students little opportunity to develop dutiful action. Avowed neutrality just means there is more responsibility on readers of the taxonomy to find any implicit values at work. Collingwood is upfront about his valuing of dutiful action, history/philosophy and Western civilisation, whereas readers of the taxonomy have to look carefully for embedded judgements such as: 'Closely allied to this concept of [intellectual] maturity and integrity is the concept of the individual as a member of a democracy'.[24] Here we might ask why intellectual maturity is equated with democracy.

In comparison with Collingwood, the epistemological foundations of the taxonomy are also naïve. First of all, Collingwood would be in agreement with Thomas F. Green's complaint of the taxonomy that the aim of education is not to change students' behaviour, but to transform behaviour — which is habitual — into action that is self-authorised or principled.[25] A second difficulty stems from the distinction in the taxonomy between behaviour and its context and content. Although Bloom's project recognised that statements of objectives should indicate both the kind of behaviour and the subject or area of life it is to be manifested in, the taxonomy lists only behaviours and disregards their content and context. For Collingwood, as for Sockett, Pring, Hirst and Ormell, behaviours are not entities that are separable from context and content. Sockett puts the point well when he considers the example of 'remembering':

> 'remembering' is unintelligible just as a psychological process (even if we lay aside its counterpart — forgetting) for we remember *something*, cases of remembering are cases of being right about what was or is the

Yearbook of the National Society for the Study of Education, Part II (Chicago, 1994), pp. 1–2.

[22] B. Bloom (ed.), *Taxonomy of Educational Objectives*, p. 14.
[23] E.J. Furst, 'Bloom's Taxonomy: Philosophical and Educational Issues', in *Bloom's Taxonomy: A Forty-year Retrospective*, ed. L.W. Anderson and L.A. Sosniak, Ninety-third Yearbook of the National Society for the Study of Education, Part II (Chicago, 1994), p. 28.
[24] B. Bloom (ed.), *Taxonomy of Educational Objectives*, p. 41.
[25] T.F. Green, 'Teaching, Acting, Behaving', *Harvard Educational Review*, Vol. 34 (3) (1964), pp. 504-24.

case. We cannot posit remembering in any sense apart from content. If remembering is thought of as content-free we have an empty concept which could not be even part of an educational objective.[26]

Hirst, too, notes along with Collingwood that elements of rational action, including concepts, principles, remembering and so on, are not detached from one another but connected.[27] Those connections are overlooked in the taxonomy. Finally, Collingwood would not hold — as is the case with the taxonomy — that cognitive, affective and psychomotor activities can be conceptually or practically separated.[28]

Thus far, Collingwood's views of education would align with a number of philosophical criticisms brought forward against Bloom's taxonomy. Collingwood alone, though, shows us that we should also ask questions of the taxonomy as a statement of foundations. While Bloom notes that there is some cultural and geographical variation in cognitive and affective behaviours, the taxonomy is clearly intended to be a solid foundation for educational practice. But how solid is it? What is the status of the objectives? Are they the atemporal categories of mind that Kant was interested in? Or do they have their origins in time? Are they subject to change and replacement? That there is no discussion or even hint of an awareness of these matters would lead Collingwood to conclude that the project is an example of a critical, scientific activity. As such, it does not represent the best that rational persons are capable of. That only comes when we recognise the historicity of the presuppositions that shape our activities, including the construction of taxonomies.

Before passing on, more needs to be said about the structure of the taxonomy. The assumption of a cumulative hierarchy in the taxonomy, organised solely on the shift from simple to complex behaviour, has generated much criticism. In his testing of the taxonomy, for instance, Ormell found a number of cases that involved inversion of objectives. For him as for other writers, it is clear that knowledge sometimes requires the prior acquisition of more 'complex' behaviours (for example, analysis). Inversions thus occur and there is fre-

[26] H. Sockett, 'Bloom's Taxonomy: A Philosophical Critique', *Cambridge Journal of Education*, Vol. 1 (1) (1971), pp. 16–25. See also R. Pring, 'Bloom's Taxonomy: A Philosophical Critique', *Cambridge Journal of Education*, Vol. 1 (1) (1971), pp. 83–91; P.H. Hirst, *Knowledge and the Curriculum*, pp. 19–20; and C.P. Ormell, 'Bloom's Taxonomy and the Objectives of Education', *Educational Research* Vol. 17 (1) (1974), p. 11.

[27] P.H. Hirst, *Knowledge and the Curriculum*, p. 26.

[28] See R. Pring, 'Bloom's Taxonomy: A Philosophical Critique', pp. 83–91.

quent overlap between the various taxonomic branches.[29] At first sight, this criticism might also be made of Collingwood's view of education. In the last chapter, we recall, education was presented as the development of dutiful action through various experiences: art, religion, science, and history/philosophy. In *Speculum Mentis*, though, Collingwood makes it clear that movement through the scale of forms of experience may not be steady. He writes:

> The life of the mind is not the rotation of a machine through a cycle of fixed phases but the flow of a torrent through its mountain bed, scattering itself in spray as it plunges over a precipice and pausing again in the deep transparency of a rock pool, to issue again in an ever-new series of adventures.[30]

Furthermore, while we know that higher forms incorporate the experiences of lower forms, Collingwood also argues that lower forms may overlap with higher ones. For example, art fosters utilitarian action. To Collingwood's view, utilitarian action tends towards dutiful action because while both are reasonable, the former ignores the 'better' parts of the latter and posits itself as the pinnacle of intellectual activity. That is, there is some part of the higher form in the lower, even at the bottom of the scale. Thus each form of experience implies others.[31] In combination, these views suggest a spiral rather than a linear view of education. As Collingwood writes in *Outlines of a Philosophy of Art* of the journey to unity of spirit through education:

> This process always takes place in time, but it is an eternal process: it is always beginning, it has always reached any given point, and it has always arrived at its conclusion, somewhat as . . . a river is always rising at its source, always flowing over each part of its course, and always discharging itself into the sea. But because the process of the spirit is a conscious process, like a river which should be aware of itself throughout its course, it does not merely travel through a fixed cycle of changes, but finds every passage past a given point altered in significance by the consciousness of what has gone before it; and hence the unity of the spiritual

[29] C.P. Ormell, 'Bloom's Taxonomy and the Objectives of Education', pp. 13–15. See also D.C. Phillips and M.C. Kelly, 'Hierarchical Theories of Development in Education and Psychology', *Harvard Educational Review*, Vol. 45 (3) (1975), pp. 351–75; L. Apt, 'Behavioural Objectives and History', *Intellect*, no. 101 (1973), pp. 445–7; P.H. Hirst, *Knowledge and the Curriculum*, p. 24; and R. Pring, 'Bloom's Taxonomy: A Philosophical Critique', p. 90.
[30] R.G. Collingwood, *Speculum Mentis*, p. 57.
[31] R.G. Collingwood, *An Essay on Philosophical Method* (Oxford, 1933), pp. 90–91. See also *Outlines of a Philosophy of Art* [1925] (Bristol, 1993), p. 94.

life resembles the unity of an infinitely increasing spiral rather than the unity of a rotating circle.[32]

This image is suggestive of Bruner's view of education, to which we now turn.

Bruner and the Process of Education

In 1959, Jerome Bruner was invited to chair a meeting of thirty-five educators under the auspices of the National Academy of Science and the National Science Foundation. One product of that meeting was the book *The Process of Education* (1960), which has had a profound impact on curriculum policy around the world, including the British National Curriculum. Four themes are presented in *The Process of Education*: structure in teaching and learning, readiness for learning, intuitive and analytic thinking, and motives for learning.

Education, Bruner tells us, is not the same as memorising discrete pieces of information for examinations. Those who equate the two should not be surprised that students are not motivated to learn.[33] If education is to engage students and serve them in the future — and help democracy to survive — then it must foster understanding of the fundamental structure or foundational principles of whatever subjects are taught.[34] And these principles, Bruner is of the belief, can be 'taught effectively in some intellectually honest form to any child at any stage of development'.[35] Schools have wasted opportunities by postponing the teaching of fundamental principles because they are held to be too complex and that students are not ready for them. What is neglected here, Bruner tells us, is that 'intellectual activity anywhere is the same, whether at the frontier of knowledge or in a third-grade classroom'.[36] These activities differ in degree, not in kind.[37] To his view, ideas can thus be visited and revisited at different stages of education; indeed, this is the best way to encourage understanding. This process of visiting and revisiting ideas forms the heart of Bruner's idea of the 'spiral curriculum'. He writes: 'A curriculum as it develops should revisit these basic ideas repeatedly, building upon them until the student has grasped the full formal apparatus that goes with them'.[38]

---

[32] R.G. Collingwood, *Outlines of a Philosophy of Art*, pp. 94–5.
[33] J.S. Bruner, *The Process of Education* (Cambridge, MA, 1960), pp. 14, 80.
[34] *Ibid.*, pp. 10–12, 17.
[35] *Ibid.*, p. 33.
[36] *Ibid.*, p. 14.
[37] *Ibid.*
[38] *Ibid.*, p. 13.

The understanding sought in education is best achieved through intuitive thinking, and to a lesser extent, through analytic thinking. Analytic thinking proceeds one step at a time, and the thinker can adequately report each step. That is, it 'proceeds with relatively full awareness of the information and operations involved'. Intuitive thinking, on the other hand, does not proceed in successive, well-defined steps and does not require awareness of the process by which an answer is arrived at. Intuitive thinkers leap from idea to idea, skipping steps and employing shortcuts to produce plausible but tentative ideas and hypotheses. It is intuitive in that it is immediate apprehension or cognition: it does not require the intervention of formal methods of analysis and proof. Analytic and intuitive thinking clearly differ, but they are not mutually exclusive, for analytic thinking often follows as a check to intuitive thinking.[39]

In some ways, Bruner's dynamic view of education is a good match for Collingwood's. As with Bruner's spiral curriculum, Collingwood seeks the development of intellectual activity through the successive approximations of the forms of experience. Artistic activities, for instance, are on the same intellectual continuum as historical/philosophical activities. The difference between them is one of degree, not kind. Additionally, both writers are against the idea of tying education to external goals such as examination results, grades or competitive ranking. Collingwood would surely agree with Bruner's vision of education as a process, not a product. Bruner writes:

> To instruct someone . . . is not a matter of getting him to commit results to mind. Rather, it is to teach him to participate in the process that makes possible the establishment of knowledge. We teach a subject not to produce little living libraries on that subject, but rather to get a student to think mathematically for himself, to consider matters as an historian does, to take part in the process of knowledge-getting. Knowing is a process not a product.[40]

We must not, however, be lured into thinking that these two writers are of like mind, for there are some fundamental differences that separate them. I would like to note two. First, we cannot be at all sure that the 'principles' and 'structural ideas' that Bruner speaks of are anything like the a priori presuppositions that Collingwood is interested in. Frustratingly, Bruner says so little on the status of principles and structural ideas that we do not, for instance, have any idea whether they are subject to judgements of truth or falsity. That is, are

[39] *Ibid.*, pp. 13–14, 57–8, 60.
[40] J.S. Bruner, *Toward a Theory of Instruction* (Cambridge, MA, 1966), p. 72.

they relative presuppositions or absolute presuppositions? Are they more like Hirst's propositions than Collingwood's presuppositions? Nor does he have anything to say about the nature and epistemological status of the relations among principles and structural ideas. Importantly, too, Bruner fails to tell us whether these principles and structural ideas are subject to cultural and temporal variation. As with Bloom, Collingwood would probably see Bruner's thoughts on the process of education as an example of a critical, scientific activity. And as with Bloom, Bruner's work falls short of the dutiful action that awareness of the historical/philosophical foundations of our world brings.

Further differences stem from Bruner's valuing of intuitive thinking above analytic thinking. Collingwood, as we have seen, clearly distinguished historical knowledge from intuitive knowledge. Historians possess no special powers of penetration that allow them to achieve identity of thoughts and emotions with historical agents. Historical thinking rests upon an awareness of the presuppositions that shape human activities — including the idea of 'identity of thought' — and the historicity of those presuppositions. Indeed, as was suggested in the last chapter, the prime task of educators is to foster self-knowledge and knowledge of others. Seen thus, historical thought is more like Bruner's notion of analytic thought. Why is there such a difference in their views? Lurking behind these claims are two very different understandings of innovation. Bruner sees fertile and shrewd ideas as arising when we take 'the courageous leap to a tentative conclusion' with our minds averted to the principles that guide us. Collingwood, on the other hand, believes that the best thinking is to be found whenever people are conscious of the principles that guide them. So we seek not escape from what we are, but better knowledge of what we are. Importantly, this is not an activity that comes at the expense of freedom, but one that epitomises it, for the thinker freely accepts the principles as rationally demanded. Freedom from principles is not possible, only freedom with principles.

Historicizing Education

The process of education can be historical in three senses. First, it may include the study of past persons, periods or events, as with the many policies and programs described in chapter one. Second, it may aim to foster an historical self-understanding, where learners come to see that their ideas, activities, abilities, skills and even identity are subject to change over time. For example, students might be asked to engage in reflective activities, where they describe changes in understanding or objectives achieved as a result of a course of study. And third, education may foster an awareness of the historical nature of the presuppositions that shape it and the wider world. While the first and the second of these two senses of history education are captured to some extent in the writings of Hirst, Bloom and Bruner, only Hirst acknowledges the third. And even then, his acknowledgement of the historicity of knowledge includes no claim that students ought to be made aware of this. That neglect is similarly carried over to policies and programs shaped by the views of these three thinkers, including the British National Curriculum. Why has this notion of an historical education in a foundational sense been neglected?

Snook puts his finger on the problem when he notes that discussions on curriculum have tended to oscillate between two extremes: in the first the bodies of knowledge that constitute the curriculum are invariant; in the second they are 'arbitrary' socio-historical constructs. In the first case, the aim of education is to help students to understand 'true' or 'objective' collections of propositions. This view can be used to reify existing curriculum subjects — like history, mathematics, or biology — as a permanent feature of Western culture. In the second case, knowledge is seen as involving more than true propositions, and can be, as Snook puts it, 'packaged' as a particular culture requires. In response, Snook argues for the careful distinction between the timeless and the time-bound in curricula. Humans participate in a wide variety of spatio-temporally variant activities. But, he notes, 'bounds are set by the nature of the world and by the nature of us as beings-in-the-world'. There are regularities in our world, and curricula are often formed out of these regularities.[41] Here, Snook approaches Hirst's position in 'The Forms of Knowledge Re-visited', where he argues that there is room for spatio-temporal variation in the forms of knowledge thesis, but it is a variation within the limits of the human form of life.

Neither writer, though, goes as far as Collingwood to grapple with and question the very distinction between the timeless and the timebound in curricula. Why? Here, I think we see evidence of the assumption first raised in chapter three that foundationalism equates with the acceptance of the timeless. As I hope is abundantly clear from arguments throughout this book, temporal foundationalism is also an option, and one that both Wittgenstein and Collingwood accept. Drawing on our earlier discussions of philosophy and the a priori, what are the implications for curricula? The curriculum is thoroughly timebound. But that does not mean that it is entirely subject to fads or to arbitrary decisions. It is shaped by presuppositions that are so long-lived and regular that any changes to them would lead to a radical transformation of the human form of life, as well as presuppositions expedient to specific historical and cultural situations. All facets of the curriculum have their origins in time, and can be subject to strain and replacement.

Nor do Snook or Hirst acknowledge that helping students to become aware of historical/philosophical presuppositions might be a key, if not *the* key aim of education. Here we see the depth of Collingwood's commitment to an historical education, a commitment unmatched by any of the other educationalists surveyed in this work. For Collingwood, history education does not require the designation of a separate subject with its own particular objectives or attainment targets and programs of study. It is, more basically, the process whereby we help students to understand the historicity of their world.

Imagination and Education

Like many writers, Hirst, Bloom and Bruner hold that imagination plays a part in education. Indeed Warnock has suggested that 'in education, we have a duty to educate the imagination above all else'.[42] Yet few would accept that they, or any other educationalists, offer an adequate account of what part imagination plays in education or how it is to be developed. As we saw in chapter one, the diversity of ways in which imagination and its cognates have been spoken of makes the task of discovering any order or coherence in the concept seem impossible. Part of the problem, I believe, arises from trying to fit the imagination into the traditional or 'sharp boundary' view of concepts described in chapter five. On the face of it, there appears to be no core or essence that is common to all instantiations of the concept of imagination. Now we could, like Egan, leave off the task of trying to explain the relation between the various activities of imagination altogether.[43] Two problems, however, arise. First, we may find ourselves back with Knight, Farmer and Lee's response to

---

[42] M. Warnock, *Imagination* (London, 1976), p. 10.
[43] K. Egan, *Imagination in Teaching and Learning: Ages 8–15* (London, 1992).

the exclusion of the term 'empathy' from the British National Curriculum. We recall that for them, the uncoupling of the activities of empathy from the conceptual label was not problematic. Indeed, Knight and Farmer preferred this uncoupling, arguing that it made the construction of concrete objectives easier. The problem is, though, that they still talked of empathy in their writings.[44] Moreover, many history educators persist in using terms like 'imagination', despite the lack of clarity. This suggests that the label 'imagination' is not empty or worthless, and that there is some link between its instantiations that warrants the use of the conceptual label. A second problem arises when the lack of an understanding of the relations between instantiations of 'imagination' leads it to become a bower for all activities. This is the case with Egan's *Imagination in Teaching and Learning*. In that work, Egan connects the imagination with the emotions, the transcendence from conventional ideas, entertaining possibilities, construction, memory, seeing others as distinct and autonomous, compassionate sympathy, visualisation, creativity, originality and the casting of our life experiences as narratives.[45] He is not too far from realising the major problem with his work when he writes: 'Perhaps you might feel that I have included too much and that the result is a sense of imagination being involved in everything of educational importance'.[46]

There is, as we have seen, middle ground between the extremes of the sharp boundary and open views of concepts just described. That middle ground is available first with Wittgenstein's 'family resemblances' view, in which instances of a concept are united by a network of overlapping similarities. So, for instance, two instantiations of the concept of imagination may not share anything in common, but may be connected by a third usage. While preferable to the two extremes, I do not think that this view of concepts suits the case of imagination in an educational context either. This is so for three reasons. First, Wittgenstein's view of concepts is still sufficiently open as to allow for the bower effect described above. All that is required for an instantiation of imagination to be labelled so is some connection with another instantiation. Where, though, do the connections end? Do all activities become those of imagination because of some connection, however distant? For instance, we can all find a connec-

[44]   A. Farmer and P. Knight, *Active History in Key Stages 3 and 4* (London, 1994), pp. 11–12; and P.J. Lee, 'History and the National Curriculum in England', *International Yearbook of History Education*, ed. P.J. Lee, A.K. Dickinson, P. Gordon and J. Slater (London, 1995), pp. 73–123.

[45]   K. Egan, *Imagination in Teaching and Learning*, pp. 48, 51, 52, 54, 58, 61, 63, 70, 74.

[46]   *Ibid.*, p. 65.

tion between the British Royal family and ourselves if we try hard enough. My point is that the use of concepts entails judgements about whether they ought to be applied or not. Second, in presenting all instances of imagination as equal, we still leave open the question of whether these instances are subject to age- and experience-related changes. More importantly, we dodge questions of value. Not all instantiations of imagination are valued equally, and not all may be present in the activities of students. Third, the issue of value introduces a temporal aspect: what is valued now in imagination may not have been valued in earlier times and it may not be valued in future.

Collingwood's view of the concept of imagination, I believe, answers these problems. Instances of the concept are united by a core — that of autonomous, dutiful reasoning — but do not embody it equally. We recall, for instance, that Collingwood holds reasoning to be minimally present in imaging, but more strongly present in critical imaginative activities. And as Collingwood openly declares his valuation of autonomous, dutiful reasoning, we can talk of some forms of imagination as higher than others. We can also, if we agree that the development of autonomous, dutiful reasoning is a key aim of education, see a developmental path that we may follow, from imaging, pure or free imagination, perceptual imagination to the historical imagination. Further, we might even follow Collingwood through the experiences of art, religion, science and history/philosophy. More importantly, the value of Collingwood's scale of forms is that it leads students to the point where they may critically consider the presuppositions that shape their activities and those of others, including Collingwood himself. They become aware of the foundations of imagination, and that they may be subject to change. All of this suggests that it is time for educators to take a closer look at what Collingwood has to say.

National and Supranational Curricula

Hirst's, Bloom's and Bruner's ideas have been employed to support educational initiatives around the world, such as the British National Curriculum described in chapter one. Many countries around the world now boast national curricula. National curriculum policies are, however, diverse. Some describe the educational traditions of a country and others mandate content. For example, the Japanese national curriculum offers only a few objectives to be achieved at each grade level, whereas in France, policies and supporting textbooks offer a detailed account of the content and objectives students are expected to master. Further, following the national curriculum in Britain is a matter of law, whereas few Australians are even aware that there is a national curriculum.[47] Looking at these curricula, it is easy to conclude that they provide a fundamental alternative to supranational and even global educational models. That is, each nation-state is seen as travelling down its own discrete educational path.

As Benavot, Cha, Kamens, Wong, Ramirez and Meyer have shown, though, all national curricula are at least implicitly supranational in character.[48] First, though societies throughout the world differ in terms of, say, their histories or economic transactions, world models of society have standardised around the idea of the nation state.[49] And this, Fiala and Langford have shown, leads to standardisation of national goals, such as the provision of mass education to achieve economic progress or educational programs that foster the integration of individuals into their community.[50] Second, most nation states are linked in larger cultural and organisational systems, whether informally or by trade agreement and treaty. For example, the British National Curriculum exists in the context of the European Union, as the Singaporean National Curriculum exists in the context of the Association of South East Asian Nations (ASEAN). Third, pressures by international agencies such as the United Nations Educational Scientific and Cultural Organisation (UNESCO), the Organisation for Economic Cooperation and Development (OECD), the World Bank and local aspirations to match the achievements of other nations leads to the copying of other educa-

---

[47] There are no global studies of national curricula available. Some information, though, can be gleaned from scanning the educational surveys conducted by the OECD (www.oecd.org) and UNESCO (www.unesco.org).

[48] A. Benavot, Y.-K. Cha, D. Kamens, J.W. Meyer and S.-Y. Wong, 'Knowledge for the Masses: World Models and National Curricula, 1920–1986', *American Sociological Review*, Vol. 56 (1) (1991), pp. 85–100; and F.O. Ramirez and J.W. Meyer, 'National Curricula: World Models and National Historical Legacies' (2002), online at Stanford University Comparative Sociology Workshop, www.stanford.edu/group/csw/PAPER2.

[49] A. Benavot *et al*, 'Knowledge for the Masses', p. 88; F.O. Ramirez and J.W. Meyer, 'National Curricula', p. 2. See also G. Thomas, J.W. Meyer, F.O. Ramirez, *Institutional Structure: Constituting State, Society, and the Individual* (Beverly Hills, CA, 1987); and B. Anderson, *Imagined Communities: Reflections on the Origin and Spread of Nationalism* (London, 1991).

[50] R. Fiala and A.G. Lanford, 'Educational Ideology and the World Educational Revolution, 1950–1970', *Comparative Education Review*, Vol. 31 (2) (1987), pp. 315–32.

tional initiatives.[51] Benavot *et al*, for instance, studied national curriculum policies from 125 countries from 1970–86 and found a global shift away from the study of history, civics and geography towards instruction in integrated social studies.[52]

National curricula are increasingly supranational in character, yet there is little acknowledgement of this in policies or curriculum theory, particularly in the area of history education. Supranational considerations are probably assumed to belong to subjects such as civics, social studies or more unusual offerings like peace studies. Here again we run up against an assumption that Collingwood tackled head on: history does not refer just to a distinct subject, profession or even national identity, but also to a wider socialising process. History is not just a preventative against insularity, as is suggested in the British National Curriculum document *History for Ages 6 to 16*.[53] It is the chief means by which we can foster the construction of a supranational and even global community. Moreover, realising this end is not an option, but a duty.

Why Collingwood?

When compared to Hirst, Bloom and Bruner and even the British idealists that preceded him, Collingwood's practical involvement in education was negligible. To the best of our knowledge, Collingwood steered clear of public debates and policy initiatives. Nor did he write a book or even lecture on the idea or principles of education, as he did for art, history, cosmology, religion and philosophy. Yet as we have seen, education is the very *raison d'être* for many of his writings. Furthermore, it has been suggested that Collingwood's views on education circumvent some of the limitations that currently dog discussions on history education, the role of imagination in education and national curricula. To apprise ourselves of his vision, though, we need to start thinking of history beyond the academy, imagination beyond the genius and education beyond the school gates. Such a broadening of vision, I hope, is worth seeking at any time, but especially in times of global trouble.

[51] P. DiMaggio and W. Powell, 'The Iron Cage Revisited', *American Sociological Review*, Vol. 48 (1) (1983), pp. 147–60.

[52] A. Benavot *et al*, 'Knowledge for the Masses', p. 91.

[53] Department of Education and Science, *National Curriculum: History for Ages 5 to 16* (London, 1990), p. 1.

Conclusion

Beyond the Academy

... historical knowledge is no luxury, or mere amusement of a mind at leisure from more pressing occupations, but a prime duty, whose discharge is essential to the maintenance, not only of any particular form or type of reason, but of reason itself.[1]

Commitment to history is usually measured by support for a distinct profession and curriculum subject. Robin George Collingwood was himself a professional historian and taught at Oxford University, but his commitment to history was far beyond the usual. When I first read his writings as an undergraduate, I assumed that I could use them simply to flesh out the frameworks of history education supplied by educational theorists and practitioners. He was the provider of methodological strategies, or tools for the history teacher's toolkit. Yet when I looked closer — and wider — that assumption began to break down. I read his lectures on metaphysics from 1935, for instance, and was amazed at how historical they were. Indeed, I wondered if any of the students he lectured were confused as to whether they were in the right class. And on reading *The Philosophy of History* (1930), I understood that I would need to broaden my understanding of history and of education.

It is increasingly recognised that history and education are to be found both inside and outside educational institutions. Writing of public history in Australia, for instance, Davison has argued that '[t]he forms in which the past are made present to us are as diverse as the forms of our national life ... The topics are diverse but they are unified by an underlying theme — the continuing power of the past

---

[1] R.G. Collingwood, *The Idea of History* [1946], rev. edn., ed. W. J. van der Dussen (Oxford, 1993).

and the need to confront its use critically'.[2] While enrolments in institutional history courses may have fallen in some places, public interest in historical films, television, novels, theme parks, museum displays, dress and music shows no signs of waning.[3] In response to this shift towards public history, historians have worked to sketch out and professionalise the theory and practice of the field. A key assumption they make is that they will keep 'a watching brief on the varieties of history . . . that circulate in the community' and refer public activities back to the academy.[4] Here, academic history is assumed to be a foundation for all historical activities.

Collingwood was interested in history beyond the academy. I do not believe, though, that his ideas can easily be matched with those of present day public historians, for at least two reasons. First, while Collingwood recognised academic history as the reference point for academic historical activities, he did not see it as the reference point for *all* historical activities. We recall that for Collingwood, 'history' refers to both the activities of academic historians and to an historical orientation towards our world. In this orientation, we seek awareness of the temporally variant a priori presuppositions that shape the human form and forms of life. Collingwood is not the first writer to claim that history underpins all of our activities. Radically, though, he suggests that this historical orientation towards the world differs from academic history in being a stronger instantiation of dutiful, autonomous reasoning and action. It grows out of academic history, but moves beyond it. Academic history is therefore not the only reference point for historical activities. Indeed, Collingwood would consider it possible that academic historians are not the best historians. What, then, are the other reference points for history? Put simply, any person, family or community can be a reference point. Collingwood sees historical education as starting not with historians or with schools, but with families. In the family community, parents guide children. Encouraged to use their imagination in artistic, religious, scientific and historical/philosophical activities, children may move from capricious action to the various degrees of rational action: utilitarian, regularian and dutiful. When they achieve dutiful, autonomous reason, they will recognise the historicity of the world and their duty to help others to achieve free-

[2]   G. Davison, *The Use and Abuse of Australian History* (St. Leonards, NSW, 2000), p. 10.

[3]   See for example H. Kean, P. Martin and S. J. Morgan (eds.), *Seeing History: Public History in Britain Now* (London, 2000); *Australian Historical Association Bulletin*, November 1997, no. 85; and *Public Historian*, 1978–.

[4]   G. Davison, *The Use and Abuse of Australian History*, p. 18.

dom of the will. Achieving freedom of the will is not an easy matter, and may take longer than the period we normally associate with schooling (say ages five to twenty five). It may even take a whole lifetime. And importantly, it is not something that others can achieve on our behalf, no matter how much they intend to help us. Ultimately then, the basic reference point for history is ourselves, located in a series of communities.

The second distinction between Collingwood and present-day public historians is to be found in their views on the use of new technologies in public and institutional history education. In 'Art and the Machine', Collingwood complains about the passivity and blind acceptance of those who listen to gramophone records compared to those who attend concerts. When we go to concerts, he tells us, we rely only on ourselves to hear the music: our experience is our responsibility. When we listen to a record, though, we abdicate responsibility to those who make the record and its player. Collingwood saw this kind of passivity as dangerous, because he held it as being in common with the blind acceptance that underpins nazism, fascism or any other kind of 'barbarism' which is the antithesis of civilisation.[5] Collingwood would probably see his complaint as extending to other technologies, including those involved in the bulk of history education today, such as films, television and the internet. While Collingwood's thesis is clearly contentious, he does direct to us an important point about responsibility in education. It is easier to accept what filmmakers and web designers tell us about our world than it is to find out for ourselves. But it is also easier to accept what anyone else tells us about our world — including our parents — than to find out for ourselves. We clearly cannot live apart from the influence of others: the social nature of our language and our selves makes that impossible. Moreover, Collingwood does believe that others can spur us along in the realisation of freedom of the will. I therefore think that Collingwood is arguing not for total self-reliance, but for greater self-reliance than we are perhaps accustomed to.

Historical education is not the responsibility of history educators or professional historians alone, nor is it the responsibility of filmmakers or web designers. It is a duty that we all must bear for our sake and for the sake of civilisation. Given this duty, 'How good an historian shall I be?' is probably the most important question we can ask.

---

[5]   R.G. Collingwood, 'Art and the Machine' [n.d.], Ms Collingwood Dep 25 (8).

Bibliography

Note: The unpublished manuscripts of R.G. Collingwood used
in this work are held in the Bodleian Library, Oxford.

Abel, T., 'The Operation Called *Verstehen*', *American Journal of Sociology*, Vol.
54 (1948–9), pp. 211–18.

Abrams, M.H., *The Mirror and the Lamp: Romantic Theory and the Critical
Tradition* (New York, NY: Norton, 1958).

Addison, J., *The Spectator*, issues 412–421, in D.F. Bond (ed.), *The Spectator*,
Vol. 3 (Oxford: Oxford University Press, 1965), pp. 535–83.

Addison, P., 'Oxford and the Second World War', *The History of the
University of Oxford*, ed. B. Harrison, Vol. 8 (Oxford: Oxford University
Press, 1994), pp. 167–88.

Aderman, D. and Berkowitz, L., 'Observational Set, Empathy and Helping',
Journal of Personality and Social Psychology, Vol. 14 (1) (1970), pp. 141–8.

Akenside, M., *The Pleasures of Imagination: and other Poems* [1744] (London:
J. Walker, 1853).

Aldrich, R. (ed.), *History in the National Curriculum* (London: Kogan Pace,
1991).

Althusser, L., 'Freud and Lacan', *Lenin and Philosophy and Other Essays*,
trans. B. Brewer (London: NLB, 1971), pp. 189–220.

Althusser, L., 'Ideology and Ideological State Apparatuses (Notes Towards
an Investigation)', *Lenin and Philosophy and Other Essays*, trans. B. Brewer
(London: NLB, 1971), pp. 127–88.

Anderson, B., *Imagined Communities: Reflections on the Origin and Spread of
Nationalism* (London: Verso, 1991).

Anon., 'Review of *The New Leviathan*', *The Scotsman*, 20 August 1942, p. 40.

Apt, L., 'Behavioural Objectives and History', *Intellect*, no. 101 (1973), pp.
445–7.

Aquinas, T., *Summa Theologica*, trans. Fathers of the English Dominican
Province (New York, NY: Benziger Brothers, 1947).

Arbuckle, J., *A Collection of Letters and Essays on Several Subjects* [1729], ed. D.
Berman and P. O'Riordan (Bristol: Thoemmes, 2002).

Ariès, P., *Centuries of Childhood*, trans. R. Baldick (London: Cape, 1973).

Ariès, P., *Hour of Our Death*, trans. H. Weaver (London: Allen Lane, 1981).

Aristotle, *De Anima*, trans. H. Lawson-Tancred (Harmondsworth: Penguin, 1986).

Aristotle, *De Memoria*, trans. G. R. T. Ross (New York, NY: Arno, 1973).

Arnold, M., *Schools and Universities on the Continent* (London: Macmillan, 1868).

Ashby, R. and Lee, P.J., 'Children's Concepts of Empathy and Understanding', in C. Portal (ed.), *History in the Curriculum* (London: Falmer, 1987), pp. 62–88.

Augustine of Hippo, *Letters*, trans. W. Parsons, Vol. 1 (New York, NY: Fathers of the Church, 1951).

Austin, J.L., 'A Plea for Excuses', *Philosophical Papers*, 3/e (Oxford: Oxford University Press, 1979), pp. 175–204.

Ayer, A.J., *Language, Truth and Logic*, 2/e (London: Victor Gollancz, 1946).

Ayer, A.J., *The Problem of Knowledge* (Harmondsworth: Penguin, 1956).

Bailey, C., 'Knowledge of Others and Concern for Others', in J. Elliott and R. Pring (eds.), *Social Education and Social Understanding* (London: University of London Press, 1975).

Balazova, J., 'Methodological Individualism in R.G. Collingwood's Philosophy of History', *Filozofia*, Vol. 47 (1992), pp. 450–63.

Baranowski, M., *A Pilgrim's Progress Through the Project*, Schools Council Occasional Paper no. 2 (London: Schools Council Publishing, 1974).

Barthes, R., 'The Death of the Author', *Image Music Text*, trans. S. Heath (London: Fontana, 1977), pp. 142–8.

Barthes, R., *Mythologies*, trans. A. Lavers (London: Paladin, 1973).

Beard, C. A. and Hook, S., 'Problems of Terminology in Historical Writing', *Theory and Practice in Historical Study: A Report of the (U. S.) Committee on Historiography* (New York, NY: Social Science Research Council, 1946), pp. 127–30.

Beattie, A., *History in Peril: May Parents Preserve It* (London: Centre for Policy Studies, 1987).

Beattie, J., *Elements of Moral Science* [1790–3], Vol. 1 (New York, NY: Garland, 1977).

Beer, S. H., 'Causal Explanation and Imaginative Re-enactment', *History and Theory*, Vol. 3 (1) (1963), pp. 6–29.

Benavot, A., Cha, Y.- K., Kamens, D., Meyer, J.W. and Wong, S.W., 'Knowledge for the Masses: World Models and National Curricula, 1920–1986', *American Sociological Review*, Vol. 56 (1) (1991), pp. 85–100.

Berkeley, G., *A Treatise Concerning the Principles of Human Knowledge*, in *The Works of George Berkeley*, ed. A.A. Luce and T.E. Jessop, Vol. 2 (London: Nelson, 1949).

Berkeley, G., *Philosophical Commentaries*, in *The Works of George Berkeley*, ed. A.A. Luce and T.E. Jessop, Vol. 1 (London: Nelson, 1949).

Berlin, I., *Vico and Herder* (London: Hogarth, 1976).

Blackburn, S., 'Reenactment as Critique of Logical Analysis: Wittgensteinian Themes in Collingwood', in H.H. Kögler, and K.R. Stueber (eds.), *Empathy and Agency: The Problem of Understanding in the Human Sciences* (Boulder, CO: Westview, 2000), pp. 270–87.

Block, J. H., 'Assessing Sex Differences: Issues, Problems, and Pitfalls', *Merrill-Palmer Quarterly*, Vol. 22 (2) (1976), pp. 283–308.

Block, N. (ed.), *Imagery* (Cambridge, MA: MIT Press, 1981).

Bloom, B. (ed.), *Taxonomy of Educational Objectives: the Classification of Educational Goals* (2 vols., London: Longmans, 1956–64).

Bloom, B., 'Reflections on the Development and Use of the Taxonomy', in *Bloom's Taxonomy: A Forty-year Retrospective*, ed. L.W. Anderson and L.A. Sosniak, Ninety-third Yearbook of the National Society for the Study of Education, Part II (Chicago, IL: University of Chicago Press, 1994) pp. 1–8.

Blyth, A., *Curriculum Planning in History, Geography and Social Science* (Glasgow: Collins, 1975).

Board of Education, *Report on the Teaching of History*, Pamphlet 37 (London: HMSO, 1923).

Boddington, T., 'Empathy and the Teaching of History', *British Journal of Educational Studies*, Vol. 28 (1) (1980), pp. 13–18.

Booth, M.B., 'Editorial', *Teaching History*, no. 27 (1980), pp. 2–3.

Booth, M.B., *History Betrayed?* (London: Longmans, 1969).

Booth, M.B., Culpin, C. and Macintosh, H., *Teaching GCSE: History* (London: Hodder and Stoughton, 1987).

Borke, H., 'Interpersonal Perception of Young Children: Egocentrism or Empathy?', *Developmental Psychology*, Vol. 5 (2) (1971), pp. 263–9.

Boucher, D., 'The Place of Education in Civilisation' (unpublished ms, 1994).

Boucher, D., 'The Significance of R.G. Collingwood's *Principles of History*', *Journal of the History of Ideas*, Vol. 58 (2) (1997), pp. 309–30.

Boucher, D., *The Social and Political Thought of R.G. Collingwood* (Cambridge: Cambridge University Press, 1989).

Bradley, F.H., *The Presuppositions of Critical History and Aphorisms* [1874], ed. G. Stock (Bristol: Thoemmes, 1993).

Braudel, F., 'The Situation of History in 1950', *On History*, trans. S. Matthews (Chicago, IL: University of Chicago Press, 1980), pp. 6–24.

Braudel, F., *The Mediterranean and the Mediterranean World in the Age of Philip II*, trans. S. Reynolds (2 vols, Glasgow: William Collins, 1972–3).

Brooks, R., Aris, M. and Perry, I., *The Effective Teaching of History* (London: Longman, 1993).

Bruner, J.S., *The Process of Education* (Cambridge, MA: Harvard University Press, 1960).

Bruner, J.S., *Toward a Theory of Instruction* (Cambridge, MA: Belkapp, 1966).

Bryant, B.K., 'An Index of Empathy for Children and Adolescents', *Child Development*, Vol. 53 (3) (1982), pp. 413–25.

Bundy, M.W., *The Theory of Imagination in Classical and Medieval Thought* (Chicago, IL: University of Illinois Studies in Language and Literature 12, 1927).

Burke, E., *A Philosophical Inquiry into the Origin of Our Ideas of the Sublime and Beautiful* [1756], in *The Works of Edmund Burke* (Oxford: Oxford University Press, 1907).

Burkitt, V., Campbell, J. and Lawton, D., *Social Studies 8–13*, Schools Council Paper 39 (London: Evans/Methuen Educational, 1971).

Burston, W.H., 'The Place of History in Education', in W.H. Burston and C.W. Green (eds.), *Handbook for History Teachers* (London: Methuen, 1964), pp. 1–14.

Burston, W.H., *Sixth Form History Teaching*, Teaching of History leaflet no. 17 (London: Routledge and Kegan Paul, 1957).

Butterfield, H., *History and Human Relations* (London: Collins, 1951).

Cairns, J., 'Some Reflections on Empathy in History', *Teaching History*, no. 55 (1989), pp. 13–18.

Campbell, A., *Enquiry into the Original of Moral Virtue* [1773] (Bristol: Thoemmes, 2000).

Carr, E. H., *What is History?* (London: Macmillan, 1961).

Catlin, G., 'Review of *The New Leviathan*', *Political Science Quarterly*, Vol. 57 (3) (1943), p. 436.

Caton, C.E. (ed.), *Philosophy and Ordinary Language* (Urbana, IL: University of Illinois, 1963).

Central Advisory Council for Education (England), *Children and their Primary Schools: A Report* (Plowden Report) (London: HMSO, 1967).

Central Advisory Council for Education (England), *Half Our Future* (Newsom Report) (London: CACE, 1963).

Cheney, D. and Seyfarth, R., *How Monkeys See the World* (Chicago, IL: University of Chicago Press, 1990).

Chisholm, R.M., 'The Truths of Reason', in P.K. Moser (ed.), *A Priori Knowledge* (Oxford: Oxford University Press, 1987), pp. 112–44.

Cicero, *Orator*, trans. G.L. Hendrickson (London: Heinemann, 1962).

Clare, J.D., 'Goodbye to all That: History in the National Curriculum', *TES*, no. 3819 (1989), p. 27.

Clark, C.K., *The Critical Historian* (London: Heinemann, 1967).

Clements, P., 'Historical Empathy — R.I.P.?', *Teaching History*, no. 85 (1996), pp. 6–8.

Cocking, J.M., *Imagination: A Study in the History of Ideas* (London: Routledge, 1991).

Code, L., 'Collingwood's Epistemological Individualism', *Monist*, Vol. 72 (1989), pp. 542–67.

Cohen, L.J., 'A Survey of Work in the Philosophy of History 1946–50', *Philosophical Quarterly*, Vol. 2 (7) (1952), pp. 172–86.

Coleridge, S.T., *Collected Letters of Samuel Taylor Coleridge*, ed. E. Griggs, Vol. 1 (London: Oxford University Press, 1956).

Coleridge, S. T., *Collected Works: Volume 7 Biographia Literaria* (London: Routledge and Kegan Paul, 1983).

Collingwood, R.G., 'Aesthetic' [Annotated Galley Proofs of a lecture published in *The Mind: A Series of Lectures Delivered in King's College, London*, ed. R.J.S. McDowall, 1927], Ms Collingwood Dep. 25 (3).

Collingwood, R.G., '*Aristotelis De Anima Libri Tres* — Translation and Commentary' [1913–14], Ms Collingwood Dep. 11.

Collingwood, R.G., 'Art and the Machine' [n.d.], Ms Collingwood Dep 25 (8).

Collingwood, R.G., 'Can Historians Be Impartial? — Paper Read to the Stubbs Historical Society, 27 January 1936', *The Principles of History and Other Writings in Philosophy of History*, ed. W.H. Dray and W.J. van der Dussen (Oxford: Oxford University Press, 1999), pp. 209–18.

Collingwood, R.G., 'Central Problems in Metaphysics: Lectures Written April 1935, for Delivery in T[rinity] T[erm] 1935', Ms Collingwood Dep. 20 (1).

Collingwood, R.G., 'Croce's Philosophy of History' [1921], in *Essays in the Philosophy of History*, ed. W. Debbins (New York, NY: McGraw-Hill, 1966), pp. 3–22.

Collingwood, R.G., 'Draft of Opening Chapters of a "Prolegomena to Logic" (or the Like)' [1920–1], Ms Collingwood Dep. 16 (5).

Collingwood, R.G., 'Fairy Tales' [n.d.], Ms Collingwood Dep. 21 (4–7).

Collingwood, R.G., 'Goodness, Rightness, Utility: Lectures Delivered in H[ilary] T[erm] 1940', Ms Collingwood Dep. 9.

Collingwood, R.G., 'Human Nature and Human History, March 1936 — First draft of a paper rewritten May 1936 and sent up for publication by the British Academy', Ms Collingwood Dep. 12 (11).

Collingwood, R.G., 'Inaugural: Rough Notes' [1935], *The Principles of History and Other Writings*, ed. W.H. Dray and W.J. van der Dussen (Oxford: Oxford University Press, 1999), pp. 143–69.

Collingwood, R.G., 'Jane Austen' [n.d.], Ms Collingwood Dep. 17 (3).

Collingwood, R.G., 'Lectures on the Philosophy of History' [1936–1940], Ms Collingwood Dep. 15 (3).

Collingwood, R.G., 'Lectures on the Philosophy of History — II C. T[rinity] T[erm] 1929', Ms Collingwood Dep. 12 (6).

Collingwood, R.G., 'Letter to Guido de Ruggiero, 3 January 1931', Ms Collingwood Dep. 27.

Collingwood, R.G., 'Notes on the History of Historiography and Philosophy of History 1936', *The Principles of History and Other Writings in Philosophy of History*, ed. W.H. Dray and W.J. van der Dussen (Oxford: Oxford University Press, 1999), pp. 219–34.

Collingwood, R.G., 'Notes Towards a Metaphysic: A' [1933], Ms Collingwood Dep. 18 (3).

Collingwood, R.G., 'Notes Towards a Metaphysic: B' [1933–4], Ms Collingwood Dep. 18 (4).

Collingwood, R.G., 'Observations on Language' [n.d.], Ms Collingwood Dep. 16 (3).

Collingwood, R.G., 'Outline of Lectures on the Philosophy of Art Delivered T[rinity] T[erm] 1924', Ms Collingwood Dep. 25 (2).

Collingwood, R.G., 'Outlines of a Philosophy of History, April 1928', Ms Collingwood Dep. 12 (4).

Collingwood, R.G., 'Reality as History' [1935], *The Principles of History and Other Writings, The Principles of History and Other Writings in Philosophy of*

History, eds W.H. Dray and W.J. van der Dussen (Oxford: Oxford University Press, 1999), pp. 170–208.

Collingwood, R.G., 'Reason is Faith Cultivating Itself', Hibbert Journal, Vol. 26 (1927), pp. 3–14.

Collingwood, R.G., 'Roman Signal-Stations on the Cumberland Coast', Transactions of the Cumberland and Westmorland Antiquarian and Archaeological Society, ns no. 29 (1920), pp. 138–65.

Collingwood, R.G., 'Rule Making and Rule Breaking: Sermon Preached in St. Mary the Virgin's Church, Oxford, 5 May 1935', Ms Collingwood Dep. 1 (9).

Collingwood, R.G., 'Science, Religion and Civilisation: A Sermon Preached in Coventry Cathedral' [1930], Ms Collingwood Dep. 1 (7).

Collingwood, R.G., 'Some Perplexities About Time: First Draft of a Paper to the Aristotelian Society, 1925', Ms Collingwood 18 (1).

Collingwood, R.G., 'The Metaphysics of F.H. Bradley, An Essay on Appearance and Reality' [1933], Ms Collingwood Dep. 29.

Collingwood, R.G., 'The Nature and Aims of a Philosophy of History' [1924–5], Essays on the Philosophy of History, ed. W. Debbins (New York: McGraw-Hill, 1965), pp. 34–56.

Collingwood, R.G., 'The Principles of History' [1939], The Principles of History and Other Writings, ed. W.H. Dray and W.J. van der Dussen (Oxford: Oxford University Press, 1999), pp. 1–116.

Collingwood, R.G., 'The Three Laws of Politics', Ms Collingwood Dep. 24 (11).

Collingwood, R.G., 'Words and Tune' [1918], Ms Collingwood Dep. 25 (1).

Collingwood, R.G., An Autobiography (Oxford: Oxford University Press, 1939).

Collingwood, R.G., An Essay on Metaphysics [1940], rev. edn., ed. R. Martin (Oxford: Oxford University Press, 1998).

Collingwood, R.G., An Essay on Philosophical Method (Oxford: Oxford University Press, 1933).

Collingwood, R.G., Outlines of a Philosophy of Art [1925] (Bristol: Thoemmes, 1994).

Collingwood, R.G., Religion and Philosophy [1916] (Bristol: Thoemmes, 1994).

Collingwood, R.G., Ruskin's Philosophy: An Address Delivered at the Ruskin Centenary Conference, Coniston 8 August 1919 (Kendal: Titus Wilson and Son, 1922).

Collingwood, R.G., Speculum Mentis (Oxford: Oxford University Press, 1924).

Collingwood, R.G., The Historical Imagination: An Inaugural Lecture Delivered Before the University of Oxford on 28 October 1935 (Oxford: Oxford University Press, 1935).

Collingwood, R.G., The Idea of History [1946], rev. edn., ed. W. J. van der Dussen (Oxford: Oxford University Press, 1993).

Collingwood, R.G., The Idea of Nature (Oxford: Oxford University Press, 1945).

Collingwood, R.G., *The New Leviathan* [1942], rev. edn., ed. D. Boucher (Oxford: Oxford University Press, 1992).

Collingwood, R.G., *The Principles of Art* (Oxford: Oxford University Press, 1938).

Collingwood, W.G., *Lake District History* (Kendal: Titus Wilson, 1925).

Coltham, J. and Fines, J., *Educational Objectives for the Study of History*, pamphlet 35 (Saffron Waldon, Essex: The Historical Association, 1971).

Cooper, H., 'Historical Thinking and Cognitive Development in the Teaching of History', in H. Bourdillon (ed.), *Teaching History* (London: Routledge, 1994), pp. 101–21.

Cooper, J.G., *Letters Concerning Taste* [1755 edition] (Bristol: Thoemmes, 1998).

Cooper, K., *Evaluation, Assessment and Record Keeping in History, Geography and Social Science* (Glasgow: Collins, 1976).

Corbin, A., *The Foul and the Fragrant: Odour and the Social Imagination*, trans. anon. (London: Macmillan, 1986).

Croce, B., *Aesthetic as a Science of Expression and General Linguistic*, trans. and ed. D. Ainslie (New York: Macmillan, 1953).

Croce, B., *Logic of the Science as a Pure Concept*, trans. D. Ainslie (London: Macmillan, 1917).

Croce, B., *What is Living and What is Dead in the Philosophy of Hegel*, trans. D. Ainslie (London: Macmillan, 1915).

Curtis, L. P., *The Historian's Workshop* (New York, NY: Viking, 1970).

D'Oro, G., 'Collingwood on Re-enactment and the Identity of Thought', *Journal of the History of Philosophy*, Vol. 38 (1) (2000), pp. 87–101.

Danto, A., *Analytical Philosophy of History* (Cambridge: Cambridge University Press, 1965).

Davidson, D., *Truth and Interpretation* (Oxford: Oxford University Press, 1984).

Davis, M., 'Measuring Individual Differences in Empathy: Evidence for a Multidimensional Approach', *Journal of Personality and Social Psychology*, Vol. 44 (1) (1983), pp. 113–26.

Davison, G., *The Use and Abuse of Australian History* (St. Leonards, NSW: Allen and Unwin, 2000).

Deegan, T., 'George Eliot's Novels of The Historical Imagination', *Clio*, Vol. 1 (1) (1972), pp. 21–33.

Deleuze, G. and Guattari, F., *Capitalism and Schizophrenia*, Vol. 1, *Anti-Oedipus*, trans. R. Hurley, M. Seem and H. Lane (New York, NY: Viking, 1977).

Derrida, J., 'Cogito and the History of Madness', *Writing and Difference* (London: Routledge and Kegan Paul, 1978), pp. 31–63.

Derrida, J., 'The Double Session', *Dissemination*, trans. B. Johnson (London: Althone, 1981).

Department of Education and Science (England), *A Framework for the School Curriculum* (London: HMSO, 1980).

Department of Education and Science (England), *Curriculum 11–16* (London: HMSO, 1977).

Department of Education and Science (England), *GCSE: National Criteria: History* (London: HMSO, 1985).

Department of Education and Science (England), *History for Ages 5 to 16: Proposals of the Secretary of State for Education and Science* (London: DES, 1990).

Department of Education and Science (England), *History in the National Curriculum (England)* (London: DES, 1991).

Department of Education and Science (England), *National Curriculum History Working Group Final Report* (London: HMSO, 1990).

Department of Education and Science (England), *National Curriculum History Working Group Interim Report* (London: HMSO, 1989).

Descartes, R., *The Philosophical Works of Descartes*, trans. E.S. Haldane and G.R.T. Ross, Vol. 1 (Cambridge: Cambridge University Press, 1969).

Deuchar, S., *History – and GCSE History* (London: CPS, 1987).

Deutsch, F. and Madle, R., 'Empathy: Historic and Current Conceptualizations, Measurement and a Cognitive Theoretical Perspective', *Human Development*, Vol. 18 (2) (1975), pp. 267–87.

Dewar, W., 'Review of *The New Leviathan*', *Time and Tide*, 15 August 1942, p. 660.

Dewey, J., *The Quest for Certainty* (New York, NY: Anchor, 1929).

Diamond, J., *The Rise and Fall of the Third Chimpanzee* (London: Vintage, 1991).

Dilthey, W., *Selected Writings*, trans. H.P. Rickman (Cambridge: Cambridge University Press, 1976).

DiMaggio, P. and Powell, W., 'The Iron Cage Revisited', *American Sociological Review*, Vol. 48 (1) (1983), pp. 147–60.

Donagan, A., 'Editor's Introduction', *Essays on the Philosophy of Art by R.G. Collingwood* (Bloomington, IN: University of Indiana Press, 1964), p. i–ix.

Donagan, A., 'The Verification of Historical Theses', *Philosophical Quarterly*, Vol. 6 (1956), pp. 193–208.

Dray, W.H., 'Broadening the Historian's Subject-Matter in *The Principles of History*', *Collingwood Studies*, Vol. 4 (1998), pp. 2–33.

Dray, W.H., 'On the Nature and Role of Narrative in History', *History and Theory*, Vol. 10 (1971), pp. 153–71.

Dray, W.H., 'R.G. Collingwood and the Acquaintance Theory of Knowledge', *Revue Internationale de Philosophie*, Vol. 2 (1957), pp. 420–32.

Dray, W.H., 'The Historical Explanation of Laws Reconsidered', in S. Hook (ed.), *Philosophy and History: A Symposium* (New York, NY: New York University Press, 1963), pp. 105–35.

Dray, W.H., *History as Re-enactment: R. G. Collingwood's Philosophy of History* (Oxford: Oxford University Press, 1995).

Dray, W.H., *Laws and Explanation in History* (Oxford: Oxford University Press, 1964).

Dussen, W.J. van der, 'Collingwood's "Lost" Manuscript of *The Principles of History*', *History and Theory*, Vol. 36 (1) (1997), pp. 32–62.

Dussen, W.J. van der, *History as a Science: The Philosophy of R.G. Collingwood* (The Hague: Martinus Nijhoff, 1981).

Dymond, R.F., 'A Scale for Measurement of Empathic Skill', *Journal of Consulting Psychology*, Vol. 14 (1) (1949), pp. 127–33.

Egan, K., *Imagination in Teaching and Learning* (London: Routledge, 1992).

Eisenberg, N. and Lennon, R., 'Sex Differences in Empathy and Related Capacities', *Psychological Bulletin*, Vol. 94 (1) (1983), p. 102.

Eliot, G., 'Historic Imagination', in T. Pinney (ed.), *Essays of George Eliot* (London: Routledge and Kegan Paul, 1963), pp. 446–7.

Engell, J., *The Creative Imagination: Enlightenment to Romanticism* (Cambridge, MA: Harvard University Press, 1981).

Ermath, M., *Wilhelm Dilthey: The Critique of Historical Reason* (Chicago, IL: University of Chicago Press, 1978).

Evans, R., *In Defence of History* (London: Granta, 1997).

Farmer, A. and Knight, P., *Active History in Key Stages 3 and 4* (London: David Fulton, 1994).

Feshbach, N. and Roe, K., 'Empathy in Six- and Seven-Year Olds', *Child Development*, Vol. 39 (1) (1968), pp. 133–45.

Fiala, R. and Lanford, A.G., 'Educational Ideology and the World Educational Revolution, 1950–1970', *Comparative Education Review*, Vol. 31 (2) (1987), pp. 315–32.

Fichte, J.G., *Addresses to the German Nation* [1807–8] (New York: Harper Torchbooks, 1968).

Fines, J. and Verrier, R., *The Drama of History* (London: New University Education, 1974).

Fines, J., 'Educational Objectives for the Study of History – Ten Years On', *Teaching History*, no. 30 (1981), pp. 8–10.

Fines, J., 'Imagination and History', *Teaching History*, no. 18 (1977), pp. 24–6.

Fischer, D.H., *Historian's Fallacies* (London: Routledge and Kegan Paul, 1971).

Fisher, H.A.L., *Education Reform Speeches* (Oxford: Oxford University Press, 1918).

Foucault, M., *Madness and Civilization: A History of Insanity in the Age of Reason*, trans. R. Howard (New York, NY: Vintage, 1988).

Foucault, M., *The Archaeology of Knowledge,* trans A.M. Sheridan-Smith (London: Tavistock, 1972).

Foucault, M., *The History of Sexuality*, trans. R. Hurley and R. McDougall (3 vols. Harmondsworth: Penguin, 1978–86).

Foucault, M., *The Order of Things: An Archaeology of the Human Sciences*, trans. anon. (London: Tavistock, 1970).

Frege, G., *The Foundations of Arithmetic*, trans. J.L. Austin, Vol. 2 (Oxford: Blackwell, 1950).

Frege, G., *The Laws of Arithmetic*, trans. and ed. M. Furth (Berkeley, CA: University of California Press, 1964).

Freud, S., 'Creative Writers and Daydreaming', *The Standard Edition of the Complete Psychological Works of Sigmund Freud*, ed. J. Strachey, Vol. 9 (London: Hogarth, 1962), pp. 99–140.

Furst, E.J., 'Bloom's Taxonomy: Philosophical and Educational Issues', in *Bloom's Taxonomy: A Forty-year Retrospective*, ed. L.W. Anderson and L.A.

Sosniak, Ninety-third Yearbook of the National Society for the Study of Education, Part II (Chicago, IL: University of Chicago Press, 1994), pp. 28–40.

Gadamer, H-G., *Truth and Method*, trans. W. Glen-Doepel (London: Sheed and Ward, 1979).

Gallie, W.B., *Philosophy and the Historical Understanding* (New York, NY: Schocken Books, 1964).

Galton, F., *Inquiries into Human Faculty and Development* (London: Dent, 1907).

Gard, A. and Lee, P.J., '"Educational Objectives for the Study of History" Reconsidered', in A.K. Dickinson and P.J. Lee (eds.), *History Teaching and Historical Understanding* (London: Heinemann, 1978), pp. 21–38.

Gardiner, P., 'The "Objects" of Historical Knowledge', *Philosophy*, Vol. 27 (1952), pp. 211–20.

Gardiner, P., *The Nature of Historical Explanation* (Oxford: Oxford University Press, 1952).

Gardner, H., *The Mind's New Science* (New York, NY: Basic Books, 1985).

Gerard, A., *Essay on Taste* [1759] (Menston: Scolar Press, 1971).

Gibbons, S., *Kant's Theory of Imagination: Bridging Gaps in Judgement and Experience* (Oxford: Oxford University Press, 1994).

Ginzburg, C., *The Cheese and the Worms: The Cosmos of a Sixteenth- Century Miller*, trans. J. and A. Tedeschi (Harmondsworth: Penguin, 1980).

Goldstein, L. J., 'Collingwood's Theory of Historical Knowing', *History and Theory*, Vol. 9 (1) (1970), pp. 13–36.

Goldstein, L. J., *Historical Knowing* (Austin, TX: University of Texas, 1976).

Goldwert, M., 'Creative Imagination in the Historian: A Leap of Faith Toward Interpreting Evolution', *Journal of Unconventional History*, Vol. 6 (2) (1995), pp. 66–70.

Good, J., 'Introduction: The Historical Imagination and the Human Sciences', *History of the Human Sciences*, Vol. 13 (4) (2000), p. 97–101.

Gordon, P. and White, J., *Philosophers as Educational Reformers: the Influence of Idealism in British Educational Thought and Practice* (London: Routledge and Kegan Paul, 1979).

Gosden, P.H. and Sylvester, D.W., *History for the Average Child* (Oxford: Blackwell, 1968).

Grant, C.K., 'Collingwood's Theory of Historical Knowledge', *Renaissance and Modern Studies*, Vol. 1 (1) (1951), pp. 65–86.

Green, T.F., 'Teaching, Acting, Behaving', *Harvard Educational Review*, Vol. 34 (3) (1964), pp. 504-24.

Green, T.H., *Lectures on the Principles of Political Obligation* [1879] (London: Longmans Green, 1937).

Green, T.H., *Prolegomena to Ethics* (Oxford: Oxford University Press, 1883).

Green, T.H., *Works*, Vol. 3 (London: Longmans Green, 1888).

Greenspan, P., *Emotions and Reasons* (New York: Routledge, 1988).

Gribble, J. and Oliver, G., 'Empathy and Education', *Studies in Philosophy in Education*, Vol. 8 (1) (1973), pp. 3–28.

Griffith, B., 'Historical Thinking as a Mode of Experience', *Becoming a Canadian Teacher* (Toronto: University of Toronto Press, 1993), pp. 32–3.

Gunning, D., *The Teaching of History* (London: Croom Helm, 1978).

Habermas, J., *Knowledge and Human Interests*, trans. J. Shapiro (London: Heinemann, 1973).

Harrington, A., 'Dilthey, Empathy and *Verstehen*: A Contemporary Reappraisal', *European Journal of Social Theory*, Vol. 4 (3) (2001), pp. 311–29.

Harrison, B., 'College Life, 1918–1939', *The History of the University of Oxford*, ed. B. Harrison, Vol. 8 (Oxford: Oxford University Press, 1994), pp. 81–108.

Hart, A. B., 'Imagination in History', in *American Historical Review*, Vol. 15 (1910), pp. 227–51.

Hayden, T., Arthur, J. and Hunt, M., *Learning to Teach History in the Secondary School* (London: Routledge, 1997).

Hegel, G.W.F., *Elements of the Philosophy of Right*, trans. H.B. Nisbet, ed. A. Wood (Cambridge: Cambridge University Press, 1991).

Hegel, G.W.F., *Phenomenology of Mind*, trans. J.B. Baillie (Cambridge: Cambridge University Press, 1931).

Hegel, G.W.F., *The Philosophy of History*, trans. J. Sibree (New York, NY: Dover, 1956).

Helgeby, S., 'Action, Duty and Self-Knowledge in R.G. Collingwood's Philosophy of History', *Collingwood Studies*, Vol. 1 (1994), pp. 86–107.

Hempel, C.G., *Aspects of Scientific Explanation and Other Essays in the Philosophy of Science* (London: Macmillan, 1965).

Henderson, H., *Versions of the Past: The Historical Imagination in American Fiction* (New York: Oxford University Press, 1974).

Herder, J.G., 'Yet Another Philosophy of History' [1774], *Against Pure Reason: Writings on Religion, Language and History*, trans and ed. M. Bunge (Minneapolis, MN: Augsburg Fortress, 1993), pp. 38–58.

Hinz, M., *Self-Creation and History: Collingwood and Nietzsche on Conceptual Change* (Lanham, MD: University Press of America, 1993).

Hirst, P.H. and Peters, R.S., *The Logic of Education* (London: Routledge and Kegan Paul, 1970).

Hirst, P.H., 'Education, Knowledge and Practices', in R. Barrow and P. White (eds.), *Beyond Liberal Education: Essays in Honour of Paul H. Hirst* (London: Routledge, 1993), pp. 184–99.

Hirst, P.H., 'Liberal Education and the Nature of Knowledge' [1965], *Knowledge and the Curriculum* (London: Routledge and Kegan Paul, 1974), pp. 30–53.

Hirst, P.H., 'The Forms of Knowledge Re-visited', *Knowledge and the Curriculum* (London: Routledge and Kegan Paul, 1974), pp. 84–100.

HMI, *A View of the Curriculum* (London: HMSO, 1980).

HMI, *History From 5 to 16* (London: HMSO, 1988).

HMI, *History in the Primary and Secondary Years: An HMI View* (London: HMSO, 1985).

HMI, *Primary Education in England* (London: HMSO, 1978).

Hobbes, T., 'The Answer of Mr. Hobbes to Sir William Davenant's Preface Before Gondibert', in *The English Works of Thomas Hobbes*, Vol. 4 (London: John Bohn, 1839), pp. 449–50.

Hobbes, T., *De Corpore*, in *The English Works of Thomas Hobbes*, Vol. 1 (London: John Bohn, 1839).

Hobbes, T., *Leviathan*, ed. R. Tuck (Cambridge: Cambridge University Press, 1996).

Hobhouse, H., 'Times Steals a March on History', *TES*, no. 3866 (1990), p. 10.

Hoffman, M.L., 'Developmental Synthesis of Affect and Cognition and its Implications for Altruistic Motivation', *Developmental Psychology*, Vol. 11 (4) (1975), pp. 602–22.

Hoffman, M.L., 'Empathy, its Development and Prosocial Implications', in C.B. Kearsey (ed.), *Nebraska Symposium on Motivation*, Vol. 25 (Lincoln, NE: University of Nebraska Press, 1977), pp. 169–218.

Hoffman, M.L., 'Sex Differences in Empathy in Empathy and Related Behaviours', *Psychological Bulletin*, Vol. 54 (4) (1977), pp. 712–22.

Hughes, H.S., 'The Historian and the Social Scientist', *American Historical Review*, Vol. 66 (1960), pp. 20–46.

Hughes, H.S., *History as Art and As Science: Twin Vistas on the Past* (London: Harper and Row, 1964).

Humboldt, W. von, 'On the Historian's Task' [1821], *History and Theory*, Vol. 6 (1967), pp. 57–71.

Hume, D., *A Treatise on Human Nature* [1739], eds. D. and M. Norton (Oxford: Oxford University Press, 2000).

Hume, D., *Enquiry Concerning the Principles of Morals* [1772], ed. L.A. Selby-Bigge (Oxford: Oxford University Press, 1975).

Husbands, C., *What is History Teaching?* (Buckingham: Open University Press, 1996).

Jenkins, K. and Brickley, P., 'Reflections on the Empathy Debate', *Teaching History*, No. 55 (1989), pp. 18–23.

Jenkins, K., *Rethinking History* (London: Routledge, 1992).

Johnson, D.H., 'W.G. Collingwood and the Beginnings of the Idea of History', *Collingwood Studies*, Vol. 1 (1994), pp. 1–26.

Johnson, P., *R.G. Collingwood: An Introduction* (Bristol: Thoemmes, 1998).

Joseph, K., *Why Teach History in Schools?* (London: Historical Association, 1984).

Kant, I., *Critique of Judgement*, trans. J.C. Meredith (Oxford: Oxford University Press, 1928).

Kant, I., *Critique of Pure Reason*, trans. N. Kemp Smith (London: Macmillan, 1929).

Kant, I., *Grounding for the Metaphysics of Morals* [1785], trans J.W. Ellington (Indianapolis, IN: Hackett Publishing Company, 1993).

Kean, H., Martin, P. and Morgan, S.J. (eds.), *Seeing History: Public History in Britain Now* (London: Francis Boutle, 2000).

Kearney, R., *The Wake of Imagination: Toward a Postmodern Culture* (Minneapolis, MN: University of Minnesota Press, 1988).

Kedourie, H., *Errors and Evils of the New History* (London: CPS, 1988).

Kelley, D.R. and Sachs, D.H. (eds.), *The Historical Imagination in Early Modern Britain* (Cambridge: Cambridge University Press, 1997).

Kenny, A., *Action, Emotion and Will* (London: Routledge and Kegan Paul, 1963).

Kenny, A., *Aquinas: A Collection of Critical Essays* (London: Macmillan, 1969).

Kenny, A., *The Metaphysics of Mind* (Oxford: Oxford University Press, 1989).

Kenny, A., *Wittgenstein* (Harmondsworth: Penguin, 1975).

Kierkegaard, S., *Fear and Trembling and Sickness Unto Death*, trans. W. Lowrie (Princeton, NJ: Princeton University Press, 1944).

Kierkegaard, S., *Training in Christianity*, trans. W. Lowrie (Oxford: Oxford University Press, 1941).

Klein, K.L., *Frontiers of Historical Imagination: Narrating the European Conquest of Native America 1890–1990* (Berkeley, CA: University of California Press, 1997).

Knight, P., 'Empathy: Concept, Confusion and Consequences in a National Curriculum', *Oxford Review of Education*, Vol. 15 (1) (1989), p. 45–60.

Knudson, K.H.M. and Kagan, S., 'Differential Development of Empathy and Prosocial Behaviour', *The Journal of Genetic Psychology*, No. 140 (1982), pp. 249–51.

Kosslyn, S., *Image and Mind* (Cambridge, MA: Harvard University Press, 1980).

Kripke, S., *Naming and Necessity* (Cambridge, MA: Harvard University Press, 1980).

Kuhn, T.S., 'Logic of Discovery or Psychology of Research', *The Essential Tension: Selected Studies in Scientific Tradition and Change* (Chicago, IL: University of Chicago Press, 1977).

Kuhn, T.S., 'Second Thoughts on Paradigms', *The Essential Tension: Selected Studies in Scientific Tradition and Change* (Chicago, IL: University of Chicago Press, 1977).

Kuhn, T.S., *The Structure of Scientific Revolutions 3/e* (Chicago, IL: University of Chicago Press, 1996).

Lacan, J., *The Seminar of Jacques Lacan*, Vol. 2, *The Ego in Freud's Theory and in the Technique of Psychoanlysis 1954–1955*, trans. S. Tomaselli (New York, NY: W.W. Norton, 1955).

Laird, J., 'Review of *The New Leviathan*', *Philosophy*, Vol. 18 (1) (1943), p. 79.

Lamont, W., 'Forget the Memory Man: "New" History', *TES*, No. 3827 (1989), p. 20.

Lawlor, S., *But What Must Pupils Know?: CPS Response to National Curriculum History Working Group, Final Report* (London: CPS, 1990).

Lawlor, S., *Proposals for the National Curriculum in History* (London: CPS, 1989).

Le Goff, J., *The Medieval Imagination*, trans. A. Goldhammer (Chicago, IL: University of Chicago Press, 1988).

Le Roy Ladurie, E., *Montaillou: The Promised Land of Error*, trans. B. Bray (New York, NY: Vintage, 1979).

Lee, P.J., 'Explanation and Understanding in History', in A.K. Dickinson and P.J. Lee (eds), *History Teaching and Historical Understanding* (London: Heinemann, 1978), pp. 72–93.

Lee, P.J., 'Historical Imagination' in A.K. Dickinson, P.J. Rogers and P.J. Lee (eds), *Learning History* (London: Heinemann, 1984), pp. 85–116.

Lee, P.J., 'History and the National Curriculum in England', in P.J. Lee, A.K. Dickinson, P. Gordon and J. Slater (eds.), *International Yearbook of History Education* (London: The Woburn Press), pp. 73–123.

Lee, P.J., 'History Teaching and Philosophy of History', *History and Theory*, Vol. 22 (4) (1983), pp. 19–49.

Leibniz, G.W., *New Essays on Human Understanding*, trans. P. Remnant and J. Bennett (Cambridge: Cambridge University Press, 1996).

Lewis, C.I., 'A Pragmatic Conception of the A Priori', in P.K. Moser (ed.), *A Priori Knowledge* (Oxford: Oxford University Press, 1987), pp. 15–25.

Lewis, P., 'Collingwood and Wittgenstein: Struggling with Darkness', *Collingwood Studies*, Vol. 5 (1998), pp. 28–42.

Leyden, W. von, 'Philosophy of Mind: An Appraisal of Collingwood's Theories of Consciousness, Language and Imagination', in. M. Krausz (ed.), *Critical Essays on the Philosophy of R.G. Collingwood* (Oxford: Oxford University Press, 1972), pp. 20–41.

Lisska, A., 'Aquinas on "Phantasia"', *Thomist*, Vol. 40 (1976), pp. 294–302.

Little, V., 'What is Historical Imagination?', *Teaching History*, No. 36 (1983), pp. 27–32.

Llewelyn, J.E., 'On Not Speaking the Same Language − II', *Australasian Journal of Philosophy* (1962), pp. 127–45.

Locke, J., *An Essay Concerning Human Understanding* (Oxford: Oxford University Press, 1975).

Longinus, *On the Sublime*, in *Classical Literary Criticism*, trans. T.S. Dorsch (Harmondsworth: Penguin, 1965).

Lord, T.C., 'R.G. Collingwood: A Continental Philosopher?', *Clio*, Vol. 29 (3) (2000), pp. 325–36.

Low-Beer, A., 'Empathy and History', *Teaching History*, No. 55 (1989), pp. 8–12.

Macaulay, T.B., 'History', in F. Stern (ed.), *The Varieties of History: From Voltaire to the Present* (New York: Vintage Books, 1973), pp. 71–89.

Maccoby, E.E. and Jacklin, C.N., *The Psychology of Sex Differences* (Stanford, CA: Stanford University Press, 1974).

Makkreel, R., *Wilhelm Dilthey: Philosopher of the Human Sciences* (Princeton, NJ: Princeton University Press, 1975).

Mandelbaum, M., 'A Note on History as Narrative', *History and Theory*, Vol. 6 (1967), pp. 413–9.

Marcus, R.F., Telleen, S. and Roke, E., 'Relation Between Cooperation and Empathy in Young Children', *Developmental Psychology*, Vol. 15 (3) (1979), pp. 346–47.

Martin Jnr, J.A., 'Collingwood and Wittgenstein on the Task of Philosophy: An Interesting Convergence', *Philosophy Today*, Vol. 25 (Spring) (1981), pp. 12–23.

Martin, R., 'Review of *Re-enactment: A Study in R. G. Collingwood's Philosophy of History* (Saari)', *Theoria*, Vol. 51 (2) (1985), pp. 121–3.

Martin, R., *Re-enactment and Practical Inference* (London: Cornell University Press, 1977).

Marwick, A., *The Nature of History* (London: Macmillan, 1970).

McCullagh, C. B., 'Narrative and Explanation in History', *Mind*, Vol. 78 (n.s.) (1969), pp. 256–61.

McGovern, C., 'How Would You Feel . . .?', *TES*, No. 3745 (1988), p. 3.

Mehrabian, A. and Epstein, N., 'A Measure of Emotional Empathy', *Journal of Personality*, Vol. 40 (4) (1972), pp. 525–43.

Miller, C., *Giambattista Vico: Imagination and Historical Knowledge* (New York, NY: St. Martin's Press, 1993).

Miller, J.C., 'Presidential Address: History and Africa/Africa and History', *American Historical Review*, Vol. 104 (1) (1999), pp. 1–32.

Mink, L.O., 'Collingwood's Historicism: A Dialectic of Process', in M. Krausz (ed.), *Critical Essays on the Philosophy of R.G. Collingwood* (Oxford: Oxford University Press, 1972).

Mink, L.O., 'Narrative Form as a Cognitive Instrument', in R. Canary and H. Kozicki (eds.), *The Writing of History: Literary Form and Understanding*, Wisconsin, WI: University of Wisconsin Press, 1978, pp. 129–49.

Mink, L. O., *Mind, History, and Dialectic* (Bloomington, IN: Indiana University Press, 1969).

Minogue, K., 'Through the Processor', *TES*, No. 3775 (1989), p. 17.

Moore, R., 'History and Integrated Studies: Surrender or Survival?', *Teaching History*, No. 18 (1974), pp. 109–11.

Morgann, M., *An Essay on the Dramatic Character of Sir John Falstaff* [1777] (New York, NY: AMS Press, 1970).

Morris, P., 'Freeing the Spirit of Enterprise' , in R. Keat and N. Abercrombie (eds.), *Enterprise Culture* (London: Routledge and Kegan Paul, 1991), pp. 21–37.

Moses Maimonides, *The Guide for the Perplexed*, trans. M. Friedlander (New York, NY: Dover, 1956).

Moss, M.E., 'The Crocean Concept of the Pure Concept', *Idealistic Studies*, Vol. 17 (1) (1987), pp. 45–50.

Munslow, A., *The Routledge Companion to Historical Studies* (London: Routledge, 2000).

Murdoch, I., *The Fire and the Sun: Why Plato Banished the Artists* (London: Chatto and Windus, 1977).

Myers, G.E., *Self: An Introduction to Philosophical Psychology* (New York: Pegasus, 1969).

Natale, S., *An Experiment in Empathy* (Slough: NFER, 1972).

National Curriculum Council (England), *National Curriculum Council Consultation Report; History* (York: NCC, 1990).

Nichol, J., 'Who wants to Fight? Who wants to Flee?: Teaching History from a "Thinking Skills" Perspective', *Teaching History*, No. 95 (1999), pp. 6–13.

Nielsen, M.H., 'Re-enactment and Reconstruction in Collingwood's Philosophy of History', *History and Theory*, Vol. 20 (1) (1981), pp. 1–31.

Nietzsche, F., *The Will to Power*, trans. W. Kaufmann and R. Hollingdale (New York, NY: Random House, 1967).

Norton, B., 'Historical Reality and the Quest for Meaning', *Journal of International and Comparative Studies*, Vol. 4 (1) (1971), pp. 28–37.

Nussbaum, M., *Aristotle's 'De Motu Animalium'* (Princeton, NJ: Princeton University Press, 1978).

O'Craven, K. and Kanwisher, N., 'Mental Imagery of Faces and Places Activates Corresponding Stimulus-Specific Brain Regions', *Journal of Cognitive Neuroscience*, Vol. 12 (6) (2000), pp. 1013–23.

Oakeshott, 'The Voice of Poetry in the Conversation of Mankind', *Rationalism in Politics and Other Essays* (Indianapolis, IN: Liberty Fund, 1991), pp. 488–542.

Oakeshott, M., 'On the Character of a Modern European State', *On Human Conduct* (Oxford: Oxford University Press, 1975), pp. 185–326.

Oliver, I., 'The "Old" and the "New" Hermeneutic in Sociological Theory', *British Journal of Sociology*, Vol. 34 (4) (1983), pp. 519–53.

Ormell, C.P., 'Bloom's Taxonomy and the Objectives of Education', *Educational Research*, Vol. 17 (1) (1974), p. 1–15.

Ostrowski, D., 'A Metahistorical Analysis: Hayden White and Four Narratives of "Russian" History', *Clio*, Vol. 19 (1990), pp. 215–36.

Paivio, A., *Imagery and Mental Processes* (New York, NY: Holt, Rinehart and Winston, 1971).

Paton, H.J., 'Plato's Theory of Eikasia', *Proceedings of the Aristotelian Society*, No. 22 (1921–2), pp. 69–104.

Phillips, D.C. and Kelly, M.C., 'Hierarchical Theories of Development in Education and Psychology', *Harvard Educational Review*, Vol. 45 (3) (1975), pp. 351–75.

Philostratus, F., *The Life of Apollonius of Tyana*, trans. F.C. Conybeare (London: Heinemann, 1912).

Pico Della Mirandola, G., *On the Imagination*, trans. H. Caplan (Westport, CT: Greenwood, 1930).

Plato, *Parmenides*, trans. L. Tarán (Princeton, NJ: Princeton University Press, 1965).

Plato, *Philebus*, trans. S. Benardete (Chicago, IL: University of Chicago Press, 1993).

Plato, *Republic*, trans D. Lee (Harmondsworth: Penguin, 1955).

Plato, *Sophist*, trans. F.M. Cornford (London: Routledge and Kegan Paul, 1935).

Plato, *Timaeus*, trans. D. Lee (Harmondsworth: Penguin, 1977).

Plotinus, *Enneads*, trans. S. MacKenna (London: Faber and Faber, 1969).

Pollan, M., *The Botany of Desire* (New York, NY: Random House, 2001).

Portal, C., 'Empathy as an Aim for the Curriculum: Lessons from History', *Journal of Curriculum Studies*, Vol. 15 (3) (1983), pp. 303–10.

Portal, C., 'Empathy as an Objective for History Teaching', in C. Portal (ed.), *History in the Curriculum* (London: Falmer, 1987).

Price, M., 'History in Danger', *History*, Vol. 53 (179) (1968), pp. 342–7.

Priestley, J., *Course of Lectures on Oratory and Criticism* [1762] (Carbondale, IL: Southern Illinois University Press, 1965).

Pring, R., 'Bloom's Taxonomy: A Philosophical Critique', *Cambridge Journal of Education*, Vol. 1 (1) (1971), pp. 83–91.

Proclus, *Proclus: A Commentary on the First Book of Euclid's Elements*, trans. G.R. Morrow (Princeton, NJ: Princeton University Press, 1970).

Quine, W.V., *Word and Object* (Cambridge, MA: MIT Press, 1960).

Quintilian, *Institutio Oratoria*, trans. H.E. Butler (London: Heinemann, 1921).

Ramachandra, G.P., 'Re-Experiencing Past Thoughts: Some Reflections on Collingwood's Theory of History', *Journal of Indian Council of Philosophical Research* (1996), pp. 67–82.

Ramirez, F.O., and Meyer, J.W., 'National Curricula: World Models and National Historical Legacies' (Stanford University Comparative Sociology Workshop, http://www.stanford.edu/group/csw/PAPER2, 2002).

Ranke, L. von, 'Preface to *Histories of the Latin and Germanic Nations from 1494–1514*', in F. Stern (ed.), *The Varieties of History: From Voltaire to the Present* (New York, NY: Vintage Books, 1973), p. 55–8.

Richard of St. Victor, *Treatise on the Study of Wisdom that Men Call Benjamin*, trans. D. Barnes (Lewiston, MN: Edwin Mellen Press, 1990).

Richards, G., 'Varieties of Historical Imagination: Imagining Life Without Freud', *History of the Human Sciences*, Vol. 13 (4) (2000), pp. 109–13.

Richardson, A., *Mental Imagery* (New York, NY: Springer, 1969).

Rickert, H., *Kulturwissenschaft und Naturwissenschaft* [1899] (Stuttgart: Reclam, 1986).

Ristau, C. (ed.), *Cognitive Ethology* (Hillsdale, MI: Lawrence Erlbaum Associates, 1991).

Ritter, H., 'Imagination', *Dictionary of Concepts in History* (Westport, CN: Greenwood Press), p. 216.

Ritter, H., 'Progressive Historians and the Historical Imagination in Austria: Heinrich Friedjung and Richard Charmatz', *Austrian History Yearbook*, Vol. 19–20 (1) (1983–4), pp. 45–90.

Roberts, M., 'Briefing for a Journey to the Past', *TES*, No. 3851 (1990), p. 70.

Rogers, P.J., *History: What and Why?* (London: Historical Association, 1987).

Rogers, P.J., *The New History: Theory into Practice* (London: Longmans, 1978).

Rorty, R., *Contingency, Irony, and Solidarity* (Cambridge: Cambridge University Press, 1989).

Rorty, R., *Philosophy and the Mirror of Nature* (Oxford: Blackwell, 1980).

Rose, D.B., 'Ned Kelly Died for Our Sins', *Oceania*, Vol. 65 (2) (1994), pp. 175–86.

Rubinoff, L., *Collingwood and the Reform of Metaphysics* (Toronto: University of Toronto Press, 1970).

Russell, C., 'Standing the Test of Time', *TES*, No. 3851 (1990), p. 69.

Ryle, G., 'Systematically Misleading Expressions', *Collected Papers*, Vol. 2 (London: Hutchinson, 1971), pp. 39–62.

Ryle, G., *The Concept of Mind* (Harmondsworth: Penguin, 1949).

Saari, H., 'R.G. Collingwood on the Identity of Thoughts', *Dialogue*, Vol. 28 (1) (1989), pp. 77–89.

Saari, H., *Re-enactment: A Study in R.G. Collingwood's Philosophy of History* (Åbo: Åbo Akademi, 1984).

Sartre, J-P., *The Psychology of Imagination*, trans. anon. (New York, NY: Citadel, 1972).

Savage-Rumbaugh, E.S. and Lewin, R., *Kanzi: The Ape at the Brink of the Human Mind* (New York, NY: Wiley, 1994).

Schelling, F.W.J., *System of Transcendental Idealism (1800)*, trans. P. Heath (Charlottesville, VA: University of Virginia Press, 1978).

Schools Council, *A New Look at History*, Schools Council History 13–16 Project (Edinburgh: Holmes McDougall, 1976).

Schools Council, *Explorations in Teaching Schools Council Projects: History 13–16* (Leeds: Holmes McDougall, 1980).

Schools Council, *Place, Time and Society 8–13: An Introduction* (Bristol: Collins Educational, 1975).

Sheffler, I., *The Language of Education* (Springfield, IL: Charles C. Thomas, 1960).

Shemilt, D., 'Beauty and the Philosopher: Empathy in History and the Classroom', in A.K. Dickinson, P.J. Rogers and P.J. Lee (eds.), *Learning History* (London, 1984), pp. 39–84.

Shemilt, D., *History 13–16: Evaluation Study* (Edinburgh: Holmes McDougall, 1980).

Simpkin, J., *Empathy in GCSE* (London: Spartacus, 1987).

Skagestad, P., *Making Sense of History: The Philosophies of Popper and Collingwood* (Oslo: Universitetsforlaget, 1975).

Skidelsky, R., 'History as Social Engineering', *The Independent*, 1 March 1988, p. 4.

Skidelsky, R., 'Mutiny at the Priory', *TES*, No. 3789 (1989), pp. 1–3.

Slater, J., *Teaching History in the New Europe* (London: Cassell, 1995).

Smith, A., *The Theory of Moral Sentiments* [1759] (Indianapolis, IN: Liberty, 1969).

Smith, R., 'Reflections on the Historical Imagination', *History of the Human Sciences*, Vol. 13 (4) (2000), pp. 103–8.

Smith, T., '"This Ring of Thought": Notes on Early Influences', *Collingwood Studies*, Vol. 1 (1994), pp. 27–43.

Snook, I.A., *Indoctrination and Education* (London: Routledge and Kegan Paul, 1972).

Snook, I., 'The Curriculum: Timeless and Time-Bound', in R. Barrow and P. White (eds.), *Beyond Liberal Education: Essays in Honour of Paul H. Hirst* (London: Routledge, 1993), pp. 94–106.

Sockett, H., 'Bloom's Taxonomy: a Philosophical Critique', *Cambridge Journal of Education*, Vol. 1 (1) (1971), pp. 16–25.

Soffer, R.N., 'The Conservative Historical Imagination in the Twentieth Century', *Albion*, Vol. 28 (1) (1996), pp. 1–17.

Solomon, R.C., *The Passions: Emotions and the Meaning of Life* (Indianaopolis, IN: Hackett Publishing Company, 1993).

Sousa, R. de, *The Rationality of Emotions* (Cambridge, MA: MIT Press, 1987).

Spinoza, B. de, *Ethics Preceded by On the Improvement of the Understanding*, trans. J. E. Woodbridge (New York, NY: Hafner, 1949).

Spongberg, M., *Writing Women's History Since the Renaissance* (London: Palgrave, 2002).

Southern Regional Examinations Board (England), *Empathy in History: From Definition to Assessment* (London: SREB, 1986).

Stanage, S., 'Collingwood's Phenomenology of Education: Person and the Self-Recognition of the Mind', in M. Krausz (ed.), *Critical Essays on the Philosophy of R.G. Collingwood* (Oxford: Oxford University Press, 1972), pp. 268–95.

Stannard, D.E., *Shrinking History: On Freud and the Failure of Psychohistory* (Oxford: Oxford University Press, 1980).

Still, A., 'Psychotherapy and the Historical Imagination', *History of the Human Sciences*, Vol. 13 (4) (2000), pp. 115–20.

Stotland, E., 'Exploratory Investigations of Empathy' in L. Berkowitz (ed.), *Advances in Experimental Psychology*, Vol. 4 (New York, NY: Academic Press, 1969).

Strawson, G., 'The Self', *Journal of Consciousness Studies*, Vol. 4 (5–6) (1997), pp. 405–28.

Strawson, P.F., *Individuals* (London: Methuen, 1959).

Sylvester, D., 'Change and Continuity in History Teaching 1900–93', in H. Bourdillon (ed.), *Teaching History* (London: Routledge, 1994), pp. 9–23.

Synesius of Cyrene, *The Essays and Hymns of Synesius of Cyrene*, trans. A. Fitzgerald (London: Oxford University Press, 1930).

Tate, N., *Countdown to GCSE: History* (London, Longmans, 1986).

Thayer, H.S., 'Plato on the Morality of Imagination', *Review of Metaphysics*, Vol. 30 (3) (1977), pp. 594–618.

Thomas, G., Meyer, J.W. and Ramirez, F.O., *Institutional Structure: Constituting State, Society, and the Individual* (Beverly Hills, CA: Sage, 1987).

Thompson, F., 'Empathy: An Aim and a Skill to be Developed', *Teaching History*, No. 37 (1983), pp. 22–6.

Toynbee, A., *A Study of History*, Vol. 9, (London: Longmans, 1954).

Trevor-Roper, H.R., 'Historical Imagination', *The Listener*, 27 February 1958, pp. 357–8, 371.

Trevor-Roper, H.R., 'History and Imagination', in H. Lloyd-Jones, V. Pearl and B. Wurden (eds.), *History and Imagination: Essays in Honour of H.R. Trevor-Roper* (London: Duckworth, 1981), pp. 356–69.

Tuveson, E.L., *The Imagination as a Means of Grace* (Berkeley, CA: University of California Press, 1960).

Vanheeswijck, G., 'Collingwood en Wittgenstein: hervormde versus deiktische metafysica', *Algemeen Nederlands Tijdschrift voor Wijsbegeerte*, Vol. 84 (3) (1992), pp. 165–81.

Vanheeswijck, G., 'Robin George Collingwood on Eternal Philosophical Problems', *Dialogue*, Vol. 40 (3) (2001), pp. 555–70.

Vico, G., *On the Most Ancient Wisdom of the Italians, Unearthed from the Origins of the Latin Language*, trans. L.M. Palmer (Ithaca, NJ: Cornell, 1988).

Vico, G., *The New Science* [1744], trans. T.G. Bergin and M.H. Fisch (Ithaca, NJ: Cornell University Press, 1968).

Wake, R., 'History as a Separate Discipline: The Case', *Teaching History*, No. 1 (1970), p. 3.

Walsh, W.H., 'Collingwood and Metaphysical Neutralism', in M. Krausz (ed.), *Critical Essays on the Philosophy of R. G. Collingwood* (Oxford: Oxford University Press, 1972), pp. 134–53.

Walsh, W.H., 'R.G. Collingwood's Philosophy of History', *Philosophy*, Vol. 22 (1947), pp. 153–60.

Walsh, W.H., *An Introduction to the Philosophy of History* (London: Hutchinson, 1964).

Warnock, M., *Imagination* (London: Faber and Faber, 1976).

Watson, J.B., *Behaviour: An Introduction to Comparative Psychology* (New York, NY: H. Hold, 1914).

Weber, M., *Economy and Society*, ed. G. Roth and C. Wittich, Vol. 1 (New York, NY: Bedminster, 1968).

Weinstein, M.A., 'The Creative Imagination in Fiction and History', *Genre*, Vol. 9 (1976), pp. 63–77.

Weitz, M., *Theories of Concepts: A History of the Major Philosophical Tradition* (London: Routledge, 1988).

White, A., *The Language of Imagination* (Oxford: Blackwell, 1990).

White, C., 'Doing the Knowledge', *TES*, No. 3851 (1990), p. 72.

White, H., 'Collingwood and Toynbee: Transitions in English Historical Work', *English Miscellany*, Vol. 8 (1957), p. 166.

White, H., 'Historicism, History, and the Figurative Imagination', *Tropics of Discourse: Essays in Cultural Criticism* (Baltimore, MD: John Hopkins University Press, 1978), pp. 48–67.

White, H., *Metahistory: The Historical Imagination in Nineteenth-Century Europe* (Baltimore, MD: Johns Hopkins University Press, 1973).

White, M., 'A Plea for an Analytic Philosophy of History', *Religion, Politics and the Higher Learning* (Cambridge, MA: Harvard University Press, 1959), pp. 61–74.

Wilson, J.R.S., *Emotion and Object* (Cambridge: Cambridge University Press, 1972).

Windelband, W., 'History and Natural Science' [1898], *Theory and Psychology*, Vol. 8 (1) (1998), pp. 5–22.

Winter, J.M., 'Oxford and the First World War', *The History of the University of Oxford*, ed. B. Harrison, Vol. 8 (Oxford: Oxford University Press, 1994), pp. 3–26.

Wisner, D. A., 'Modes of Visualisation in Neo-Idealist Theories of the Historical Imagination (Cassirer, Collingwood, Huizinga)', *Collingwood Studies*, Vol. 6 (1999), pp. 53–84.

Wittgenstein, L., *On Certainty*, ed. G.E.M. Anscombe and G.H. von Wright (Oxford: Blackwell, 1969).

Wittgenstein, L., *Philosophical Grammar*, ed. R. Rhees, trans. A. Kenny (Oxford: Blackwell, 1974).

Wittgenstein, L., *Philosophical Investigations*, trans. G.E.M. Anscombe, ed. G.E.M. Anscombe, R. Rhees and G.H. von Wright (Oxford: Blackwell, 1953).

Wittgenstein, L., *Remarks on the Foundations of Mathematics*, ed. G.H. von Wright, R. Rhees and G.E.M. Anscombe (Oxford: Blackwell, 1964).

Wittgenstein, L., *Remarks on the Psychology of Philosophy*, ed. G.E.M. Anscombe and G.H. von Wright, Vol. 2 (Oxford: Blackwell, 1992).

Wittgenstein, L., *The Blue and Brown Books* (Oxford: Blackwell, 1958)

Wittgenstein, L., *Zettel*, ed.G.E.M. Anscombe and G.H. von Wright (Oxford: Blackwell, 1967).

Wordsworth, W., 'Tinturn Abbey', *Ode on Immortality and Lines on Tinturn Abbey* (London: Cassell, 1885), II. 95–9.

Wordsworth, W., *Prelude* [1805] (London: Macmillan, 1932).

Wordsworth, W., *Prose Works*, eds. W.J.B. Owen and J.W. Smyser (Oxford: Oxford University Press, 1974).

Yates, F., *The Art of Memory* (Chicago, IL: University of Chicago Press, 1966).

Index

D

E

Q

R

S

T

U

V